GOD'S SECRET

The Gospel of God's Kingdom Unveiled

Jesse Nelms

GOD'S SECRET

The Gospel of God's Kingdom Unveiled

By Jesse Nelms
© Copyright 2011, by Jesse Nelms

No part of this book may be reproduced or copied in any form
or by any means without written permission of the author.

Unless otherwise noted, Scripture quotations are from The New King James Version
Copyright © 1979, 1980, 1982 by Thomas Nelson, Inc.
Used by permission. All rights reserved.
ISBN 978-0-615-60498-5

Edited by: Dr. Henry Oursler
Formatting & Layout by: Brandi Gonsman
Front Cover Illustration by: Lazaro Ruiz

Various citations have been made from E-Sword, Version 9.7.2; Copyright © 2000-2010,
Rick Meyers, all rights reserved.
www.e-sword.net

Table of Contents

Acknowledgements
Forward
Preface

Section 1: Understanding the Kingdom

1. The King and the Kingdom............3
2. Anticipation of the Kingdom: Blessed to Be a Blessing............11
3. Extension of the Kingdom: Creating a Nation of Priests............21
4. Inauguration of the Kingdom: Flesh and Blood............33
5. Fulfillment of the Kingdom: Mission Accomplished - All Praise............47

Section 2: Experiencing the Kingdom

6. Entering the Kingdom of God............57
7. The Glory of God through the Blood of the Lamb............67
8. Experiencing the Kingdom of God............83
9. The Marriage of Christ and the Church............93
10. Kingdom Life vs. Religious Life: It's a Relationship Not a Religion............115
11. Kingdom life: Living Like Jesus............133
12. Kingdom Citizenship: What Kingdom Citizens Are Not............151
13. Kingdom Citizenship: What Kingdom Citizens Are............163

Section 3: Extending the Kingdom

14. Exercise Your Kingdom Calling............185
15. Jesus Christ: Kingdom Divider............205
16. A Call to Kingdom Action!............229

Appendix 1: Becoming a Kingdom Citizen and Growing as a Kingdom Citizen............241

Acknowledgements

As I sit here alone in my quiet living room at 10:00 pm, I am amazed how quickly and simply God allowed this book to come together. At the same time, I could not even begin to explain to you the blood, sweat, tears, and years it took me to get to the point where I could sit down and write this book with a sincere and honest heart. I am just a sinner saved by the grace of God. I thank Jesus Christ every single day for His broken body and shed blood. Because He lives, I can face yesterday, today and tomorrow with faith, hope, and love … and even joy! So, thank You, Lord, for your blessings on me.

I also want to thank and acknowledge my wife Sara. If God had not brought Sara into my life in my younger days, the Lord only knows where I'd be. I'm still not convinced she is not an angel! The name Sara means princess, and I have never seen another woman fit that word as perfectly as my wife does. She is more than my wife and the queen of my home. She is one with me in spirit and I thank God every single day for her love, support, encouragement, and accountability to stay on the path that God has for our family.

Finally, I would like to acknowledge and thank Dr. Henry Oursler who edited this book and was an immense help to me. *God's Secret* is the first book the Lord has allowed me to author and I am positive that God placed Dr. Oursler in my life at this exact time to bring this book to completion. Thank you Henry.

Forward

"The kingdom of God is here now, change the way you perceive things and believe this good news." **Mark 1:15**

These are the first words uttered by Yeshua el Nazarene, the man we have come to know as Jesus Christ. While on earth, He was a *"tekton,"* the Greek word for a builder, who according to believers and unbelievers alike, appeared and demonstrated power to manipulate particle-based matter and worked primarily as an exorcist, healer, and teacher for approximately three years. Crucified under Pontius Pilate, one thing is agreed upon by all scholars in all schools of sophisticated inquiry and thought: on the third day, no one could find His broken body.

So many manifestations, political and religious (and even the marriage of both) have claimed His name in the last two thousand years. For the common man such as I, the quest to know who He was and is takes commitment beyond a Sunday morning show and perfunctory prayers; as well as sorting through the spiritual pabulum being dealt by the Jesus junk in bookstores and the idea that to know what He meant by his initial words is like joining some elite special sector or "team" of society.

During those three years of recorded public ministry, interwoven into all He said and did was that there was no building or observable place where the kingdom of God was. Rather, He insisted indefatigably that *"the kingdom of God does not live in buildings made with men's hands-it is within and among you."* This idea of God having a kingdom was not new. That it was going to be inside of people was foreshadowed by the Torah and the prophets for many generations. That He was, in a real, phenomenally, empirically, and verifiable manner Himself going to manifest it now was earth shaking.

Also, as St. Paul asserted, this kingdom would be literally ruling over all earthly distraction and drama, giving meaning to the impermanence and suffering we are surrounded and engulfed by in our humanity (this kingdom being among us as we speak the truth in love to each other) and took the matter to an entirely new level as the "church" was born and literally turned the world upside down from the bottom up.

In the book you are about to read, you are going to experience the first toddling steps of a credentialed, thoroughbred, evangelical minister, who on both sides of his biological origin has a litany and legacy of longtime preachers, teachers, singers, administrators and, above all, highly refined and disciplined characters, who have committed their lives, fortunes and their inner selves to the work of the Lord.

The assertions made in this book reflect analogically a young boy, coming of age as a proven, master's degreed, credentialed and highly respected executive pastor of one of America's most generous and mission-minded mega churches. These pages resound with the author's burning passion and own experience of some form of supernatural awakening to the words spoken by Jesus Christ so many years ago.

Written with a fearless, daunting stream of consciousness reflecting his own experience, he inspires, motivates and encourages all of us to dare to return to the original foundations of the Jesus Christ teachings. He explains with simplicity the commencement and connection of conscious contact between creation and its Creator accomplished through the finished work of Jesus Christ's death, burial and resurrection. Taking off the rose-colored glasses he dares to believe and demonstrate how each one of us really can return to what Jesus Christ's original intentions were: *"to seek and to save that which was lost;"* that is, each person's joyous and free state of being not only with Christ in them but also they in Christ. This book shows us corporately and individually the facts of our present miserable state and our own way back to discovering our divine destiny.

Taking us from toddling steps into full stride action, he explains clearly the present day state of the North American church, pulling out root and branch and every misconception with a heartfelt cry seldom seen in a minister of any age and echoing like one of the Hebrew prophets of old.

If you know there is something more to life in any way, shape, form or fashion, this book is an integrous, authentic and, above all else, life-changing, soul shout out that explains what was, what is and what can be if you will but dare to "...*change the way you see things and believe the good news*" (Mark 1:15).

In my own personal life and ministry of over 35 years, it has become quite apparent that with increasing desperation the western church continues along a dying path as if we can declare enough statistics, attract enough people and erect enough self-serving, celebrity-producing, outwardly visible constructs, so that perhaps eventually we could convince God that what we are experiencing is the kingdom.

The pages within reflect a young boy becoming a man, leading an exemplary, blameless life and deciding not to curse the darkness but rather to light a candle. With the dawn of artificial intelligence yet unable to think our way out of the global catastrophe at hand, we continue creating machines to further our attempts to think our way out of the monstrosity our ego-driven lives have built. Echoing the simple Builder's words and using factual evidence to make his case, Jesse Nelms insists that this thinking should stop (knowing that the still mind is able to hear the divine mind – the mind of Christ). He not only points out that the emperor has no clothes but bids us in the simplest way, showing us how it can be done, to be clothed with the Light of God Himself; simply stating what he has seen and heard and knows resolutely and confidently, "*The kingdom of God is here,*" and shows us how to "*change the way we know things and believe the good news.*"

Jesus Christ built no organization. Rather, He "*conferred upon us a kingdom,*" (Luke 22:29). If you are ready to witness and have proven that this kingdom is real, if you're ready not only to enter it but also see it unite, then you are in for the experience of a lifetime.

Rev. Dr. Rick Amato
November, 2011

Preface

Dear reader, I want to let you in on a little secret ...

There is a war going on out there. We are in the midst of a cosmic war far greater than any mind has ever conceived. This is a war between light and darkness that pre-dates our world history. It is war on a global, galactic, and possibly even a universal scale being fought by hundreds of millions of highly advanced beings and creatures with technology and weapons that are still beyond our wildest dreams. This war between light and darkness is not a dualistic struggle where equal opponents are in constant struggle to get the upper hand over each other. The light is eternal, while the darkness has source, beginning, and will have an end. The light will prevail and has not lost control. [1]

Even more interestingly, the earth – and more specifically, humanity – is positioned smack dab in the bull's eye of the battle zone. In fact, planet earth is caught in the middle of an ancient war mostly fought in realms and dimensions [2] that science is just

---

[1] I agree with Gregory Boyd who notes that *"One cannot deny that the warfare motif of the New Testament presupposes a dualistic world-view of sorts. At the very least, there is clearly a God/non-God duality of power. In other words, significant powers exist with some measure of autonomy over against God, with whom God must therefore work or against whom God must genuinely fight. But this dualism, as intense as it is, never crosses into metaphysical dualism in the New Testament. That is, never does the New Testament come close to affirming that the forces that oppose God are metaphysically ultimate, such as later Zoroastrianism and Manichaeism affirmed. Rather, the powers that oppose God are uniformly understood to be created by God. They are not eternal, and they are not infinite. Hence, while they can and do generally oppose God and wreak destruction throughout the cosmos, they never pose a threat of overthrowing God."* Gregory A. Boyd, God At War (Downer's Grove: Intervarsity Press, 1997), p. 284.

[2] The word *"dimension"* is defined by the American Heritage Science Dictionary (www.dictionary.com) as *"any one of the three physical or spatial properties of length, area, and volume. In geometry, a point is said to have zero dimension; a figure having only length, such as a line, has one dimension; a plane or surface, two dimensions; and a figure having volume, three dimensions. The fourth dimension is often*

now discovering and trying to explore. Still, these other interdimensional forces and beings have sometimes manifested themselves in our three dimensional experience of reality. In fact, all of the major religions of the world (Christianity, Roman Catholicism, Islam, Hinduism, Buddhism, New Age, Occult, etc.) believe that these highly skilled, powerful, wise, and illuminated beings for better or worse either manipulate, control, or influence the world and world events.

The Battle Throughout The Ages

For example, in Psalm 82, the author Asaph inspired by the Spirit of God asks how long the *"gods"* in charge of administrating justice and overseeing the world affairs are going to rule and administrate by injustice and corruption. The Hebrew word translated *gods* is *Elohim*, literally, *"strong ones,"* which is the most common name for God – though it also can refer to false gods and demonic beings.

Psalm 82:1-2 *God stands in the congregation of the mighty; He judges among the gods. How long will you judge unjustly, and show partiality to the wicked?*

People throughout the ages have experienced these beings and often worshipped them as "gods," building temples to worship and exalt them. From the beginning of time, many people in every country, tribe, culture, during every time period of world history, have claimed to have seen and even interacted with these beings. Just as human beings, some of the beings appear to be kind and gracious, while others are malevolent and violent bent on destruction. In his book, *God at War*, Gregory A. Boyd

---

said to be time, as in the theory of General Relativity. Higher dimensions can be dealt with mathematically but cannot be represented visually." We all live in one *"dimension"* and we know that we don't really know where heaven is. It is some other realm or reality that is "other-worldly" and is "another plane or reality" closely connected but still separated from ours, and therefore I have chosen to use the word "dimension" often in this book to describe the "spiritual realm" referred to as "heavenly places" in the New Testament Scriptures.

notes,

> The Bible from beginning to end presupposes spiritual beings exist 'between' humanity and God and whose behavior significantly affects the human existence, for better or for worse. Indeed, just such a conception ... lies at the center of the biblical worldview. Furthermore, one is hard pressed to find any culture, prior to or contemporary with our own, that does not assume something like this perspective. From a cross cultural perspective, the insight that the cosmos is teeming with spiritual beings whose behavior can and does benefit or harm us is simply common sense. It is we modern Westerners who are the oddballs for thinking that the only free agents who influence other people are humans. [3]

In addition, the diversity of the appearance, shape, size, and teaching from these beings are as diverse as the earth's animal kingdom, ranging from beings looking exactly like human beings to downright bizarre-looking creatures and beasts. Some UFO-ologists and extraterrestrial religions have classified and labeled multiple races of alien *"gods"* or intelligent life forms with names like *Reptilians, Dracos, Serpents, Pleidians, Greys, Annunaki, Lyrans,* [4] and others from other locations and dimensions in the multiverse [5] we live in. [6] Below is one account of some of the warrior-beings described in our ancient Hebrew Scriptures:

2 Kings 6:15-18 *And when the servant of the man of God arose early and went out, there was an army, surrounding*

---

[3] Boyd, p. 11.

[4] Chuck Missler and Mark Eastman, *Alien Encounters: The Secret Behind the UFO Phenomenon* (Coeur d'Alene, ID: Koinonia House, 1997), pp. 299-301. I would recommend to the readers to read Missler and Eastman's whole book for a very biblical, scholarly, and scientific discussion on the *"alien phenomenon"* from a Biblical perspective.

[5] I am using the term *multi-verse* to describe the universe with layer upon layer of dimensions or "spheres" of reality; we live in one "sphere" or "plane" of that reality)

[6] There are many scientists within the field of physics and quantum physics who believe is such things. For example, see J.D. Barrow, P.C.W. Davies, & C.L. Harper eds., Cambridge University Press (2003), and *Parallel Universes*. Max Tegmark; Dept. of Physics, Univ. of Pennsylvania, (January 23 2003). http://space.mit.edu/home/tegmark/multiverse.pdf.

the city with horses and chariots. And his servant said to him, "Alas, my master! What shall we do?" So he answered, "Do not fear, for those who are with us are more than those who are with them." And Elisha prayed, and said, "LORD, I pray, open his eyes that he may see." Then the LORD opened the eyes of the young man, and he saw. And behold, the mountain was full of horses and chariots of fire all around Elisha. So when the Syrians came down to him, Elisha prayed to the LORD, and said, "Strike this people, I pray, with blindness." And He struck them with blindness according to the word of Elisha.

This is one of many examples in Scripture where a person sees or experiences spiritual military forces involved in overseeing and interacting in human affairs. The question that I want to discuss here is NOT whether or not supernatural beings with divine power and wisdom exist. That fact is *presupposed* by the Bible as well as by most other religions around the world. However, the difficult thing we encounter is that these beings are referred to as "angels," a term that simply means messenger. Further, we as twenty-first century readers of Scripture read accounts of these "angelic" beings which were seen and described for us by men and women who lived thousands of years ago in agrarian societies with no concept of technology which is now commonplace to us. Therefore, the descriptions of these beings or "gods" is vague and described in ways that seems almost cartoonish or like a fairy tale to modern readers. The challenge this creates for modern students of the Bible is to perceive angels, demons, and God in an almost mythological way, yet our Bibles that we love and cherish teach the exact opposite!

Do We See What God Sees?

You don't believe me? What would happen in your local church today if three eight-foot-tall angelic beings, with shields, swords, glowing luminescent white hair, and eyes of red hot fire manifested on your stage behind the preacher, while several large, reptile like, demonic beings stood in the aisles and hissed at the people in the church? How would you or your fellow brothers and sisters in Christ respond? I'm positive that the common reaction would be paralyzed fear, shock, trauma, and inexpressible terror. Why? Don't Christians believe in angels and demons? Don't the pastors, elders, deacons, Sunday school teachers, and small group leaders teach that demons and angels are real?

First of all, most of us for some reason understand angels and demons to be cookie-cutter type beings: all demons are the same (dark, hooded, faceless beings) with a grim-reaper like appearance. Likewise, all "good" angels have the appearance of a caucasian white man, dressed in white, short blond curly hair, with a kind of glow – gentle, loving, and soft, with a bright warm smile. I'm afraid the Bible doesn't paint such a picture. In fact, the very angels who hover above God's throne day and night are very bizarre in appearance and beastly looking ... they appear rather terrifying, if you ask me. One looks bird-like in his face, one looks like a lion or large cat-like being in face and body characteristics, one like a bull, and one like a man. Each being is covered with eye balls. That might not fit well with your perception of the appearance of angels, but it is what the Bible says (see Revelation 4:5-11 for more details). Even more, some say Lucifer was probably one of the most magnificent angels of God's creation. But, if the Bible is to be taken literally, he is described as having a dragon, reptilian, or serpent type of appearance. Jesus referred to evil spirits as *"serpents and scorpions"* in Luke 10:19.

What is interesting about the above scenario is that most people understand the above description to be ridiculous. They see it as an unrealistic, hypothetical situation concocted by someone with an uneducated and delusional imagination. They would never believe someone who said that they saw something like that happening in a church service. That person would be labeled crazy and dangerous by "the normal people." Ironically, the so-called "normal people" will then open their Bible to 2 Kings 6:15-18 and read about Elisha with awe and wonder and believe every *jot and tittle* as the inspired Word of God. See my point? Am I saying that we should walk around believing every person who says they "see things?" Should we spend our time trying to open up our spiritual eyes to be able to see into the spiritual realm? Absolutely not. If God wants you to see angels, He'll let you seem them. If not, we ought not be concerned with such gifts and abilities. Usually, the individuals who are able to see into other dimensions have a hard time dealing with reality and actually view their ability as more of a curse than a gift.

The response of the main-line, status-quo church to the supernatural realm is very disturbing. We leave the supernatural realm to something that is talked about in the Bible. As long as we only *read* about the spiritual realm, angels, demons, cosmic warfare, and the powers and technologies associated with the other realms, then everything is fine and dandy. Meanwhile, our entire world-view, belief system, and moral values about sin and righteousness are based upon the supernatural realm. *Our constructs are supposed to be based on the supernatural,* but when it comes down to daily life, we don't really seem to believe that the supernatural realm actually intersects into our lives, families, or homes.

Spiritual Battle and the Kingdom of God

What does all of this have to do with the Kingdom of God? Everything! We have already seen that humanity and planet earth are smack dab in the middle of a massive cosmic confrontation and convergence unlike ever before. The grand finale is just beyond the horizon and fast approaching. Even more, this *"multi-verse"* we live in is filled with hundreds of millions of supernatural beings fighting against each other. They are organized in extremely complex rankings, orders, and factions. The beings who belong to the *"darkness"* are led by one of God's created Cherubim beings, the most brilliant and illuminated of God's created beings: Lucifer.

According to Donald Grey Barnhouse, Lucifer was possibly, at his height, the *top administrator* over God's entire creation (all realms, all spheres, all places). Essentially, underneath the Godhead, the "morning star" and "light bearer" (Lucifer) was "number two" in God's cosmic kingdom. He was created and ordained to be God's vice-regent to rule and oversee all things. However, somewhere along the way, pride and lust for power developed in Lucifer's heart. Then, he actually rebelled against the Creator, *Yahweh* (the most holy and revered name we speak only in honor and praise), in the most outrageous act of rebellion and treachery of all time. He desired to usurp God's control, reign, and glory. His plan was to create his own kingdom and to be "number one." Before his rebellion, there was no sin or evil in God's Kingdom. God's Kingdom was based upon love, justice, holiness, beauty, truth, and perfection. There was only one will and one agenda – the will, rules, and agenda of our eternal Creator and God. Everything was in perfect harmony, balance, and God's kingdom functioned with absolute glory and perfection as it was always intended to operate.

When Lucifer (*Satan, the adversary*) rebelled, he managed to lead a sizeable portion of God's created angelic beings (possibly entire races of angelic beings) and species [7] to join his futile and temporary attempt to be independent of God's will. What Satan did accomplish was to create a new agenda and will opposing

---

[7] Using the word "species" to describe a particular type of angel may seem odd to you. However, the word species (again see www.dictionary.com) can be defined as *"a class of individuals having some common characteristics or qualities; distinct sort or kind."* In Scripture we see different types of angels (seraphim, cherubim, etc.) We also see fallen angels (or demons) described in animalistic ways – such as three "frog-like" spirits in the book of Revelation. Therefore just taking the Bible literally, it seems that there are a variety of types or groups of angelic *beings "of a similar kind"* and therefore I have chosen to the word *"species,"* not to be weird or different, but because the word itself defines well the thought I'm trying to convey.

God's will and agenda. However, unlike God's everlasting Kingdom of Light which transcends time and space, Satan's kingdom is temporary. It has a beginning and an end. In essence, in the span of eternity, his kingdom will be but a tiny parenthesis in the infinite timeline. His ignorant and arrogant attempt to take control and usurp the throne of the Most High God is only being allowed by the infinite and eternal God – not because God has lost His grip and is in a serious and nervous effort against a formidable enemy. HARDLY! God created all things by the mere thought and word of His Being. He could speak a few words and all of His opponents would cease to exist in a nanosecond. Instead, God has given His children free-will. He did not create a bunch of mindless, unthinking robots incapable of love, feeling and decision-making.

Therefore, God allowed Lucifer's rebellion to play out to the very end as an object lesson to the entire heavenly (and earthly) community to prove once for all that HE IS GOD, HE IS CREATOR. HIS KINGDOM, HIS WILL, HIS AGENDA, HIS WAYS, HIS RULES, WILL NEVER END, AND HE HIMSELF ALONE IS WORTHY OF GLORY, HONOR, AND PRAISE. Amen!

Are You Shocked into Reality Yet?

There was a time when people would have labeled me a crazed and obsessed conspiracy theorist who is stuck on demonology and miracles or UFOs. Nothing could be further from the truth! I challenge you to simply open up your mind to **take the truth revealed in the Scripture** (which is inspired, infallible, and inerrant), and understand it from a new paradigm. We must get rid of the *disconnect* that exists between "*our reality*" and the *Bible*. Newsflash: the Bible is historical reality … all of it. We are still living in the same world, surrounded by the same forces that were at work during the days of the Bible characters! We must wake up!

Furthermore, my goal is to awaken your senses to the *actuality* and *reality* of the Bible. It is not a cartoon, mythology, or fairy-tale story. It is not a nice novel to read next to the fireplace on a rainy day. It contains a story, a real historical story. It makes sense. It is the story of our ancestors on this earth and it answers the questions that we all want answered: *"who, what, when, where, why, and how?"* Everyone is asking, *"What in the world is going on and where are we headed as a global community? Is there any hope for mankind?"* The answer is that God is in complete control. We have a sure and solid hope. Our hope is one of the best kept secrets in the world. It is the hope of eternal glory, everlasting life, everlasting prosperity, and godliness, in a perfected world and universe living in perfect harmony in God's eternal Kingdom. And the beautiful thing is - it's free.

There is no monetary cost to be part of this Kingdom – God simply requires you to put your faith in the shed blood of Yeshua (Jesus Christ) of Nazareth, believing that He died and was resurrected back to life. He is still alive and well, now in authority over all realities at the right hand of God. Jesus Christ is Messiah and the Lord of the world. The time is now! It is such a beautiful Kingdom and system to be a part of. It just makes sense.

I'd like to warn you: I'm a little crazy, a little smart, and a little fun all at the same time – so sit back, relax, and enjoy the ride because when we're done, you're going to have a lifetime of work to do!

See you in the Kingdom!

Questions for Reflection and Response:

- What if it's all true? What difference does the reality of angels and demons make in your everyday life?

- How does the on-going spiritual battle affect your understanding of the mission of the Kingdom of God?

- What new perspective does the reality of spiritual warfare (all around you everyday) place in your personal life and calling?

Section One

Understanding the Kingdom

Chapter One

The King and the Kingdom

Introduction

Jesus talked a lot about the Kingdom. The message that He preached was inundated with Kingdom references. Over sixty times in the Gospels, He talked about *"the Kingdom of heaven being at hand," "entering the Kingdom,"* and *"Your Kingdom come."* His stories (parables) often began with the phrase, *"The Kingdom of God is like …"* Yet the Kingdom of God is a foreign concept to many Christians. We hear much about the Gospel, and a lot about the mission of the Church. But the Kingdom? Not so much. As a result, many are clueless about what the Kingdom of God even means, while others have wrong or unbiblical understandings about what the Kingdom really is.

Understanding the Kingdom is over-complicated by some while over-simplified by others. Growing up in the church, going through seminary, and reading books as a pastor, I have often heard the common phrase that *"the Kingdom of God simply refers to God's rule in your heart."* I also have heard many times that the Kingdom of God is real but it has not yet come in its fullest extent, that it is *"now, but not yet."* That is, God's Kingdom which is alive and well in heaven, promised to the people of Israel for a millennia, will be established in Jerusalem when the Lord Jesus returns to earth in bodily form and sets up a theocratic world government which will be administered from His royal throne in Jerusalem. Though Christians disagree of the timing, the nature, and the manner in which He comes, all Christian's nonetheless believe that He is coming in the future to setup His literal Kingdom on the earth. [8]

The Gospel and the Kingdom

Though both of these concepts are correct, they have not had a major impact or influence on my everyday thinking until recently. In addition, my concept of the Gospel and the Kingdom of God for many years were never closely connected. For example, I viewed the Gospel as the good news of Jesus Christ coming from heaven, shedding His blood for the sins of the world, dying, being buried, and resurrecting. Anyone who put his faith in Jesus Christ, His shed blood, death, burial, and resurrection will be saved ... period. To most people, that is the message of the Gospel. Ask anyone in an evangelical church in America what the Gospel is, they will likely say the good news of Jesus Christ, involving Jesus' sacrifice for mankind on the cross so that people can be saved from death and hell.

In essence, we have knowingly or unknowingly divorced *the Gospel message* from the *Kingdom of God*. However, in Jesus' teaching, the proclamation of the Kingdom of God was intricately connected and inseparable from the Gospel of salvation. The blood of God's Son was required for the forgiveness of our sins and the cross, resulting in the death of Jesus Christ, was required to deal with the curse of sin itself. *Essentially, to be born again (or "saved") was to enter the Kingdom of God and to enter the*

---

[8] Many covenant/reformed leaders may take exception at this statement, as if I'm implying Christ is not already reigning on the earth now through His Church. Is Jesus reigning now over all human and cosmic rulers, authorities, principalities, and powers? Of, course! Just look at Matthew 28:18 for proof. However, all of us would agree that righteousness is not overpowering evil in the earth at this time, nor has it appeared that way since the ascension and exaltation of Christ. Clearly, there is an event coming in the future (or near future) when Christ Jesus is going to break into earth, in our reality in real-time, and topple the human and spiritual forces of darkness and continue His reign and rule on earth!

Kingdom of God was equivalent to receiving salvation and new life. Thus, the Gospel is not only about "being forgiven of your sins and being justified (declared *"not guilty"*) before the Lord."

The Gospel is the total package. The Gospel is the good news of Jesus Christ and His salvation. Salvation from what? Salvation from sin, death, condemnation, *and* the kingdom of darkness! Salvation thrusts all of its initiates into a new realm of reality. Salvation and spiritual rebirth enter us into God's Kingdom of light and power and lead us into a new way of thinking and living. Thus, Jesus not only proclaimed His ability to forgive people of their sins, He preached that the Kingdom of God was at hand. Look at the verses below and see what Jesus preached and proclaimed as a divine herald to the people of Israel and the world.

Matthew 4:17 *From that time Jesus began to preach and to say, "Repent, for the kingdom of heaven is at hand."*

Matthew 9:35 *Then Jesus went about all the cities and villages, teaching in their synagogues, preaching the gospel of the kingdom, and healing every sickness and every disease among the people.*

Mark 1:14-15 *Now after John was put in prison, Jesus came to Galilee, preaching the gospel of the kingdom of God, and saying, "The time is fulfilled, and the kingdom of God is at hand. Repent, and believe in the gospel."*

Luke 4:42-43 *Now when it was day, He departed and went into a deserted place. And the crowd sought Him and came to Him, and tried to keep Him from leaving them; but He said to them, "I must preach the kingdom of God to the other cities also, because for this purpose I have been sent."*

Luke 8:1 *Now it came to pass, afterward, that He went*

through every city and village, preaching and bringing the glad tidings of the kingdom of God.

Jesus' message was the Kingdom of God. As you begin to see this, you will notice all throughout the four Gospels (the books of Matthew, Mark, Luke, and John) Jesus' teaching and story-telling (the parables) often related to God's Kingdom: Kingdom values, Kingdom requirements, Kingdom truths, etc. The challenge we have as believers two thousand years later is that we don't pay much attention to the Kingdom of God. For most of us, the Kingdom is either neglected or remains a vague and abstract idea. It is not really important to our everyday lives. However, nothing could be farther from the truth. But before moving on, let us take a moment and think about what the Kingdom of God means. What did Jesus mean when He spoke about the Kingdom of God?

The King of the Kingdom

Jesus' birth was the birth of a King. Luke 1:32-33 records the angel's prophecy, *"He will be great, and will be called the Son of the Highest; and the Lord God will give Him the throne of His father David. And He will reign over the house of Jacob forever, and of His kingdom there will be no end."*

When John the Baptist appeared, he came preaching a message of repentance and preparation for the Kingdom. He stated, *"Repent, for the kingdom of heaven is at hand"* (Matthew 3:2). He was saying, *"Get ready, the King is about to show up."* Jesus' miracles, teaching, offering of forgiveness, and resurrection were a "breaking in" of God's sovereign rule into this dark, evil age.

The crucifixion of Jesus was perceived as the death of a king.

Mark 15:25-32 *Now it was the third hour, and they crucified Him. And the inscription of His accusation was written above:* **THE KING OF THE JEWS.** *With Him they also crucified two robbers, one on His right and the other on His left. So the Scripture was fulfilled which says, "And He was numbered with the transgressors." And those who passed by blasphemed Him, wagging their heads and saying, "Aha! You who destroy the temple and build it in three days, save Yourself, and come down from the cross!" Likewise the chief priests also, mocking among themselves with the scribes, said, "He saved others; Himself He cannot save. Let the Christ, the King of Israel, descend now from the cross, that we may see and believe." Even those who were crucified with Him reviled Him.*

Peter reminded his listeners at Pentecost that a descendent of David would occupy the King's throne forever, a promise that was fulfilled in the resurrection of Christ, a direct physical descendant of King David.

Acts 2:30-32 *Therefore, being a prophet, and knowing that God had sworn with an oath to him that of the fruit of his body, according to the flesh, He would raise up the Christ to sit on his throne, he, foreseeing this, spoke concerning the resurrection of the Christ, that His soul was not left in Hades, nor did His flesh see corruption. This Jesus God has raised up, of which we are all witnesses.*

When men and women come to Christ for salvation, they are *"delivered from the power of darkness and conveyed into the kingdom of the Son of His love"* (Colossians 1:13).

The ultimate fulfillment of the Kingdom will be when Jesus comes back to reign as King of Kings and Lord of Lords. When that day arrives, the will of God will be done throughout the earth just as it is now done in heaven.

Revelation 19:11-16 *Now I saw heaven opened, and behold, a white horse. And He who sat on him was called Faithful and True, and in righteousness He judges and makes war. His eyes were like a flame of fire, and on His head were many crowns. He had a name written that no one knew except Himself. He was clothed with a robe dipped in blood, and His name is called The Word of God. And the armies in heaven, clothed in fine linen, white and clean, followed Him on white horses. Now out of His mouth goes a sharp sword, that with it He should strike the nations. And He Himself will rule them with a rod of iron. He Himself treads the winepress of the fierceness and wrath of Almighty God. And He has on His robe and on His thigh a name written: KING OF KINGS AND LORD OF LORDS.*

The Message of the Kingdom

As part of their training, Jesus sent the twelve out *"preaching the kingdom of God"* (Luke 9:1-2). The good news of the Gospel was to be proclaimed to the whole world. Extending the Kingdom of God to the ends of the earth was to be their major preoccupation.

Jesus also instructed the disciples to pray, *"Your kingdom come, Your will be done on earth as it is in heaven"* (Matthew 6:10). The throne room of heaven is filled with the light and glory of God. Out from God's throne come flashes of lightning and rolling thunder while brilliant beings hover around His throne, each with six wings, three of them animal like in appearance (Revelation 4). While hovering and flying without effort, they cry out *"Holy, Holy, Holy is the Lord God Almighty!"* The ultimate hope in the pages of the Bible is that one day all the people on earth, the called out ones, will praise God with the same passion and fervency as the angels praise God in heaven right now as we speak.

1 Chronicles 16:31-34 *Let the heavens rejoice, and let the earth be glad; and let them say among the nations, "The LORD reigns." Let the sea roar, and all its fullness; let the field rejoice, and all that is in it. Then the trees of the woods shall rejoice before the LORD, for He is coming to judge the earth. Oh, give thanks to the LORD, for He is good! For His mercy endures forever.*

One day *"every knee shall bow and every tongue confess that Jesus is Lord"* (Philippians 2:9-10). Even now, we long for that day and pray … *"Come! Come quickly, Lord Jesus!"*

Questions for Reflection and Response:

- In what ways were you made for a kingdom? In what ways does the story of the Kingdom answer all the questions you've ever had?

- Why is it so hard to submit to a king? What should you know about the New King to whom you belong that should cause you to trust Him, submit to Him, and spread His message?

Chapter Two

Anticipation of the Kingdom: Blessed to Be a Blessing

Psalms 89:5-11 *And the heavens will praise Your wonders, O LORD; Your faithfulness also in the assembly of the saints. For who in the heavens can be compared to the LORD? Who among the sons of the mighty can be likened to the LORD? God is greatly to be feared in the assembly of the saints, and to be held in reverence by all those around Him. O LORD God of hosts, who is mighty like You, O LORD? Your faithfulness also surrounds You. You rule the raging of the sea; when its waves rise, You still them. You have broken Rahab in pieces, as one who is slain; You have scattered Your enemies with Your mighty arm.* **The heavens are Yours, the earth also is Yours; the world and all its fullness, You have founded them.**

The concept of the Kingdom of God did not originate with Jesus and His apostles. As seen in the above passage, the ancient Israelites understood that the God of Israel, the Lord of the armies of heaven, was the creator and ruler of all things. Hebrews 11:3 states "*By faith we understand that the worlds were framed by the word of God, so that the things which are seen were not made of things which are visible.*"

So before moving right to Jesus, we need to get a little bit of *perspective* and *context* in order to understand Jesus and His message about the Kingdom of God from an Israelite's point of view. After all, Jesus was Jewish and was born in Israel! Many people in America seem to think of Jesus as an American and a Republican. Not exactly! We must relate to Jesus according to who He actually was, where He came from, and what He was about. Jesus' life and message fit into a cohesive story, plot, and message from *God's greater story*, which is really what we call *history*.

The Old Testament lays the foundation for examining Jesus' message and revelation about the Kingdom of God. In this chapter and the next, we will take a super fast-forward synopsis through the Old Testament to give you a snap-shot of *how* the nation of Israel came to be, *why* the nation of Israel came to be, and then tell you what in the world that has to do with Jesus, the Kingdom of God, and you in the 21st Century!

A Covenant of Promise

After God destroyed the world with water and restored mankind on the earth through Noah, many generations passed by. Mankind began to spread about the earth, build cities and multiply. But just as in the beginning, people strayed away from their Creator to worship other idols and gods and created things. Meanwhile, nations were developing and expanding on the earth. It was at that point that God decided to break into human history and create His own nation of people. He would use this group of people to be a model for the rest of the world. This nation would be instructed directly by the Most High God of the Universe and would do things in their nation on the earth the way God had things organized and done in heaven. He would give the nation a law, a temple, an offering system, and He would be their God. He would even live among them in a specialized temple. Then in the future, the Creator would eventually send a promised *"Messiah"* or *"Anointed One"* to be christened as the Eternal King and ruler of the nation of people on earth for all time. His name was Yeshua (Jesus the Christ), but we'll get to Him later!

God chose to start His nation through a man named Abram. Abram was from what is now modern day Iraq. Contrary to most people's understanding, Abram was not a *Jew*, because there was no such thing yet! There was no nation of Israel at all. Abram seems to have been a fairly wealthy man from Ur of Chaldea. Before he met the Most High God face-to-face, Abram most likely worshipped the moon god *Sin*. He was what we would nowadays call a pagan. He did not know about the Most High God Yahweh. However, one day, Abram had an other-worldly experience like few people have ever experienced. Abram encountered the Most High God of the Universe who made this incredible promise to him:

> **Genesis 12:1-7** *Now the LORD had said to Abram: "Get out of your country, from your family and from your father's house, to a land that I will show you. I will make you a great nation; I will bless you and make your name great; and you shall be a blessing. I will bless those who bless you, and I will curse him who curses you; and in you all the families of the earth shall be blessed." So Abram departed as the LORD had spoken to him, and Lot went with him. And Abram was seventy-five years old when he departed from Haran. Then Abram took Sarai his wife and Lot his brother's son, and all their possessions that they had gathered, and the people whom they had acquired in Haran, and they departed to go to the land of Canaan. So they came to the land of Canaan. Abram passed through the land to the place of Shechem, as far as the terebinth tree of Moreh. And the Canaanites were then in the land. Then the LORD appeared to Abram and said, "To your descendants I will give this land." And there he built an altar to the LORD, who had appeared to him.*

This passage is perhaps the most critical, foundational section of the Old Testament. Yahweh, the covenant-keeping God, makes a one-sided promise to Abram (later named Abraham), whose fulfillment extends throughout the rest of the Bible. This promise, or covenant, is completely dependent on God to fulfill – it does not depend on Abram's obedience but is completely based on God's faithfulness. On that day the LORD made a covenant with Abram, saying, *"To your offspring I give this land, from the river of Egypt to the great river, the river Euphrates"* (Genesis 15:18). As the covenant promise was made, animal sacrifices were laid out and *"a smoking fire pot and a flaming torch passed between these pieces"* (15:17). These items, representing God's very presence, passed through the sacrifices alone – symbolizing a commitment on God's part that He would forever keep His promise to Abraham and his descendants.

From the beginning, Abraham knew that this was not a covenant to be selfishly kept to himself. He had been *"blessed to be a blessing."* God was going to do something to bless all the peoples of the earth. It would start with Abraham – but it wouldn't end there. The focus was always outward, always missional.

Though he didn't know it, and many generations after Abraham didn't know it, God seems to be foreshadowing in His covenant promise to Abraham that His original intention and plan was not to save just one race of people on earth, but rather to use one race of people to gather many people out of every nation, race, ethnicity, and people groups, to become a multi-ethnic beautiful mosaic collective nation of people from all over the earth. God was ultimately going to take a hopelessly divided, tribal-like species, and bring all of them together into one new nation composed of a new type of man – regenerated, renewed, and perfected. When you read the Bible as a single book, you'll see this beautiful story unfold. We as followers of Jesus Christ are still involved in the same story. It's not over yet!

If you are going to be the head of a great nation, you have

to start having children. Abram was seventy-five years old – and childless – when God first appeared to him. However, God told him *"Do not be afraid, Abram. I am your shield, your exceedingly great reward"* (15:1). Yahweh promised Abram millions of descendants, as many as the stars in the heavens, *"and Abraham believed the Lord, and He counted it to him as righteousness"* (15:4-6).

A Son of Provision

God promised … Abraham believed … and it was a done-deal. Except for the fact that he had to wait another twenty-some years before Isaac was born. But after years and years of waiting, Abraham was eventually given God's *child of promise*. Through the experiences of his life, Abraham learned to trust God with everything – even to the point where he was willing to sacrifice Isaac on Mount Moriah, the spot where Jerusalem would later be built, and possibly the location where Jesus would ultimately be sacrificed. The writer to the Hebrews records Abraham's reasoning:

> **Hebrews 11:17-19** *By faith Abraham, when he was tested, offered up Isaac, and he who had received the promises offered up his only begotten son, of whom it was said, "In Isaac your seed shall be called," concluding that God was able to raise him up, even from the dead, from which he also received him in a figurative sense.*

The child of blessing was given back to Abraham … and the lineage continued. Isaac later had twin sons, Jacob and Esau. *As Jacob began to have children, we see the birth of a nation.* Esau was the older twin brother because he came out of the womb first, which meant by custom and tradition, He was the *"first-born son,"* and thus as his birthright, he would continue on the covenant promises from God…that is, he and his offspring, like Abraham and Isaac, would be set apart as God's covenant people. His descendants should be the people of God with land and blessing as promised Abraham and his father Isaac. However, just as God sovereignly picked and "elected" Abram out of the nations to create his own nation, God chose the younger brother Jacob to be the Patriarch and possessor of God's covenant promise instead of Esau. Paul commented on this interesting story in Romans 9:10-13:

> *And not only this, but when Rebecca also had conceived by one man, even by our father Isaac (for the children not yet being born, nor having done any good or evil, that the purpose of God according to election might stand, not of works but of Him who calls), it was said to her, 'the older shave serve the younger.' As it is written, 'Jacob I have loved, but Esau I have hated.'*

Thus, as Jacob began to have children, we begin to see the birth of a nation. Without getting into all of the details and the story, you must know that it was Jacob, who, after a sleepless night on the eve of meeting his brother Esau, wrestled with the "angel of the Lord" face to face, hand to hand, all night long (Genesis 32:24-30). Subsequently, God gave Jacob a new name: Israel (Genesis 32:28). Jacob, now re-named Israel, in time had twelve sons, each son becoming the patriarch of one of the twelve tribes (families/clans) which comprised the nation of Israel. After the years passed, Jacob and his sons, who lived in the land of Canaan, what is now called Israel (including parts of Palestine, Jordan and Syria) , were forced to migrate down to Egypt as a result of a severe drought in the land of Canaan. Thankfully, despite the treachery and betrayal of Jacob's sons towards their younger brother Joseph, God saved his covenant people (the nation of Israel) from extinction.

Thus, Joseph is a key figure in the over-arching story of Israel and in order to understand the roots of Israel and the roots of your faith in Jesus Christ today, you need to know a little bit about Joseph.

A Demonstration of Providence

Early in his life, Joseph made the mistake of telling his brothers about his destiny which God had revealed to him in one of his dreams. Joseph told his brothers that one day his entire family (including mother and father) would bow down to him. This was absurd and evil in the minds of his brothers. Joseph was perceived as arrogant, disrespectful and dangerous. They felt Joseph was a threat and an annoyance to the family. Also, they couldn't understand why their father liked Joseph so much. Therefore, while the young men were away from home one day working, they ganged up on Joseph to kill him. But the eldest of the brothers, Reuben, stepped in and stopped them, telling them to just push him down into a large hole in the ground from which Joseph couldn't get out (see Genesis 37:18-36).

After pushing Joseph into the hole, the brothers noticed a caravan of slave traders coming down the road and decided to sell Joseph to some merchants/slave traders. Joseph was then taken down to Egypt. Throughout the following years, Joseph, even though he was a slave, a prisoner, the object of treachery/abuse and deception, somehow always had God's protection from the plots of people around him. God was with Joseph and made Joseph successful in everything he did. He was the golden child of his day. Joseph was obviously a very sharp and brilliant man that stood head and shoulders above his fellow workers in intelligence, class and savvy. He was a diamond in the rough. God handpicked him from the beginning to be a sign and wonder to the world for the rest of history. Joseph was so very special and yet so very despised by others.

Joseph knew who he was and what he was to be according

to the revelation God had shown to him as a child. But after he was betrayed and sold into slavery, he must have thought that his dream was just his own imagination. How was he to know whether or not the dream was his own sub-conscious thinking or if it was God showing him his future? His life didn't match his dream, so he must be crazy.

That would be logical according to worldly or carnal thinking. But Joseph remained faithful to God. Genesis tells the story of Joseph being a man of high morals and faith despite his circumstances. He was a deeply spiritual man who knew God and prayed to God, even though his dreams had never come true. Nothing made sense about his life, but he somehow kept trusting God's plan and purposes. When Potiphar's wife tried over and over to seduce him, Joseph resisted. That shows a lot about Joseph's character.

In the end, Joseph became the most respected leader in Egypt, second only to Pharaoh. How extraordinary is that? How insane is that? Joseph rose from slavery to royalty among a foreign people group. That is the power of God to turn a mess into a miracle. God can work any situation out for His own glory and His own purpose and His own story…even using the evil motives, sins, plots, and schemes of jealous and perverse people to do it. God does the impossible with Joseph.

Once Joseph was a ruler in Egypt, God sent a drought to Canaan. Joseph, knowing by divine revelation that the drought was coming, made preparations to store food and grain to provide for the people in Egypt. The drought also forced Joseph's long-lost family to come to Egypt to get food. In His providence, God raised Joseph up to a position of royalty so that the Israelites would be protected and nourished and grown into a healthy body of people and a great nation. He allowed the evil and treachery in Joseph's life only to end up being the greatest blessing and joy for Joseph for the rest of eternity. In fact, Joseph later responded to his brothers, *"But as for you, you meant evil against me; but God meant it for good, in order to bring it about as it is this day, to save many people alive"* (Genesis 50:20).

Questions for Reflection and Response:

- In the midst of building a great nation, God developed Abraham's faith. How is He developing your faith?

- How has God used the circumstances of your life to be a blessing and provide for others?

Anticipation of the Kingdom: Blessed to Be a Blessing

Chapter Three

Extension of the Kingdom: Creating a Nation of Priests

Exodus 19:5-8 *Now therefore, if you will indeed obey My voice and keep My covenant, then you shall be a special treasure to Me above all people; for all the earth is Mine. And* **you shall be to Me a kingdom of priests and a holy nation.'** *These are the words which you shall speak to the children of Israel." So Moses came and called for the elders of the people, and laid before them all these words which the LORD commanded him. Then all the people answered together and said, "All that the LORD has spoken we will do." So Moses brought back the words of the people to the LORD.*

Revelation 5:9-10 *And they sang a new song, saying: "You are worthy to take the scroll, and to open its seals; for You were slain,* **and have redeemed us to God by Your blood out of every tribe and tongue and people and nation, and have made us kings and priests to our God;** *and we shall reign on the earth."*

Joseph died while in Egypt. More than four hundred years passed by and Jacob's small family had now turned into a huge clan of people numbering more than six hundred thousand men. At some point, the government of Egypt changed and the new leadership had no ties to Joseph. They didn't know or care about

Extension of the Kingdom: Creating a Nation of Priests

Israel's story. They saw this huge clan of strong people as a threat, so they took them hostage and by force made *them "prisoners without bars"* in the land they were living. The Pharaoh of Egypt forced them to do hard labor and build up the cities and do work for the Egyptian government. The people of Israel submitted to the oppressive and brutal Egyptian government for years. It was the accepted way of life, the status quo. It was the way things had always been for these people ... and then God stepped into a man's life named Moses.

A Man Torn Between Two Cultures

Exodus is the second book of the Torah and it is a story about God, Moses, and the people of Israel. Moses was a Jewish boy born in Egypt. He was born into a hostile, scary, oppressive life to a people group called the Israelites who had no land of their own. Pharaoh was enacting infanticide against the male children of the Israelites so that he could keep the people oppressed with no chance of raising up strong men that may try to buck the system and rebel. It was smart on Pharaoh's part – though evil to the very core and beyond horrific to the mothers and fathers living in Israel. Can you imagine living that way?

The story of Moses' birth is very familiar. He was hidden in a special basket and placed in a river to float downstream. Providentially, Pharaoh's daughter was bathing down by the river and saw Moses in the basket and took him home.

Moses was raised up in an Egyptian home with Egyptian culture and customs. He was trained in Egyptian religion, foods, cultures, social norms, and slang. As a youth he played the games the other Egyptian boys played. He was raised in the most cutting-edge and hi-tech country in the entire known world. But perhaps the most amazing fact was that Moses was raised as an Egyptian elite. The most powerful people in the world were his family. They were the affluent and connected in their society. Moses heard the old stories the men of Egypt told. He learned all about all the gods of Egypt and the afterlife and the secrets and mysteries of the universe.

Moses was born during a confusing time and had a very dysfunctional upbringing. Talk about an identity crisis: who was he supposed to be? Genetically, he knew he was an Israelite (a "Hebrew"). But culturally, he was Egyptian –trained and raised by Egyptians who were oppressing the Hebrews. His friends were probably racist towards the Hebrews; the Hebrews hated the Egyptians deeply – and as a result Moses was totally confused in the deepest part of his being. God saw Moses and loved him from the beginning and was going to use this confused and tormented young man to separate the Hebrews from the Egyptians.

Disastrous Choices

When Moses was a grown man, he was strong and tough. One day he saw one of his fellow Egyptian countrymen abusing a Hebrew. It stirred up a murderous anger and rage inside of Moses that he could not control. He went berserk, attacking his fellow Egyptian and murdering him in front of a few nearby Hebrews. He took the man's life – most likely a father, a brother, a husband, and son to a family who was going to be devastated at his death. Shocked and terrified at what he had done, Moses fled the scene, just as criminals on the street would today, with blood on his hands.

Moses was now a murderer. Witnesses had seen him do it. They knew who Moses was – didn't everyone know about the royal Hebrew-Egyptian man? He did the only thing he could do: he ran. He got out of town as fast as his Egyptian sandals would flap. Scared for his life, he knew he was a dead man if he got caught. I'm sure he spent many lonely nights crying and weeping and wondering why his life was so terrible. He moved on to a new land and people and settled down to simply live a normal life. He got married, had children, and fought with his in-laws.

God Invades the Normal

But one day, something extraordinary happened. Moses was walking in the desert, minding his own business, when he saw a bush that was on fire. Not unusual ... except the bush was not burned up. It stayed the same. Mind-boggling! Moses knew something was happening, and when he went closer, a voice spoke to him from the bush, calling him by name.

> **Exodus 3:4-10** *So when the LORD saw that he turned aside to look, God called to him from the midst of the bush and said, "Moses, Moses!" And he said, "Here I am." Then He said, "Do not draw near this place. Take your sandals off your feet, for the place where you stand is holy ground." Moreover He said, "I am the God of your father—the God of Abraham, the God of Isaac, and the God of Jacob." And Moses hid his face, for he was afraid to look upon God. And the LORD said: "I have surely seen the oppression of My people who are in Egypt, and have heard their cry because of their taskmasters, for I know their sorrows. So I have come down to deliver them out of the hand of the Egyptians, and to bring them up from that land to a good and large land, to a land flowing with milk and honey, to the place of the Canaanites and the Hittites and the Amorites and the Perizzites and the Hivites and the Jebusites. Now therefore, behold, the cry of the children of Israel has come to Me, and I have also seen the oppression with which the Egyptians oppress them. Come now, therefore, and I will send you to Pharaoh that you may bring My people, the children of Israel, out of Egypt."*

This was not an encounter with one of the impersonal Egyptian gods, but the true God who knew him by name. Moses was terrified. He was probably thinking, *"Why is the God of the Hebrews contacting me? How did He know where I was? Was He watching me? From where was He watching me? How is that even possible? Where does He live?"*

That day Moses experienced something almost no one on earth could say had ever happened to them: *he talked with God.* And God began to develop an actual relationship with Moses and made Himself known to him. It must have been beyond baffling. This was not a common thing. People probably thought he was crazy when he told them what had happened. His wife must have been perplexed. And we read this today like it's a nice story. But *it actually happened!* This is historical fact with an entire historical context.

On Mission with God

In the context of their discussion, Moses found out why God had communicated with him. God had chosen Moses to go back to Egypt, his homeland, and free the entire clan of Israelites – not only bringing them out of slavery, but bringing them back to their God.

What a story! Can you imagine being asked to do something like that? *"Hi, my name is Jesse and for years, this invisible God who created our entire reality has been coming to me and talking to me. And he is telling me to go to the President of the United States and tell him that the Creator God says 'Let My people go!'"*

Even with God speaking directly to him, Moses was borderline adamant about not going through with it. He came up with excuse after excuse. He was afraid; he felt inadequate; he couldn't imagine how in the world he would do it; he didn't have any relationships with the Israelites to lead them; it had been decades since he was in Egypt; most likely, he could never even get a meeting with the Pharaoh – and even if he did, would they still try to kill him for the murder he committed so many years back?

Moses knew God was talking to him, but even so, he was so freaked out that he wanted to get his brother Aaron to help him do the talking. In the end, God actually used Moses and Aaron to deliver the entire Israelite population out of the nation of Egypt single handedly with no weapons, no fighting, no money, no nothing. It is beyond miraculous! God raised up Moses, who marched back into his old stomping grounds and somehow got permission to go speak directly to the *top dog*, the PHAROAH, *the most powerful man in the world,* and demanded that He let the Hebrews go … all because their God said so.

From the record of Scripture, it seems that Pharaoh didn't even recognize or know about the Hebrews' God or even give it consideration. He had an entire religious worldview and pantheon of gods which he personally worshipped. He was immersed into the occult powers and realities of their powers far beyond any human's comprehension. Pharaoh was their representative on earth. Now Moses stood in front of him and said, *"The true God commands you and your gods* (that must be implied) *to let my people go!"* What an outrage! What a shock! What a down-right explosive thing to say in the quarters of the most powerful man in the world. Even more, Pharaoh was utilizing the Hebrews to expand and grow his empire. He had the sweetest deal in the world: free labor.

How did Pharaoh respond? He objected and insulted Moses and his God over and over again. Apparently he truly believed that his gods were more powerful than the God of Moses. However, the systematic and well-thought-out plagues designed and enacted by Yahweh were chosen to deconstruct and destroy everything the Egyptians believed about their gods and the powers theirs gods possessed. Without breaking a sweat or lifting a finger, God humiliated the most powerful nation and the most powerful known gods in all the world and universe through a confused Hebrew-Egyptian man named Moses. This was not just about Moses or Egypt. This was a sign to the entire world that God is *large and in charge* and *what God says, God does – plain and simple. Nothing is impossible with God!*

Moses quickly becomes a household name among all the Hebrews. An instant celebrity, he rises to the top of the food chain and becomes the instant leader of an entire nation of people who came to be known as Israel, a unique nation of people who lived their entire existence as forced laborers with no real land of their own to claim. Where were they supposed to go? What were they supposed to do? They were surrounded, with nowhere to go.

God ends up leading the people out of Egypt, through the Red Sea, into a barren wilderness to a mountain called Sinai. At Sinai, God made himself known to Moses directly, face to face, on a mountain. The entire nation of Israel saw God's glory and presence descend from the sky onto the top of the mountain. This spectacular divine Person, who could not be seen due to the blinding light came from 'somewhere' out of 'nowhere' into our world. They must have had a lot of questions: *"Where did this God come from?" "Are there other gods more powerful than Him?" "How is that possible? It doesn't make sense, but it just happened and it's real."*

A Place for God to Live

God's arrival and presence was bright and fiery, and loud like trumpets blasting. God commanded that no person or animal touch the entire mountain upon which He descended. He was to be totally set apart from these earth people. Moses was the only one allowed to speak with God. God gave Moses instructions about what to do and how to do it. He told Moses that He was going to live among the Hebrews – in this present reality, in the middle of their campsite. Moses was to construct a proper dwelling place called the Tabernacle. The Bible tells us that this tabernacle is an exact copy and design of the place that Yahweh lived in His abiding place in the sky (Hebrews 8:5). He showed Moses what it was supposed to look like – possibly through a vision, picture, hologram, or video/visual tour. Moses was shown everything exactly and thoroughly. He studied it and examined every little detail for many days. For all we know, God may have had a flat-screen TV to show Moses exactly what everything in the heavenly realm looked like so that Moses could copy it and re-create it in the earthly realm. God promised Moses to put His Spirit in some of the Israelites to give them special artistic and constructive abilities to work the crafts and designs needed to make the tabernacle just perfect. Moses wrote the entire blueprint, design, and parameters down. God was going to use the materials that the Israelites already had in their possession or what they could gather in the geographical area they were located.

Moses did exactly what God told him to do. He had the people gather and construct the Tabernacle just as God had described. God's presence dwelled with the people in the Tabernacle as they slowly journeyed through the wilderness for forty years ... almost a lifetime.

These things actually happened. It was real-life ... scientific, historical fact. God was giving to Moses and Israel the land that He originally told Abraham He would provide for Abraham's descendants. The only problem was that there were literally giants and terrifying warriors now living in the land. Pretty wild stuff! But according to the Bible, what we perceive as normal in the twenty-first century in regards to people, beings, parallel universes (other-worldly realms) or extraterrestrials (what we would now "consider" extraterrestrials at least), was not the same in Moses' day. In fact ancient Sumerian, Egyptian, and Babylonian mythologies and religious documents speak directly about such phenomena as if they were normal. Because these things have not happened for several thousand years, it has been forgotten and turned into comical myths for people to laugh at today. This may sound strange to the modern reader, but this particular aspect of Israel's story and the exodus to the Promised Land is very important to understand. It is part of the true miracle of Israel's "exodus" and entrance into the land of Canaan.

The Old Testament speaks of the *Nephilim* who were dwelling in the land of Canaan (already referenced in the days of Noah in Genesis 6:1-4, who just happened to have something to do with God's flooding and destroying the entire planet). These same *Nephilim (giants)* people were now conveniently located smack dab in the middle of land God promised to Abraham generations earlier! Talk about bad luck for Moses! First, he had to get the people out of Egypt only to lead them to their new "homeland" full of scary, barbaric, fierce and powerful giant people groups. To read about the "giants," refer to Numbers 13 (especially verses 27-33).[9] This is ironic, as the Muslim holy site, the "Dome of the Rock," is located on the original temple mount where God desired His temple to be built. History, like a silent witness, seems to repeat itself over and over.

God also gave Moses rules, regulations, procedures and laws that He wanted Moses and Israel to abide by. They were not going to be out-of-order like the other nations. He was going to make the Israelites do things His way, not like the way the Israelites had done while in Egypt. Obviously, the Israelites had been influenced by the Egyptians. The Hebrews were not religious or godly people. They had no reference point to know who God was and was not. They had no holy Scriptures

---
[9] See also: (NKJV) Genesis 6:4; Numbers 13:33; Deuteronomy 2:11; 2:20; 3:11; 3:13; Joshua 12:4; 13:12; Joshua 17:15

or commandments given to them yet. God was starting from scratch, washing the slate clean and telling Israel how to be a true nation and how to please the Most High God. They were a special nation. They were going to be a symbol to all the other nations and Kingdoms, modeling to the nations of the world how God intended humanity to exist and live on the earth. He gave them a law, a temple and a sacrificial system to atone for sins, and promised them that in the future He would send a "Messiah" or "Anointed One" to rule over His Kingdom directly.

But instead of considering this the most valuable and important privilege they could have ever imagined, the people grumbled and complained because they were tired, hungry, and living in a desert! Go figure?! Are we any different today?

Questions for Reflection and Response:

- How does the story of Moses encourage you? What do you learn about God's faithfulness through his story?

- How does God's deliverance of Israel out of Egypt and ultimately into the Promised Land demonstrate the Kingdom of God on Earth?

If you're interested in doing research on your own, the concept of the *Kingdom of God* can be found in certain key Old Testament passages like Psalm 2:1-12; 22:8; 47:1-9; 83:18; 103:19; 113:5; 145:11-13; 1 Chronicles 29:11; Daniel 4:3, 25-26; 5:21; and Obadiah 21. [10] As noted above, the main theme throughout the writings of the prophets in the OT is that Israel's God rules over a divine Kingdom and is therefore the legitimate King of Israel as well as the entire world. [11] Furthermore, there is a sense in the Old Testament that God's kingdom is both present and future. Yes, the prophets believed God was sovereign and in control of all things, but they also looked forward to a specific time when God would make it evident to the entire world that He is King of all. [12]

It is not clear in the Old Testament whether the hope for that earth shattering moment, when God's Kingdom would manifest into earthly reality, would be realized by the revival and restoration of a progeny of the ancient King David ruling in Jerusalem or whether it would be the invasion and manifestation of some kind of apocalyptic *heavenly* kingdom breaking into this present dimension (Daniel 7).[13]

While living in captivity in Babylon, the prophet Daniel prophesied that after a succession of multiple powerful world kingdoms there would come a supernatural kingdom which would smash the authority of all other kingdoms and would keep control: *"And in the days of these kings the God of heaven will set up a kingdom which shall never be destroyed; and the kingdom shall not be left to other people; it shall break in pieces and consume all these kingdoms, and it shall stand forever"*

---

[10] See also: Evans, W. & Coder, S.M., *The Great Doctrines of the Bible* (Electronic edition), Chicago: Moody Press, 1974, pp. 302-303; Zuck, R.B., *A Biblical Theology of the New Testament* (Electronic edition), Chicago: Moody Press, 1994), pp. 27, 202-205; Enns, P. P., *Moody Handbook of Theology* (Electronic edition), Chicago: Moody Press, 1989), p. 33.

[11] Donald Guthrie, *New Testament Theology* (Inter-Varsity Press, 1981), 410. Guthrie lists certain passages to prove this point: Exodus 15:18, Deuteronomy 33:5, Isaiah 43:15; Jeremiah 46:18.

[12] Ibid.

[13] Ibid.

(Daniel 2:44). Later, Daniel had a spectacular vision of the "*son of man*" coming with the "*clouds of heaven*" approaching the Ancient of Days seated on His glorious throne: "*Then to Him was given dominion and glory and a kingdom, that all peoples, nations, and languages should serve Him. His dominion is an everlasting dominion, which shall not pass away, and His kingdom the one which shall not be destroyed*" (Daniel 7:14)

Chapter Four

Inauguration of the Kingdom: Flesh and Blood

Isaiah 9:6-7 *For unto us a Child is born, unto us a Son is given; and the government will be upon His shoulder. And His name will be called Wonderful, Counselor, Mighty God, Everlasting Father, Prince of Peace. Of the increase of His government and peace there will be no end, upon the throne of David and over His kingdom, to order it and establish it with judgment and justice from that time forward, even forever. The zeal of the Lord of hosts will perform this.*

The history of Israel is disappointing. Over and over, they broke God's covenant. After Solomon's reign as king, the twelve tribes broke into two separate nations (ten forming the northern kingdom known as Israel, two forming the southern kingdom of Judah). Both nations were conquered and rebuilt. There were occasionally good kings in the southern kingdom, but for the most part, these leaders were far from God and led the people astray. [14] God raised up prophets to warn the nation of judgment, [15] but in most cases their message fell on deaf ears.

They were supposed to be unlike any nation in the world. But instead of being a light in the world and a witness of the glory

---
14 Their history is recorded in 1 – 2 Kings and 1 – 2 Chronicles.
15 In your Bible, these are the Old Testament books from Isaiah to Malachi.

of God to the nations, they became just like all the other nations around them. They were no different at all. They didn't make a difference at all.

But the Jews did have one thing going for them: they had the Scriptures. God had spoken to them – and He had promised them that one day, a Messiah – a Savior and King – would come and set them free and make them the people He wants them to be. This freedom was not simply a political freedom, but a spiritual freedom – setting them free *from themselves and their sin* – and setting them on a mission that would change the world and bring great glory and honor to God.

But after the prophet Malachi's ministry, God stopped sending prophets to the nation. Nothing. No Messiah, no deliverance, and very little hope. Until...

Jesus the Messiah Arrives

If you were a Jew in the first century, your major preoccupation was *survival*. Rome was in charge – and that meant you were, at the least, marginalized, and at the worst, persecuted. Every Sabbath you would faithfully attend Synagogue services, praying for Messiah to come. It is true that your concept of Messiah had devolved into a physical deliverer from Rome's oppression – but you longed for His coming nevertheless.

It was into this environment that John the Baptist appeared. Notice how Luke sets his ministry in the context of the harshness of Rome's rule: *"In the fifteenth year of the reign of Tiberius Caesar, Pontius Pilate being governor of Judea, and Herod being tetrarch of Galilee, and his brother Philip tetrarch of the region of Ituraea and Trachonitis, and Lysanias tetrarch of Abilene, during the high priesthood of Annas and Caiaphas, the word of God came to John the son of Zechariah in the wilderness"* (Luke 3:1-2).

This wild-man preacher had one goal: to prepare the way for the coming Messiah. But notice: it was not the outward preparations that mattered. It was all about heart-preparation.

Luke 3:3-9 *And he went into all the region around the Jordan, preaching a baptism of repentance for the remission of sins, as it is written in the book of the words of Isaiah the prophet, saying: "The voice of one crying in the wilderness: 'Prepare the way of the LORD; make His paths straight. Every valley shall be filled and every mountain and hill brought low; the crooked places shall be made straight and the rough ways smooth; and all flesh shall see the salvation of God.' "*

Then he said to the multitudes that came out to be baptized by him, "Brood of vipers! Who warned you to flee from the wrath to come? Therefore bear fruits worthy of repentance, and do not begin to say to yourselves, 'We have Abraham as our father.' For I say to you that God is able to raise up children to Abraham from these stones. And even now the ax is laid to the root of the trees. Therefore every tree which does not bear good fruit is cut down and thrown into the fire."

He became so popular that the crowds started wondering if John might be the promised Messiah. John quickly extinguished those thoughts by saying, *"I baptize you with water, but He who is mightier than I is coming, the strap of whose sandals I am not worthy to untie. He will baptize you with the Holy Spirit and fire. His winnowing fork is in His hand, to clear His threshing floor and to gather the wheat into His barn, but the chaff He will burn with unquenchable fire"* (Luke 3:16-17).

The King has finally arrived … and the people must be ready.

The Make Up of the Kingdom

What is the Kingdom like? How would its coming be announced? A world-renowned theologian and historian on Jewish culture in the first century, N. T. Wright, has written extensively on the historical Jesus and the Kingdom of God. In his book *The Original Jesus*, Wright tells us,

> *Jesus joined in with John's movement and bided His time. Then, when the authorities came for John, as they were bound to do sooner or later, Jesus took a deep breath and began his own independent movement. Now is the time, he said; the days of preparation are over. This is the moment when our God is at least becoming king. Jesus went through Galilee, village by village, telling people that the kingdom of God was happening now. Now, at last, Israel's oppression would be over. God would come home to save the people. Now, at last, with the world at its lowest point, evil would be defeated and justice would triumph. No wonder they followed Him. No wonder they hung on his words. He was telling them the story they wanted to hear, the story of justice and hope at last."* [16]

The New Testament, through the lips of Jesus Christ and His Apostles, heralds the realization and beginning of the Kingdom of God on earth which the Old Testament prophets spoke of and saw thousands of years earlier. However, the establishment and initiation of this Kingdom is not exactly what the people of Israel were looking for. At the time of Christ's entrance to the world, the Jewish people were living under the oppressive Roman government seeking liberation. They were waiting for their Messiah to come, to drive the Romans out of their land and setup a Theocratic Kingdom, the King's throne being in Jerusalem. Their Messiah and King would restore Israel's former glory and be recognized, loved, and admired by the entire world. Israel,

---
[16] N.T. Wright, *The Original Jesus: The Life and Vision of a Revolutionary,* (Grand Rapids: Wm. B. Eerdmans Publishing Co, 1996), p. 31.

particularly Jerusalem, would finally be that beautiful *"shining city on a hill"* which the Lord God had promised to His people so many years earlier.

Even after His resurrection, Jesus' disciples did not yet understand the nature of Jesus' Kingdom. They had a glimpse of the truth about the Kingdom but did not yet fully comprehend the "whole picture." For example, the book of Acts reveals that after Jesus' resurrection, He spent the next 40 days *"speaking of the things pertaining to the Kingdom of God"* (Acts 1:3). Regardless, the disciples did not yet fully comprehend everything that Jesus was trying to teach them, for they had not yet received the illuminating Spirit of God. *"Therefore, when they had come together, they asked Him, saying, "Lord, will You at this time restore the kingdom to Israel?" And He said to them, "It is not for you to know times or seasons which the Father has put in His own authority"* (Acts 1:7). Wright comments:

> … What was original about Jesus' version of this message? Well, as He told the story, He was also adjusting it in a number of ways. Justice and peace wouldn't come, as many had supposed, through military revolt against Rome. They wouldn't come through Israel simply having every aspiration endorsed and underwritten. Like the prophets of old, and like John the Baptizer himself, Jesus warned His contemporaries that when the Kingdom of God arrived it would be a double revolutionary event. Yes, it would overturn all the power structures of the world; but it would also overturn all the expectations about how that would happen…. [17]

Before leaving earth, Jesus taught His disciples how to pray: *"Our Father, Who art in heaven, hallowed be thy name. Thy Kingdom come, Thy will be done on earth as it is in heaven."* Later, Jesus told Pilate at the trial before His death: *"'My kingdom is not of this world. If My kingdom were of this world, My servants*

---

[17] Ibid, pp. 31-32.

would fight, so that I should not be delivered to the Jews; but now My kingdom is not from here.' Pilate therefore said to Him, 'Are You a king then?' Jesus answered, 'You say rightly that I am a king. For this cause I was born and for this cause I have come into the world, that I should bear witness to the truth"* (John 18:36-37).

It is important to note that from Jesus' perspective the Kingdom He proclaimed was not *of this physical world.* According to Jesus, His Kingdom is a heavenly Kingdom. It is a heavenly dominion in which He is King ruling with His Father. Jesus prayed for His Father's Kingdom to break forth into the earth so that the will of the Father would be done on the earth just as the will of God was done in the heavenly realms of God's Kingdom.

Therefore, Jesus longed to see the rule of God and administration of God's government in heaven to break forth into the earth and spread from Israel to the rest of the world. Essentially, Jesus' prayer was to see heaven and earth merges into one system; one Kingdom under one Head. This sounds rather simple, but the truth is, the merging of heaven and earth into a unified system is a deep mystery that was not revealed to the people of the world for thousands of years. It was even a mystery that was kept secret from Satan and his own evil governmental system which dominates the earth to this day.

When it came time for the King to give His Great Commission to His disciples, He began by reminding them that He possessed all authority in the universe:

Matthew 28:16-18 *Then the eleven disciples went away into Galilee, to the mountain which Jesus had appointed for them. When they saw Him, they worshiped Him; but some doubted. And Jesus came and spoke to them, saying, "All authority has been given to Me in heaven and on earth ...."*

The Apostle Paul wrote about the mystery (literally, *secret*) of

God's will, describing the Father's plan to bring everything into submission to Jesus Christ in the future. [18]

> **Ephesians 1:9-10** *...having made known to us the mystery of His will, according to His good pleasure which He purposed in Himself, that in the dispensation of the fullness of the times He might gather together in one all things in Christ, both which are in heaven and which are on earth—in Him.*

This word *mystery* refers to a truth previously hidden but now made known by divine revelation and is now fulfilled in the life of the Church. [19] The King will ultimately consummate all things together under His purpose and plan. He will be able to do this because, as Paul said …

> **Philippians 2:9-11** *Therefore God also has highly exalted Him and given Him the name which is above every name, that at the name of Jesus every knee should bow, of those in heaven, and of those on earth, and of those under the earth, and that every tongue should confess that Jesus Christ is Lord, to the glory of God the Father.*

> **Colossians 1:19-20** *For it pleased the Father that in Him all the fullness should dwell, and by Him to reconcile all things to Himself, by Him, whether things on earth or things in heaven, having made peace through the blood of His cross.*

Kingdom of Darkness vs. the Kingdom of Light

Now, to understand Jesus' vantage point and perspective of the world, you've got to understand the *very beginning of mankind* and what happened to mankind and the earth as a result of the choices of Adam and Eve. God placed our first parents

---
18 Tom Constable, *Expository Bible Study Notes*, Electronic Edition, (Sonic Light Publishers, 2010).
19 Matthew 13:11; Luke 8:10; Romans 11:25; 16:25-26.

into a beautiful garden with limitless possibilities and perfect relationships, both with Him and the world around them. They were the crowning achievement of God's creation. He gave them one simple command:

> *"You may surely eat of every tree of the garden, but of the tree of the knowledge of good and evil you shall not eat, for in the day that you eat of it you shall surely die:* (Genesis 2:16-17).

Tempted by the serpent (the Devil in snake-disguise), they questioned God's goodness and authority, and ate the fruit. [20] The results were, in a phrase, not so good. The earth and all of humanity were cast into a downward spiral of sin, death and judgment. [21]

From the fall of Adam to the present day, all of humanity has rejected God's rule and God's way of living and *"being."* Because of this, they have lost the relationship, union, and conscious contact with their Maker. They lost their contact with the divine nature and no longer reflected and imaged God's glory and radiance in the world (Romans 3:23). To *know* God is to have life (John 17:3) for God is the source of all life (John 1:4). Sin and rebellion by man instantly separated him from God. Man instantaneously lost his life and was cursed, therefore, with death.

All human beings, at the moment of conception, are already dying. The day we are born is one day closer to our death. In addition, when men rejected God's rule and relationship, they became subject and hostage to a powerful ruler formerly known as Lucifer. This lesser being, who we call Satan or the Devil, had already rebelled against his Master and Creator. Therefore, all beings whether in heaven or earth serve a master. They either serve the Lord God of Heaven or they chose to follow in the way of the dark lord Satan.

---

[20] Genesis 3:1-7.
[21] Genesis 3:8-19.

What does all this mean? The meaning is that Scripture reveals two opposing kingdoms and systems which currently exist: The Kingdom of God and the kingdom of Satan; the Kingdom of Light and the Kingdom of Darkness. These two Kingdoms transcend space, time and matter. It doesn't matter which way you look at it, from any angle, dimension, or perspective, everyone and everything is willingly or unwillingly in the Kingdom of God or the kingdom of Satan – period.

The Apostle Paul, in 2 Corinthians 4:4 referred to Satan as the *"god of this age"* (age or aeon, "the period or dispensation of time"). In John 12:31 Jesus referred to Satan as the *"ruler of this world,"* and the *"prince of the world"* in John 16:11. In a similar fashion, Paul again called Satan the *"prince of the power of the air"* in Ephesians 2:2.

In Luke chapter 4, we find an interesting story of Jesus fasting for 40 days in a desert wilderness after his baptism. He was alone, tired, and weary. I have personally traveled through the dry desert area east of Jerusalem near the Jordan River where Jesus stayed and it does not look like a very nice place to stay. It is dry, arid, hot, and dusty. I don't think I could survive even a week out there on my own with no food or water. Jesus was quite a strong man. At his weakest moment, Satan came to Jesus and very seductively tempted Jesus to sin in three distinct ways:

Luke 4:5-8 *Then the devil, taking Him up on a high mountain, showed Him all the kingdoms of the world in a moment of time. And the devil said to Him, "All this authority I will give You, and their glory; for this has been delivered to me, and I give it to whomever I wish. Therefore, if You will worship before me, all will be Yours." And Jesus answered and said to him, "Get behind Me, Satan! For it is written, 'You shall worship the LORD your God, and Him only you shall serve.' "*

During this aspect of the temptation, Satan showed Jesus all

Inauguration of the Kingdom: Flesh and Blood

the kingdoms of the world. Satan revealed that all the nations and kingdoms on earth were under his control. In fact, Satan noted that *"this has been delivered to me and I will give it to whomever I wish."* Interestingly, Jesus didn't argue with Satan about whether or not he controlled the kingdoms of the earth. Jesus knew that Satan was telling the truth. Even though God is ultimately in control of everything and infinitely more powerful than any other person, angel, or thing, He has temporarily allowed the Evil One to control and rule over the nations and kingdoms of the world. I guess, it's really just the illusion of control. Nonetheless, this is exactly what Satan wanted and desired.

Satan fell from his position and place in heaven when he became proud and jealous of God's rule and glory. Satan's aim was and still is to create his own worldly kingdom or system that rivals God's kingdom, leaving God out of the equation. Essentially, Satan wants to be God with his own worshippers and servants. He became proud and hated God's authority over him. Thus, this world is not God's Kingdom and is not ruled by righteousness and justice.

In fact, the world as we know it is influenced and manipulated from "behind the veil of visibility" by evil forces from other realms or dimensions called *"rulers, against the authorities and cosmic powers"* (Ephesians 6:12). These other-worldly beings (demons or fallen angels) are called rulers because they rule. Some are called authorities, because they really do have some type of authority and power. Cosmic powers imply that there are real powerful forces (way beyond human understanding) which are in direct conflict with the people who follow Jesus Christ as Lord and Savior. Therefore, if the rulers, authorities, and cosmic powers controlling the world hate God and are damned to sin, what should we expect of our world?

This world is corrupt from the top to the bottom. It is dark. It is a counterfeit of the true and glorious Kingdom which God rules. Even more, *"this world is passing away"* and soon it will be no more (1 John 2:17). This is why the Apostle James instructed all believers to *"keep yourself unstained from the world"* (James 1:27) and that *"friendship with the world hostility toward God"* (James 4:4 NASB).

The Heart of the Problem

Now here is the major problem and curse of all humanity: all of us are born into this fallen, dark, and corrupt Kingdom which is under the rule and subjection of an evil spiritual dictator because the original man and woman of our species sinned after being tempted by Satan. We all were born into Satan's Kingdom. Because of the original sin in the garden when Adam and Even followed the serpent and broke God's one simple rule, all people are born into this world with a disease ... a disease which has no cure. Our disease is a curse which is eating away at our core. It is called sin.

We are not just sinners because we sin. We are born sinners, actually corrupted and sinful in our very being at the moment we are conceived, which is the cause of actual realized sin in our lives. As many people understand it, mankind is born with a "sinful nature." This problem separates us from our true Creator and God. As a result, all men and women are born slaves to sin. We are slaves to sin, death, and Satan. There is no hope for freedom and no chance to escape death. No hope of escaping the kingdom of darkness and entering into the Kingdom of light. This is God's perspective of mankind. As God looked over His world, creation, and humanity, He saw and still sees prisoners locked in unbreakable chains. Almighty God saw His creatures, human beings, as helpless and dumb sheep being led to their slaughter; a school of fish all caught in a large net being carried away to death with no hope. Even worse, the people were blind and deaf to the truth of this spiritual condition. While man resists

God's path of light to pursue *"freedom"* and *"liberty,"* he foolishly pursues an eternity of death, slavery, and chains of darkness.

Freedom

Thank God that He did not leave us without hope. God, through Jesus Christ, came to His creation to set the captives free. Jesus was not just a man. He was not just a prophet, religious leader, or even an angel. Jesus is the name of the one-and-only God-man. Jesus was *Emmanuel*, which means *"God with us."* *"In the beginning was the Word and the Word was with God and the Word was God. He was in the beginning with God. All things came into being through Him, and apart from Him nothing came into being which has come into being. In Him was life, and the life was the light of men … and the Word became flesh, and dwelt among us, and we saw His glory, glory as of the only begotten from the Father, full of grace and truth"* (John 1:1-4, 14).

Yes, there are an innumerable host of *"sons of god"* (or angels) and yes, all the children of God are referred to in Scripture as *"sons of God."* But Jesus Christ was the *"one and only," "unique,"* or *"begotten"* Son of God – set apart and distinct from all others (John 3:16). The *"begottenness"* of Jesus Christ is so important to understand. Hebrews 1:1-14 brilliantly explains how much greater Jesus Christ was than the angels of heaven.

Of Jesus Christ, Philippians 2 states that *"Christ Jesus, who, although He existed in the form of God, did not regard equality with God a thing to be grasped, but emptied Himself, taking the form of a bond-servant, and being made in the likeness of men"* (2:5b-7). Colossians 1:15-17 reveals that *"He is the image of the invisible God, the firstborn of all creation. For by Him all things were created, both in the heavens and on earth, visible and invisible, whether thrones or dominions or rulers or authorities*

– all things have been created through Him and for Him. He is before all things, and in Him all things hold together."

Do you realize what this means? *Yeshua Ha Mesheach* ("Jesus the Messiah") was and is the visible manifestation and image of the invisible God. The eternal God of creation is everywhere and seemingly totally intangible and incomprehensible to a finite and human mind. We cannot even begin to fathom or comprehend God. Scriptures state that no man has ever seen the *"invisible God"* as He truly is in His radiance and glory. Jesus Christ, however, allows humans with a finite and limited mind to *"see"* in real time and in living form, the visible, walking-and-talking God in a comprehensible way. This is similar to the way a singular and simple desktop icon on your computer screen can take an almost infinite matrix like the internet and represent it by a simple icon. The "Internet Explorer icon" takes a complicated system like the internet and makes it visible and tangible for us.

Though He humbled Himself to take on the likeness and form of His own creation, the eternal "Son of God" is the *Word who was with God and was God* in the beginning. He was One with God in substance and essence. Many people today argue that if God was real and truly did love His people then He would come and set things straight. He would come to us, announce Himself, and fix everything.

God has already revealed Himself to us – two thousand years ago through the Lord Jesus Christ of Nazareth. He came and showed us what humanity was intended to be like from the very beginning. God came to us and taught humanity what is right and what is wrong. He interpreted His own law for His people. He modeled a life of righteousness, love, compassion, truth, and justice. He was a revolutionary. The Lord of the Heavens covertly broke through enemy lines and entered into His enemies very own kingdom and dominion one of the prisoners. He then began preaching a message of good news everywhere He went.

One day early in His earthly ministry, Jesus preached a sermon at a local synagogue. Quoting from Isaiah 61, He read the job description of the Messiah – *His* job description. Here is what He came to do:

> **Luke 4:16-20** *So He came to Nazareth, where He had been brought up. And as His custom was, He went into the synagogue on the Sabbath day, and stood up to read. And He was handed the book of the prophet Isaiah. And when He had opened the book, He found the place where it was written:*
>
> *"The Spirit of the LORD is upon Me, because He has anointed Me to preach the gospel to the poor; He has sent Me to heal the brokenhearted, to proclaim liberty to the captives and recovery of sight to the blind, to set at liberty those who are oppressed; to proclaim the acceptable year of the LORD."*
>
> *Then He closed the book, and gave it back to the attendant and sat down. And the eyes of all who were in the synagogue were fixed on Him.*

Think about that: *on that very day, the Old Testament Scripture was fulfilled* … because Messiah came. And because He came, our world will never be the same.

Questions for Reflection and Response:

- How is our world different because Messiah came? How is *your* world different?

- What is God doing in the world *today*?

Chapter Five

Fulfillment of the Kingdom: Mission Accomplished – All Praise

Revelation 11:15 *And there were loud voices in heaven, saying, "The kingdoms of this world have become the kingdoms of our Lord and of His Christ, and He shall reign forever and ever!"*

The Coming Kingdom

We have seen that Christ inaugurated the Kingdom in His earthly ministry. [22] That inaugurated Kingdom continues today in the hearts of believers and the life of the Church. [23] As a result, the prime mission of the Church as a whole is to tirelessly and powerfully proclaim the Gospel of the Kingdom of God throughout the world by making disciples (other Kingdom Citizens) and thus bring glory and fame to Jesus Christ and His Father in heaven. In this chapter we are going to take a look into the future where the Kingdom will reach its ultimate end when Christ returns in glory.

The church at Corinth had many questions about the resurrection and the afterlife. Paul spent the entire chapter of 1 Corinthians 15 answering their concerns. At the end of the chapter, he concludes by comparing our former identity in Adam

---
[22] Matthew 2:2; 4:23; 9:35; 27:11; Mark 15:2; Luke 16:16; 23:3; John 18:37.
[23] Matthew 24:14; Romans 14:16-17; 1 Corinthians 4:19-20; Colossians 4:11.

with our future inheritance in the Kingdom by saying, *"Just as we have borne the image of the man of dust, we shall also bear the image of the man of heaven"* (15:49). We were made to be image-bearers – reflectors of the divine nature. I like what evangelist and close friend, Rick Amato, often says: *"When we understand Jesus' humanity, we can begin to understand His divinity in our humanity."*

Paul goes on to talk about how the Kingdom will ultimately be fulfilled in Christ and what will happen to those of us who are alive when that happens:

> **1 Corinthians 15:50-57** *Now this I say, brethren, that flesh and blood cannot inherit the kingdom of God; nor does corruption inherit incorruption. Behold, I tell you a mystery: We shall not all sleep, but we shall all be changed— in a moment, in the twinkling of an eye, at the last trumpet. For the trumpet will sound, and the dead will be raised incorruptible, and we shall be changed. For this corruptible must put on incorruption, and this mortal must put on immortality. So when this corruptible has put on incorruption, and this mortal has put on immortality, then shall be brought to pass the saying that is written: "Death is swallowed up in victory." "O Death, where is your sting? O Hades, where is your victory?" The sting of death is sin, and the strength of sin is the law. But thanks be to God, who gives us the victory through our Lord Jesus Christ.*

When that day finally comes, Paul tells us that two things will happen: death will be defeated – it will be swallowed up in the victory of God, and our perishable bodies will be transformed into imperishable, eternal bodies. The final enemy will be defeated, and there will be joy and celebration throughout eternity. At that point, the reality of Revelation 11:15 will be totally fulfilled: *"The kingdoms of this world have become the kingdoms of our Lord and of His Christ, and He shall reign forever and ever!"*

Mission Accomplished

At the beginning of His earthly ministry, when Jesus went to His home-town synagogue and claimed to be the Messiah, He read the job description of the Messiah from Isaiah 61 and said, *"Today this Scripture has been fulfilled in your hearing"* (Luke 4:21). He came to inaugurate the Kingdom. At the end of His earthly ministry, He gave His disciples the mission of going into all the world, proclaiming the Gospel. [24] Earlier He told them, *"This gospel of the kingdom will be proclaimed throughout the whole world as a testimony to all nations, and then the end will come"* (Matthew 24:14).

We'll talk more about this later, but it is important to realize that the mission of the Church is to proclaim the Gospel of the Kingdom – and it will be successful. *"The gates of hell will not prevail against it"* (Matthew 16:18). There will be trials, persecutions, hard times – but the message of the Gospel will prevail. The whole world will know of Jesus the Messiah. There has been a great surge and renewed emphasis in recent years in world evangelization. Through church planting efforts like *The Timothy Initiative*, [25] founded and led by David Nelms (my dad and hero), senior pastor of Grace Fellowship, West Palm Beach, innovative evangelistic tools like *The Jesus Film*, [26] and visionary leaders that God has raised up around the world, the Kingdom is growing.

Jesus taught a series of stories about the Kingdom of God in Matthew 13. One of those stories was about a very tiny seed known as the mustard seed:

Matthew 13:31-32 *Another parable He put forth to them, saying: "The kingdom of heaven is like a mustard seed, which a man took and sowed in his field, which indeed is the least of*

---

[24] Mark 16:15.

[25] See ttionline.org.

[26] JesusFilm.org.

all the seeds; but when it is grown it is greater than the herbs and becomes a tree, so that the birds of the air come and nest in its branches."

A mustard seed is TINY! But here's the thing most people usually don't think about: mustard trees aren't very big. Have you seen mustard trees? I was expecting to see some kind of oak tree or sycamore tree or something, but on a recent trip to Israel, I was disappointed to find out that mustard trees really don't grow to be that large. What was Jesus saying? Did he fall asleep in botany class back in Nazareth? No, I don't think so. His point was that the Kingdom of God is not like anything else. It is different! One day it's just a little tiny mustard seed that was planted into the ground (by King Jesus). But when you come back a few years later to see your five or six foot tall mustard tree, you find this huge solid tree with massive branches, and all these birds are nesting in it! You would stand there and scratch your head asking, *"What kind of mustard seed was that? Some kind of mustard seed on steroids or something? What in the world is going on? This needs to be in the Guiness Book of World Records! That just doesn't happen! It's impossible!"*

That was the point. When the message of the Kingdom of God is "caught," it is like Jack and the Bean Stalk. It can't be stopped. It is going, going, gone! It just takes off in revival fire in an unnatural, other-worldly way, because it is what everyone is groaning for. That's why Satan and his submissive world "government" wants to keep the lid on it! Let's open the lid up and let the people of the world know how wonderful and fun God's Kingdom really is.

The Kingdom is growing and expanding. Nothing can compare to its value. Therefore, nothing we can do can be as important as involvement in its mission. In another parable about the Kingdom, Jesus said, *"Again, the kingdom of heaven is like a merchant in search of fine pearls, who, on finding one pearl of great value, went and sold all that he had and bought it"* (Matthew 13:45-46). We were made for involvement in God's Kingdom Mission.

All Praise to Jesus

Revelation 21 and 22 tell us that at the end of the age, the present heaven and earth will be burned up; the New Jerusalem will descend from heaven to a newly reformed earth, and the eternal dwelling place of God will be eternally among men on a new and re-created earth.

N.T. Wright wrote a book entitled *Surprised By Hope*, which corrects the commonly held belief among Christians and non-Christians that the hope of the New Testament is for Christians to *"die and go to heaven for all of eternity."* That idea alone is not totally true and accurate. Left alone, it could even be considered *unbiblical*. The true hope of the New Testament is for unregenerate people to enter into the Kingdom of God and one day join in the resurrection of Jesus Christ with a new, perfected body, in a perfected world system (ruled by King Jesus Christ), on a totally new and re-created perfect world, bringing all humanity back to the "Edenic state of mankind" (that is, the Garden of Eden) originally purposed by God when He created mankind. The story of the Bible is *From Paradise to Prison* [27] and then *From Prison to Paradise* by the remnant of humanity saved and redeemed by the atoning blood of God's Son! The King will reign and the will of God will be done throughout the earth just as it is done in heaven.

> **Revelation 21:2-7** *When I, John, saw the holy city, New Jerusalem, coming down out of heaven from God, prepared as a bride adorned for her husband. And I heard a loud voice from heaven saying, "Behold, the tabernacle of God*

---
[27] *Paradise to Prison* is the title of a commentary on Genesis by John J. Davis.

is with men, and He will dwell with them, and they shall be His people. God Himself will be with them and be their God. And God will wipe away every tear from their eyes; there shall be no more death, nor sorrow, nor crying. There shall be no more pain, for the former things have passed away." Then He who sat on the throne said, "Behold, I make all things new." And He said to me, "Write, for these words are true and faithful." And He said to me, "It is done! I am the Alpha and the Omega, the Beginning and the End. I will give of the fountain of the water of life freely to him who thirsts. He who overcomes shall inherit all things, and I will be his God and he shall be My son.

The book of Revelation, though known for its prophetic and futuristic description of coming tribulations, is filled with praise. Whenever the veil is pulled back and we are allowed to see into heaven, we hear the chorus of great praise resounding from the citizens of heaven:

Revelation 4:8 The four living creatures, each having six wings, were full of eyes around and within. And they do not rest day or night, saying: "Holy, holy, holy, Lord God Almighty, Who was and is and is to come!"

Revelation 5:9-10 And they sang a new song, saying: "You are worthy to take the scroll, and to open its seals; for You were slain, and have redeemed us to God by Your blood out of every tribe and tongue and people and nation, and have made us kings and priests to our God; and we shall reign on the earth."

Revelation 19:6-8 And I heard, as it were, the voice of a great multitude, as the sound of many waters and as the sound of mighty thunderings, saying, "Alleluia! For the Lord God Omnipotent reigns! Let us be glad and rejoice and give Him glory, for the marriage of the Lamb has come, and His wife has made herself ready." *And to her it was granted to be arrayed in fine linen, clean and bright, for the fine linen is the righteous acts of the saints.*

God is not narcissistic nor is He self-centered. He is, however, worthy of all praise, glory and honor. Not only were we made for missional involvement, we were made to bring praise to His glorious name. Hebrews 13:15 states, *"Therefore by Him let us continually offer the sacrifice of praise to God, that is, the fruit of our lips, giving thanks to His name."*

Obviously, God is worthy to be praised. I don't think that God is forcing those angels to praise Him non-stop. It is just an automatic response of any and every creature, person, or thing, who comes into actual face to face contact with the Most High God. Our God is awesome! He is powerful! He can do all things! No one can stop Him! If big, powerful angelic beings are compelled to fall down and shout out praises and songs, how much more should we praise and worship God every chance we get? Yes, God desires for us to constantly be on mission advancing His Kingdom, but if we will just intentionally stay in His Presence and be near to Him, we can do nothing other than stop and praise God.

If you catch fire, you're instructed to stop, drop, and roll. When you get a moment to be still and be alone, where ever you are, stop, pause, pray, believe, and experience the presence of God with you at all times. When you experience God, all you can do is stop, drop, and praise His name! I'm serious – try it out, there is nothing better than being in the presence and company of the Lord and singing praises to Him from your heart knowing that He doesn't care how off tune or out of pitch your voice is … He just loves you because He loves you and you are free.

Questions for Reflection and Response:

- How can the church best communicate the Gospel to people around the world? How can you be sensitive to their cultures and background, yet maintain the integrity of the Gospel message? How can you sensitively communicate both His love and His judgment?

- Since praising God is one of the great themes of the book of Revelation, how does that affect the quality of our personal and corporate worship now? How can you mature in your ability to praise and worship God?

Section Two

Experiencing the Kingdom

Chapter Six

Entering the Kingdom of God

Two Kingdoms – Two Births

There are two kingdoms: God's Kingdom and the kingdom of this world. You are either a part of one or the other. Which one you are in makes an eternal difference.

In John chapter three, Jesus told Nicodemus that *"unless one is born again, he cannot see the Kingdom of God"* (John 3:3). When questioned about this by Nicodemus, Jesus again said that *"unless one is born of water and the Spirit, he cannot enter the Kingdom of God"* (3:5). Some have suggested that when Jesus talked about *"seeing"* and *"entering"* the Kingdom of God, He was referring to what happens when believers die … they go to heaven, *entering and seeing* the Kingdom of God. Not so fast! A better understanding is that if you have been *"born again,"* then truly, you are able see the Kingdom of God. Yes, you are able to *see* the Kingdom of God … right now, right here.

Jesus began His discussion with Nicodemus by talking about a topic he could relate to: birth. Nicodemus could understand being born. That's a common, everyday occurrence. But he became confused when Jesus talked about being *"born again."* This great teacher of the Law couldn't *"see"* the spiritual reality of the Kingdom of God.

All Are Born into the Kingdom of This World – Some Are Also Born Again into God's Kingdom

When we are born again, God opens our eyes and enables us to see the reality of the spiritual life. If you have been born again, then you have been baptized by the Spirit into Christ, and you have entered into the Kingdom of God. How do I know this? In Colossians 1, Paul explained to the believers that Jesus *"delivered us from the domain of darkness and transferred us into the kingdom of His beloved Son"* (v.13). In Philippians 3:20 Paul wrote that *"our citizenship is in heaven."* Later in the New Testament we read,

Revelation 1:4-6 *Grace to you and peace from Him who is and who was and who is to come, and from the seven Spirits who are before His throne, and from Jesus Christ, the faithful witness, the firstborn from the dead, and the ruler over the kings of the earth. To Him who loved us and washed us from our sins in His own blood, and has made us kings and priests to His God and Father, to Him be glory and dominion forever and ever. Amen.*

Revelation 5:9-10 *And they sang a new song, saying: "You are worthy to take the scroll, and to open its seals; for You were slain, and have redeemed us to God by Your blood out of every tribe and tongue and people and nation, and have made us kings and priests to our God; and we shall reign on the earth."*

1 Peter 2:9-10 *But you are a chosen generation, a royal priesthood, a holy nation, His own special people, that you may proclaim the praises of Him who called you out of darkness into His marvelous light; who once were not a people but are now the people of God, who had not obtained mercy but now have obtained mercy.*

So then, the first step to incorporation into and understanding of the reality of the Kingdom of God is to *enter the Kingdom*. However, according to Jesus, no one can "*see*" or "*enter*" the Kingdom of God without first experiencing a "spiritual re-birth." What was Jesus talking about? Entrance into God's Heavenly Kingdom is initiated by a spiritual rebirth and resurrection which occurs *internally*. At this very beginning stage, a person hears of King Jesus Christ who left His throne and dominion in heaven to set all of the captives free. All of us were locked in chains of spiritual darkness under Satan's rule. Jesus made liberty and deliverance possible by canceling the debt and condemnation all of the captives owed to God, through his own shed blood. Jesus took the totality of sin (past, present and future sin) on His own back and thus appeased God's wrath, punishment, and death which was required of all men. In so doing, he broke the curse, and the guilt. Jesus once and for all wiped away the sin that was on the backs of all humanity. Romans 8:1 tells that *"there is now no condemnation for those who are in Christ Jesus."* Jesus shed his blood, died, was buried, but then overcame death by God's Power. He did what no other human being has ever done by His own might. He resurrected from death to life. But He didn't just come back to life, He was transformed from a regular mortal body into a glorified eternal body. Then the Lord Jesus ascended back into His heavenly home and placed Satan's authority (over the earth) underneath His own authority.

Now, Jesus offers freedom and life to all who would follow Him. When this message is accepted by any man or woman, the Lord Jesus transfers His resurrection life and power by means of His Spirit, to fuse together and indwell that person's own spirit (which was formerly dead and separated from God's omnipresent Spirit – see Ephesians 2). When the Spirit of Christ enters our own spirit, He quickens, recreates, and resurrects our own spirit to life, joining us intimately with Christ's actual Spirit. This literally happens! Do you believe it? When this occurs, each disciple and follower of Christ becomes an actual extension of Christ in the physical world, enabling Christ to continue His rule and reign and work in this three dimensional realm through us ... the extension. Each disciple actually becomes a member of the Body of Christ. This miracle and divine act of creation inside of us at salvation and this spiritual baptism joins us with Christ and initiates us into a real, live, heavenly kingdom and nation with Christ. We instantly become citizens and partakers of the heavenly Kingdom of God: the divine government and administration of Jesus Christ which rules over all the earth, the universe, the dimensions, the heavenly places, and all creation in this current age and in the age to come.

What God started in Abram He finished through Jesus Christ. He chose Israel to be His holy nation, but God's plan was never just to bless one country. Rather, His plan was to bring about salvation to all the world – all people, all places, all races, all faces, all colors, throughout all time, through His holy nation Israel. Jesus Christ is the Lord [28] and the perfect representative and King of Israel, [29] King of the world, and King of all Kings [30] whether in heaven, on earth, or below the earth. He is the only mediator between God and man, [31] He himself being God in the flesh. [32] Now all people from any place of any ethnicity can be grafted into the nation of Israel [33] and become God's Kingdom citizens while still living on earth!

Understanding Re-birth and Re-Generation

I like to use a simple illustration to show people in a visual way what happens during spiritual re-birth or "regeneration." Imagine there was a ten gallon aquarium full of water – the size of a fish tank – on a small table. Now, suppose I take a small dry

---
28 Philippians 2:11.
29 John 1:49.
30 1 Timothy 6:15.
31 1 Timothy 2:5.
32 John 1:14, 18.
33 Romans 4:13-18; 11:1-25.

sponge and seal it inside of a zip-lock bag. When I place the sealed zip-lock bag and place it into the water, what happens to the sponge? Nothing, of course. Why? Because the sponge is separated from the water by the plastic bag. Now if you were to take the sponge out of the bag and place it in the water, the sponge would immediately fill up and be saturated with water. The sponge however does not become the water and the water does not become the sponge . Rather, the sponge is filled up with the water and *"immersed into the water"* at the same time.

    This is a shoddy but helpful picture of what happens during our spiritual re-birth. The Spirit of God is omnipresent, meaning He is everywhere at all times, through all things, and transcends time and space. Before salvation, we are like the sponge in the zip-lock baggie. We are surrounded by God's presence and sometimes come into contact with God's influence and Spirit tugging on our heart, speaking to us, drawing us to Him, but we ourselves are not changed or indwelt by His Spirit because our sin disconnects us from uniting spiritually with God's Spirit. Our flesh separates us, just like the plastic bag separated the sponge from the water. However, when a person hears about the Man, the message, and the sacrifice of Jesus Christ on the cross and puts his faith in Jesus Christ, His shed blood, death, and resurrection, the power of the blood of Jesus Christ covers over all sin. God is able to justify each and every one of us – legally, according to His own perfect law. The Holy Spirit then unites with our spirit and re-creates and resurrects our spiritual man inside of our body, and our spirits meld and join to become a harmony of spirits in intimate fellowship. In effect, we are *"immersed"* into Christ. Every human being who is indwelt by the Spirit of God becomes one member or part of the collective *"body of Christ."* The body of Christ is then called the Church. The only problem with this analogy of the sponge is the fact that it just shows how the Spirit comes and lives within our own Spirit, but Scripture seems to teach that God actually brings our dead spirit to life as well.

Entering the Kingdom of God

This spiritual re-birth is illustrated in the Church by a sacrament and holy institution called baptism. Jesus commanded that all of His disciples be baptized (Matthew 28:18-20). Paul wrote about the true meaning of baptism in several places, especially Romans 6. Further, Jesus taught in John chapter three that *"unless one be born again, He cannot enter the Kingdom of God."* Paul taught that from the moment we believed in Jesus, we have been transferred into the Kingdom of Light and placed in heavenly places (Colossians 1:13; Ephesians 2:6; Hebrews 12:22-28). This implies that spiritual re-birth through the blood of Jesus Christ is our *"ticket"* into the Kingdom of God.

The Kingdom of God is not of this world. It is a spiritual or heavenly Kingdom. One could even say that God Himself is the true essence of the Kingdom itself. Being filled with God's Spirit is the same thing as walking in the Kingdom. That means, Kingdom life really has a totally different meaning than just being on earth and living on earth in the future when Jesus literally brings and establishes His Kingdom. Therefore, those who are born again will dwell in the Kingdom of God … those who are not born again will not.

It is important that each new believer catch this vision and mindset. It is a paradigm shift that needs to occur. We don't all need to be able to recite what was just said above or even word it that way. The symbol and acting out of *"baptism"* is a beautiful and perfect picture in and of itself which teaches all followers of Christ the wonderful spiritual regeneration that occurred. *Each follower and lover of Jesus Christ needs to understand that he is not just a member of a local religious club or organization. He is not just part of a local church team. His job is not to come to church or read a few chapters of the Bible in the morning. He is a citizen of the most prestigious, powerful, and eternal Kingdom which will ever be and ever has been.*

Yes, the local church is important because it is the only way to make the Kingdom of God on earth tangible and manifest, but when a person views himself as a soldier and officer in a real, tangible and true Kingdom, it will change his worldview and outlook on his purpose and calling. He is not a mechanic, business man, or school teacher. He is a Spirit-filled representative and Kingdom official for the Lord Jesus Christ who is working to build up and strengthen God's Kingdom on earth, while also attacking Satan's kingdom. It is his job to see God's Kingdom take more and more ground, and more and more root in his life, his home, his workplace, his neighborhood, his county, state, nation, and the entire world!

This is the worldview (mindset) and calling which creates a true sense of fellowship and camaraderie between believers inside and outside of the local church. It allows believers to stop viewing themselves as members of *"such and such church"* and instead view themselves as fellow citizens of the Kingdom of God, members of the holy nation and people of God. We are one entity … spiritually grafted into Israel as descendants of Abraham but not replacing Israel. We are an organism indwelt by One and the same Holy Spirit of God … each individual partaking, living, and being from the same Spirit. We are members of the ecclesia; "the Church." The word church really has nothing to do with a structure or building, but rather implies a congregation or assembly of people. Essentially what we now call a "church" is really just a community of Kingdom Citizens biblically organized according to the pattern and teachings of the Apostles and first group of disciples directly under Jesus' teaching and influence in the first century.

What is a Local Church?

I like *The Timothy Initiative's* (TTI) definition of a local church: *"A group of believers, who meet together regularly, to worship the Father, study and communicate the Word of God in the power of the Holy Spirit, pray and fellowship together, observe the ordinances, and then sent out to share the love of Christ to the lost world, all of this under the authority of Biblically qualified leadership. A church can meet in a building, in a house, under a tree, or anywhere!* [34]

TTI suggests that every church that is involved in the TTI network of churches have at least 2 or 3 unrelated individuals as members. *These "churches" could really simply be called fellowships, communities, clusters, small groups or whatever, because in reality there is only One Church ... the body of Jesus Christ. The church of Jesus Christ is a diverse ocean of people who have been plucked out of the world and transferred into a different Kingdom. We are "the called out ones."*

Dear friend, you are a member of THE CHURCH, not just "a church." You are part of something so much greater than yourself. You are part of a greater sum. You are not just an isolated believer or hermit but a partaker of an unbreakable and eternal circle of spiritually united brothers and sisters united by the same Holy Spirit of God.

---

[34] http://ttionline.org/#/our-mission/strategy.

Questions for Reflection and Response:

- What would you say if a modern-day Nicodemus came to you and asked you to describe how one becomes a Christian? How would you describe your relationship with Jesus Christ in language that someone not familiar with Christianity could understand?

- How should the Church aid in the mission of the Kingdom of God? In what ways have you seen churches *help* the mission of the Kingdom of God? In what ways have you seen churches *hinder* the mission of the Kingdom of God?

Entering the Kingdom of God

Chapter Seven

The Glory of God Through the Blood of the Lamb

Exodus 33:18 *Moses said, "Please, show me Your glory."*

Matthew 17:1-2 *Now after six days Jesus took Peter, James, and John his brother, led them up on a high mountain by themselves; and He was transfigured before them. His face shone like the sun, and His clothes became as white as the light.*

Simple Word ... Deep Meaning

There are many words that we use in everyday conversation ... they are somewhat common and familiar, and we *think* we know what they mean ... but we really don't. The word *glory* is one of those words. If you put ten people in a room and asked them to come up with a definition, they might say things like *"praise," "light,"* and *"power."* Close ... but not quite. Each of those definitions fall short of the rich and deep meaning that the Bible ascribes to the glory of God.

The Evangelical Dictionary of Theology is a great and reliable source for Bible study. It defines God's "glory" the following way:

The principle word in the Hebrew for this concept is kābôd, and in the Greek doxa, which is derived from dokeō, "to think" or "to seem." These two meanings account for the two main lines of significance in classical Greek, where doxa means opinion (what one thinks for one's self) and reputation (what others think about that person), which may shade into fame or honor or praise.... In the Old Testament: since kābôd derives from kābed, "to be heavy," it lends itself to the idea that one possessing glory is laden with riches (Gen. 31:1), power (Isa 8:7), position (Gen. 45:13), etc....

But kābôd also denoted the manifestation of light by which God revealed himself, whether in the lightning flash or in the blinding splendor that often accompanied theophanies. Of the same nature was the disclosure of the divine presence in the cloud that led Israel through the wilderness and became localized in the tabernacle....

At times kābôd had a deeper penetration, denoting person or self. When Moses made the request of God, "show me Your glory" (Exodus 33:18), he was not speaking of the light-cloud, which he had already seen; rather, he was seeking a special manifestation of God that would leave nothing to be desired (cf. John 14:8). Moses had a craving to come to grips with God as He was in Himself. In reply, God emphasized His goodness (Exodus 33:19). The word might be rendered in this instance as moral beauty. Apart from this, the eternity of God as a subject of human contemplation might be depressing. This incident involving Moses is the seed plot for the idea that God's glory is not confined to some outward sign that appeals to the senses, but is that which expresses His inherent majesty, which may or may not have some visible token. [35]

---

[35] *The Evangelical Dictionary of Theology, Second Edition*, edited by Walter A. Elwell, (Grand Rapids: Baker Book House, 2001), pp. 484-485. Article on "Glory" by E. F. Harrison.

God's glory is ours through the blood of the Lamb. Do you realize what I just said? Do you? God's glory is ours through the blood of the Lamb! And as Harrison said in the above quote about glory, when we see that glory, *"it will leave nothing to be desired."*

Do you know how valuable God's glory is? Do you like gold? Do you like diamonds? One microscopic spec of God's glory makes the world's most brilliant diamond look like a piece of charcoal. There is no earthly way to compare something to God's glory. God's glory is invaluable …. but more valuable than the appearance of God's glory is the experience of God's glory. His glory is the whole package. It is the greatest experience, the greatest sight, the greatest smell, the greatest taste, the greatest music, the greatest energy, the greatest essence there is. It is God's glory.

The only definition for God's glory could be perfection in every way. God's glory satisfies every need: spiritual, physical, and emotional. His glory is love, peace, holiness, righteousness, goodness, grace, mercy, truth, and beauty. God's glory is the essence of God Himself. God's glory is God's light. God's manifest presence, His Shekinah glory, is the height and pinnacle of consciousness.

Now that is a mouthful! But there is a problem – God's word says *"all have sinned and fall short of the glory of God"* (Romans 3:23).

The Seriousness of Glory

In the beginning God created man to be perfect. Academic editor of the famous *Logos Bible* Software and Ph. D. in Hebrew Scriptures and Semitic languages, Michael Heiser,[36] makes the

---
[36] http://www.michaelsheiser.com, www.thedivinecouncil.com

argument that we are more than simply *"made in the image of God."* We are image-bearers – God's imagers, reflecting and manifesting His glory in this world. Imagine if you took a big *blob* of God's glory and swallowed it down into your stomach where it settled. Let's imagine that it turned your body into a bright, shinning glorious luminescent looking being – radiating energy, love, beauty, truth, and peace. You might be able to understand how God intended human beings to exist and be – in a perfect state of being in a perfect place called the Garden of Eden, walking with our God who Himself was the source of our glory.

But then we all know what happened. Sin happened. Cosmic rebellion against God's authority and rule. God didn't create a bunch of robots. He made us real. He made us with the ability to pick and choose and make decisions. I'm glad … but that means we can choose the wrong thing. The glory of God departed from mankind and was gone … what a terrible situation. God's glory was too precious and too holy to be corrupted and come near sin. It was kept hidden until a suitable place was built for God's glory to manifest, first at Mt. Sinai in the wilderness for all of Israel to see in a tabernacle, and then a temple – the most beautifully designed, structured, and orderly temple, made as an exact replica of a temple that exists in the heavenly realm where God dwells.

If I didn't know anything about God and the Bible but you explained to me what the glory of God was and you asked me where God could let His glory dwell on earth, I would probably tell you to build a temple, the most beautiful temple imaginable, and keep it as clean and holy and sanctified as possible. That's exactly where God chose to allow His glory to dwell – in the Holy of Holies of the Temple. The Holy of Holies was the innermost chamber of the Tabernacle and then later in Solomon's Temple. God's glory dwelt in that small, private room that contained the Ark of the Covenant. The room was closed off to the public. No one was allowed to enter – except the High Priest of Israel. And he could come into that place only one day a year for only a few moments.

You don't even want to know the rituals that he had to go through in order to be prepared to go in. The High Priest had to be covered by the ritualistic washing, purification, repentance, and blood of animals ... sprinkled and "covered by blood" of an innocent sacrifice, because even the High Priest was not worthy to be in the presence of God's glory. He even had to wear clothing with bells and rope on because if he was not "right" when he went in, he would die. The rope tied to him would be used to pull him out and he'd be buried outside the city. I'm talking about the real deal: *God's presence is Holy and awesome and powerful!* See for yourself in these passages below.

> **Exodus 40:34-38** *Then the cloud covered the tent of meeting,* **and the glory of the LORD filled the tabernacle. And Moses was not able to enter the tent of meeting because the cloud settled on it, and the glory of the LORD filled the tabernacle.** *Throughout all their journeys, whenever the cloud was taken up from over the tabernacle, the people of Israel would set out. But if the cloud was not taken up, then they did not set out till the day that it was taken up. For the cloud of the LORD was on the tabernacle by day, and fire was in it by night, in the sight of all the house of Israel throughout all their journeys.*

Here we see that God's presence was so *thick* and *powerful* that Moses was not even able to enter the tent of meeting. We also see that all the people of Israel were able to see the cloud and the fire. Imagine that – such a powerful visual that could be seen by perhaps a million people. The people were constantly reminded that God was holy – and they were not. They also saw the presence of God with them, but were reminded that they were individually separated from Him ... by the walls of the tent, by the doors to the Holy of Holies, and by the necessity of the priest as intercessor for them. They saw a powerful, awesome God ... but lived in fear of Him.

1 Kings 8:1-13 *Then Solomon assembled the elders of Israel and all the heads of the tribes, the leaders of the fathers' houses of the people of Israel, before King Solomon in Jerusalem, to bring up the ark of the covenant of the LORD out of the city of David, which is Zion. And all the men of Israel assembled to King Solomon at the feast in the month Ethanim, which is the seventh month. And all the elders of Israel came, and the priests took up the ark. And they brought up the ark of the LORD, the tent of meeting, and all the holy vessels that were in the tent; the priests and the Levites brought them up. And King Solomon and all the congregation of Israel, who had assembled before him, were with him before the ark, sacrificing so many sheep and oxen that they could not be counted or numbered. Then the priests brought the ark of the covenant of the LORD to its place in the inner sanctuary of the house, in the Most Holy Place, underneath the wings of the cherubim. For the cherubim spread out their wings over the place of the ark, so that the cherubim overshadowed the ark and its poles. And the poles were so long that the ends of the poles were seen from the Holy Place before the inner sanctuary; but they could not be seen from outside. And they are there to this day. There was nothing in the ark except the two tablets of stone that Moses put there at Horeb, where the LORD made a covenant with the people of Israel, when they came out of the land of Egypt.* **And when the priests came out of the Holy Place, a cloud filled the house of the LORD, so that the priests could not stand to minister because of the cloud, for the glory of the LORD filled the house of the LORD. Then Solomon said, "The LORD has said that he would dwell in thick darkness. I have indeed built you an exalted house, a place for you to dwell in forever."**

I have just described for you God's glory and then the place where God allowed His glory to dwell. But there is one big problem. God's glory was not accessible to anyone. No one was allowed into the Holy of Holies. It was the most sacred of all rooms in the world. The whole temple and sacrificial system was created so that God could even remain in the midst of the people He chose to redeem and make His own nation.

Keeping the Cross and the Blood of Jesus Christ at the Heart of our Lives and Theology

Let's take a look at some helpful passages on this subject from the Epistle to the Hebrews. They are lengthy, but all Kingdom citizens MUST know, understand, and remember these important passages! I encourage you to take the necessary time to read the passages prayerfully, reflect upon them, and even memorize them if you're able to in the future.

> **Hebrews 9:1-28** *Then indeed, even the first covenant had ordinances of divine service and the earthly sanctuary. For a tabernacle was prepared: the first part, in which was the lampstand, the table, and the showbread, which is called the sanctuary; and behind the second veil, the part of the tabernacle which is called the Holiest of All, which had the golden censer and the ark of the covenant overlaid on all sides with gold, in which were the golden pot that had the manna, Aaron's rod that budded, and the tablets of the covenant; and above it were the cherubim of glory overshadowing the mercy seat. Of these things we cannot now speak in detail.*
>
> *Now when these things had been thus prepared, the priests always went into the first part of the tabernacle, performing the services. But into the second part the high priest went alone once a year, not without blood, which he*

offered for himself and for the people's sins committed in ignorance; the Holy Spirit indicating this, that the way into the Holiest of All was not yet made manifest while the first tabernacle was still standing. It was symbolic for the present time in which both gifts and sacrifices are offered which cannot make him who performed the service perfect in regard to the conscience— concerned only with foods and drinks, various washings, and fleshly ordinances imposed until the time of reformation.

But Christ came as High Priest of the good things to come, with the greater and more perfect tabernacle not made with hands, that is, not of this creation. Not with the blood of goats and calves, but with His own blood He entered the Most Holy Place once for all, having obtained eternal redemption. For if the blood of bulls and goats and the ashes of a heifer, sprinkling the unclean, sanctifies for the purifying of the flesh, how much more shall the blood of Christ, who through the eternal Spirit offered Himself without spot to God, cleanse your conscience from dead works to serve the living God? And for this reason He is the Mediator of the new covenant, by means of death, for the redemption of the transgressions under the first covenant, that those who are called may receive the promise of the eternal inheritance.

For where there is a testament, there must also of necessity be the death of the testator. For a testament is in force after men are dead, since it has no power at all while the testator lives. Therefore not even the first covenant was dedicated without blood. For when Moses had spoken every precept to all the people according to the law, he took the blood of calves and goats, with water, scarlet wool, and hyssop, and sprinkled both the book itself and all the people, saying, "This is the blood of the covenant which God has commanded you." Then likewise he sprinkled with blood both the tabernacle and all the vessels of the ministry. And *according to the law almost all things are purified with blood, and without shedding of blood there is no remission.*

Therefore it was necessary that the copies of the things in the heavens should be purified with these, but the heavenly things themselves with better sacrifices than these. For Christ has not entered the holy places made with hands, which are copies of the true, but into heaven itself, now to appear in the presence of God for us; not that He should offer Himself often, as the high priest enters the Most Holy Place every year with blood of another— He then would have had to suffer often since the foundation of the world; but now, once at the end of the ages, He has appeared to put away sin by the sacrifice of Himself. And as it is appointed for men to die once, but after this the judgment, so Christ was offered once to bear the sins of many. To those who eagerly wait for Him He will appear a second time, apart from sin, for salvation.

Hebrews 10:12-23 *But this Man, after He had offered one sacrifice for sins forever, sat down at the right hand of God, from that time waiting till His enemies are made His footstool. For by one offering He has perfected forever those who are being sanctified. But the Holy Spirit also witnesses to us; for after He had said before, "This is the covenant that I will make with them after those days, says the LORD: I will put My laws into their hearts, and in their minds I will write them," then He adds, "Their sins and their lawless deeds I will remember no more." Now where there is remission of these, there is no longer an offering for sin. Therefore, brethren, having boldness to enter the Holiest by the blood of Jesus, by a new and living way which He consecrated for us, through the veil, that is, His flesh, and having a High Priest over the house of God, let us draw near with a true heart in full assurance of faith, having our hearts sprinkled from an evil conscience and our bodies washed with pure water. Let us hold fast the confession of our hope without wavering, for He who* *promised is faithful.*

These passages talk a lot about the blood that Jesus shed on the cross for us. What does all this talk about blood mean? Why do we talk so much about the cross and the blood? Whenever I have the opportunity to talk with someone about the Gospel, I read to them John the Baptist's description of Jesus as *"the Lamb of God who takes away the sin of the world"* (John 1:29). I ask them what they think that means. Many have never thought through the concept of a blood-payment for sin.

Leviticus 17:11 states, *"For the life of the flesh is in the blood, and I have given it to you upon the altar to make atonement for your souls; for it is the blood that makes atonement for the soul."* This is one of the most central, foundational, and significant statements from our God about the importance of blood in the sacrificial system He set up for the people of Israel to deal with sin. Notice that this was God's provision for people and not vice-versa. Man was not buying God's favor by giving God blood. In contrast, God told man that He would accept this sacrifice and only this sacrifice. But the blood of animals never pleased God. I think it devastated God in the very beginning when He killed the first animal in the garden for Adam and Eve's sin – in order to give them covering for their naked bodies.

The use of the blood in the sacrificial system was a price-paying act to make atonement for sin. It was the *"redemption price"* for the offense committed. It was a life (an innocent life) for another life (a guilty life). Most of us think God grades on the curve – that if my good works outweigh my bad works, God will accept me and I'll be okay. However, it was one sin – just one – that required the life to be taken away from the guilty party. An animal was killed on the human's behalf as a sacrifice so the human didn't have to be put to death every time he knowingly or unknowingly sinned. The life of the flesh is in the blood. Thus, to shed blood is to kill and take life away.[37]

Doesn't that sound strange in today's world? As strange as all of it sounds, it is of the utmost importance! It sets the stage for the Messiah, the sacrificial lamb of God who came into the world to be that once-and-for-all blood offering for sin … our Lord and Savior Jesus Christ.

Notice in the passage below the significance of the word *light* and the idea of light (or glory) coming into a dark world through the *man* who John describes as *"the Word."*

> **John 1:1-10, 14, 18 (NET Bible Translation)** *In the beginning was the word, and the word was with God, and the word was God. He was with God in the beginning. All things were created by Him, and apart from Him not one thing was created that has been created. In Him was life, and the life was the light of mankind. And the light shines on darkness, but the darkness has not mastered it. A man came, sent from God, whose name was John. He came as a witness to testify about the light, so that everyone might believe through him. He himself was not the light, but he came to testify about the life. The true light, who gives light to everyone, was coming into the world. He was in the world, and the world was created by Him, but the world did not recognize Him … Now the word became flesh and He took up residence among us. We saw his glory – the glory of the one and only, full of grace and truth, who came from the Father ... No one has ever seen God. The only one, Himself God, who is in closest fellowship with the Father, has made God known.*

Essentially, Jesus was a walking, talking temple – or embodiment of God Himself. In an abstract way, He was the Holy of Holies personified. At His transfiguration, Jesus became radiant

---
[37] For more information, please see *"Blood, Sacrificial Aspects of,"* J. A. Motyer, in Elwell, Walter A. *The Evangelical Dictionary of Theology, 2nd Ed* (Downers Grove, Grand Rapids: 2001), p. 176.

[38] and a cloud of glory formed around Him. Light came out of Him and He shined like the sun. His veiled deity was shining through ... and the three disciples with Him (Peter, James and John) were so drawn to the experience that they never wanted it to end. Do we understand ... this is what we long for! But the glory of God, as magnetic and attractive as it is, only comes through a cross.

Do we really know what the cross and the blood are all about? If we did, we would be changed forever. We couldn't stop thinking about it – or talking about it. John the Baptist understood the importance of sacrifice ... that's why when he first saw Jesus, he said *"Behold the lamb of God, who takes away the sins of the world"* (John 1:29).

It wasn't a good time to be a lamb when Passover was approaching in Israel. Each family was to choose a spotless lamb and take it to the priest for sacrifice. The priest would inspect the lamb, insuring its suitability as an offering, and then place his hand on the lamb, symbolizing the transfer of sin from the guilty people to the innocent lamb. The lamb's throat would then be cut quickly, allowing the blood to flow upon the altar. 1 Peter 1:18-19 states that *"knowing that you were ransomed from the futile ways inherited from your forefathers, not with perishable things such as silver or gold, but with the precious blood of Christ, like that of a lamb without blemish or spot."*

Our High Priest, our perfect High Priest, being Himself God in the form of man, became God's sacrificial lamb for us. He bled, died, and was buried into a lifeless tomb. He went into heaven itself as our High Priest on our behalf. He defeated death and was raised back to life and transformed into a new, GLORY-FILLED BODY! His body was glorious because it was full of glory.

On this subject, N. T. Wright has said,

---

[38] Matthew 17:1-2; see also Hebrews 12:1-2; Revelation 1:12-20.

All that the temple had stood for would now be summed up in the cross, the last great symbolic event of Jesus' life…. What the temple stood for – the saving presence of Israel's God at the very center of the world – would be summed up in the violent death, at the hands of the pagans, of the young Jew who carried on His shoulders the pain and grief of the whole world. This was how sins would be forgiven. This was how the real Exodus would happen. This would be how the shameless, reckless love of the creator-God would come running down the road to embrace the whole world. [39]

The Really Good Part for All of Us

Colossians 1:19-27 teaches us the following truth about the Lord Jesus Christ and the glory of God:

> *For it pleased the Father that in Him all the fullness should dwell, and by Him to reconcile all things to Himself, by Him, whether things on earth or things in heaven, having made peace through the blood of His cross. And you, who once were alienated and enemies in your mind by wicked works, yet now He has reconciled in the body of His flesh through death, to present you holy, and blameless, and above reproach in His sight— if indeed you continue in the faith, grounded and steadfast, and are not moved away from the hope of the gospel which you heard, which was preached to every creature under heaven, of which I, Paul, became a minister. I now rejoice in my sufferings for you, and fill up in my flesh what is lacking in the afflictions of Christ, for the sake of His body, which is the church, of which I became a minister according to the stewardship from God which was given to me for you, to fulfill the word of God, the mystery which has been hidden from ages and from generations, but now has been revealed to His saints.* **To them God willed to make**

---
[39] N. T. Wright, *The Original Jesus*, p. 63.

known what are the riches of the glory of this mystery among the Gentiles: which is Christ in you, the hope of glory.

Hebrews 2:10 states: *"For it was fitting for Him, for whom are all things and by whom are all things, in bringing many sons to glory, to make the captain of their salvation perfect through sufferings"* We are saved and forgiven only by the blood of Jesus! You can be saved on no other grounds, no other merit, your justification only comes from the precious, perfect, cleansing, royal red blood of Jesus Christ. Unfortunately, many have turned the Gospel into something we do .… we "pray to God," or we say "we're saved because we love Jesus," or "because we go to church we're not going to hell anymore." Many say they're going to heaven because one day they "asked Jesus into their heart." Where did those terms ever come from? Not the Bible!

Hebrews 2: 1 says *"Therefore we must give the more earnest heed to the things we have heard, lest we drift away."* Salvation is impossible for any man, woman, or child – eternal life, the presence of God, the glory of God, is forever lost without the blood of Jesus Christ. Without the shedding of blood, there is no forgiveness of sins - period! Jesus did all the work. We must put our faith in the work of Jesus Christ on the cross. Do you understand the glory of Jesus Christ's suffering on the cross? He was tortured, wounded, bruised, hurt, stabbed, struck, flogged, mocked, rejected, and killed for us. The blood that flowed out of His veins paid the price for our sins … and we are bathed in His blood … perfected and purified in God's sight by His blood.

What does this mean? It means that the glory of God is now ours! God's glory, His presence, His life, He Himself is our inheritance, because of the blood of Jesus Christ. If and when you truly put your faith in Him, His blood, and His resurrection from the dead, confessing with your mouth that Jesus Christ is the Lord, you are given the gift of God's Spirit – God's essence

Himself. God's glory is placed inside of you. You become God's Tabernacle. You become God's Temple.

God showed this visibly on the day of Pentecost by putting flames of light, or flames of "fire," inside of the disciples (Acts 2:1-4). Throughout the Old Testament, the presence of God was identified with burning fire. [40] When God came to permanently live inside His people in the New Testament, those around them saw tongues of fire rest upon their bodies. The light of God has come to live inside of us to change us from the inside, to transform us. We become a new creation, children of the light. We have a new Father. Our new spirit in us is not given to us from our parents, but is birthed inside of us directly out of God's essence Himself, and we become united in Spirit with God and with one another! It means that we are in Christ and Christ is in us. We have been given the glory of God.

The moment Jesus died on the cross, the earth quaked and the temple mount shifted and caused the huge thick veil in front of the holy of holies to tear in two from top to bottom (Matthew 27:51). God's glory came to permanently dwell within and around the saints who are washed in the blood of the lamb. Something new had begun … and it changed everything.

---

[40] Exodus 3:2; 13:21; 1 Kings 18:38.

Questions for Reflection and Response:

- What does the cross mean to you? Why is it so necessary?

- The idea of blood sacrifices seems primitive and superstitious to many. Why is the idea of "blood" so central to Christianity?

Chapter Eight

Experiencing the Kingdom of God

"The Gospel of the kingdom is the Gospel of grace, with the additional element of the powers of the age to come." Watchman Nee [41]

The "Right Now-ness" of Our Faith

This is the point where the "rubber meets the road." Everything that has been discussed up to this point refers to a state of being, where we are in a right relationship with God through His Son, Jesus. Because of what He did on the cross in our place, there were *positional* changes which have occurred in our lives at a spiritual level when we believed. We have been changed from the inside out. We have been forgiven of our sins, cleansed by the powerful blood of Jesus Christ, raised from death to life, and have been brought forth into the everlasting government and rule of God's Kingdom. Now what? What does it mean for your life today?

The moment we believed in the Lord Jesus Christ, we were saved (Romans 10:9-13). Our eternal destiny and our relationship with God were guaranteed through the shed blood of Christ and

---
[41] Watchman Nee, *Secrets to Spiritual Power* (Whitaker House: New Kensington, PA: 1998), p. 233.

the forgiveness found in Him. We became members of the body of Christ, the Church. But besides our "once-and-for-all" salvation in Christ, there is the "here-and-now" relationship with Him. This "right-now-ness" is centered on what it means to be part of the Kingdom of God.

The Kingdom of God is the realm in which we are called to be disciples. Entering into the Kingdom enables us to begin enjoying and experiencing the privileges of God's government right here and right now as we follow Christ Jesus and His plan for our lives.[42] After describing how we are saved only by grace through faith in Christ, Paul told the Ephesians, *"For we are His workmanship, created in Christ* **Jesus for good works, which God prepared beforehand that we should walk in them**" (Ephesians 2:10).

What are those good works? They are the works of the Kingdom that God designed for us to participate in.

The night before His crucifixion, Jesus gathered His disciples into a small, second-story room where He told them many insights into the Kingdom. One of the most profound was, *"In that day you will know that I am in My Father, and you in Me, and I in you"* (John 14:20). What day is He speaking about? And when is "that day"? He is not talking about someday far into the future when we get to heaven, but that day when He comes to indwell His people permanently. That occurred at the day of Pentecost fifty days after the resurrection. The very same union that He had with the Father was one that believers would enjoy both with the Son and the Father.

While preaching and teaching His "Sermon on the Mount," Jesus said *"Blessed are the poor in spirit for theirs is the kingdom of heaven"* (Matthew 5:3). Greek scholar Spiros Zodhiates explains,

---
[42] See Ibid. p. 234.

The Lord tells us that we can be blessed here and now. The Kingdom of God can be ours here and now. This is why in the Beatitudes, whenever Jesus speaks of the Kingdom of God or the Kingdom of Heaven, the promise is always in the present tense, while all His other promises are in the future. It's to indicate that this blessedness, this being indwelt by God, is for here and now. [43]

Did you catch that? *"For here and now!"* Our union with God and His Son Jesus is not something for "later." It is something for here … now. He indwells His people, and calls us to Kingdom involvement.

The Veil is Torn Down

Earlier, we saw some of the incredible events that occurred immediately after Jesus' death. Matthew 27:50-51 records, *"And Jesus cried out again with a loud voice and yielded up his spirit. Then, behold, the veil of the temple was torn in two, from top to bottom; and the earth quaked, and the rocks were split."* This veil was the veil that separated the holy place of worship in the Temple from the Holy of Holies. Matthew goes into great detail when he says that the veil was torn *"from top to bottom."* This signifies that it was *God Himself* who tore the veil. It began *in heaven* and extended *to earth*. God was sending the world His change of address: He was saying, I don't live here anymore. I now live within My people.

God now lives within us. *"For through Him we both have access by one Spirit to the Father"* (Ephesians 2:18). Walvoord and Zuck have written, *"The word "access" can mean "introduction" in the sense that Christ is a believer's "introduction" to the Father. But it seems better to understand*

---
[43] Spiros Zodhiates, *Jesus and the Demon World* (AMG Publishers: Chattanooga, TN, 109), p. 109.

Experiencing the Kingdom of God

that Christ gives believers access. [44] Because of what Jesus has done, we now have access into His holy place ... into the Holy of Holies. But more than that, we **are** that holy place. 1 Corinthians 6:19-20 says, *"Or do you not know that your body is a temple of the Holy Spirit within you, whom you have from God? You are not your own, for you were bought with a price. So glorify God in your body."* He lives within us ... and that makes all the difference in how we live for Him.

Kingdom Citizens

When the Apostle Paul wanted to communicate the reality of what happens to a person when they become part of the Kingdom of God, he wrote these words:

> **Ephesians 2:1-7** *And you He made alive, who were dead in trespasses and sins, in which you once walked according to the course of this world, according to the prince of the power of the air, the spirit who now works in the sons of disobedience, among whom also we all once conducted ourselves in the lusts of our flesh, fulfilling the desires of the flesh and of the mind, and were by nature children of wrath, just as the others.* **But God, who is rich in mercy, because of His great love with which He loved us, even when we were dead in trespasses, <u>made us alive together with Christ</u> (by grace you have been saved), <u>and raised us up together, and made us sit together in the heavenly places in Christ Jesus</u>, that in the ages to come He might show the exceeding riches of His grace in His kindness toward us in Christ Jesus.**

This passage contains so much rich truth ... but I want you to first notice one little phrase repeated three times in verses five and six. It is the phrase *"with Christ"* or *"with Him."* Paul seems

---

[44] Walvoord, J. F., Zuck, R. B., & Dallas Theological Seminary, *The Bible Knowledge Commentary: An Exposition of the Scriptures*, Eph 2:17–18, (Wheaton, IL: Victor Books, electronic edition, 1983).

preoccupied with the idea that our new identity has to do with our new relationship *"with Christ."* Being with the King means we are thrust into the Kingdom and all that He is doing there.

As we've already discussed above, we are truly "alive" (John 17:3) because God's Spirit has resurrected our own spirit and indwelt us (Ephesians 2:6, Colossians 3:1). The same Spirit which raised Jesus Christ from death to life also brought *us* from death to life and has taken residence inside of our own spirits (see Romans 8:9-11; Ephesians 1:19-20). By becoming spiritually "alive in Christ," we simultaneously entered into the heavenly Kingdom. Though our mortal and physical bodies still remain in this three-dimension plane of existence, our spirits were brought forth into God's invisible realm of operation and government. We instantly were forced into a dual experience of reality. On the one hand we see, hear, smell, taste, and touch the physical world all around us. It is what we know and experience on a daily basis for the duration of our lives on this earth. However, by entering the Kingdom, a new realm is opened up to us **through faith**. The keyword there is faith, for many people will not live the Kingdom life in faith. Essentially, all born again believers are living in two parallel universes at the same time. As weird and mystical as that sounds, it is the truth. Please give me a chance to explain.

Before salvation, we could not truly "know" God. Yes, we could know of God intellectually, but we could not know Him experientially. Therefore, according to Jesus, we had no life. Jesus said in John 17:3, *"And this is eternal life, that they may know You, the only true God, and Jesus Christ whom You have sent."* Prior to coming to faith in Christ, all of us were dead, dying, and condemned. But now we have come to life. We can experience the presence of God. We can "see the Kingdom" (John 3:3) of God through spiritual eyes … the eyes of our heart. New spiritual gifts are imparted to us by the Holy Spirit. New dynamic and divine power is made available to us through God's Spirit (Acts 1:8). All of the sudden, communication, conversation, and direct relationship with Almighty God, the Most High is available. The ability to enter the very throne room in God's heavenly temple is open and available to all believers (Hebrew 4:16).

Because we are alive *(together with Christ)* and have been saved we have been *"raised up"* and *"seated"* with Christ in the heavenly places. This is not a figure of speech. This is not a metaphor or mere symbolism. It is the truth of God's word. This begs the question then, what and where are heavenly places? The phrase "heavenly places" is unique to the apostle Paul and used several times in the book of Ephesians:

Ephesians 1:3 *Blessed be the God and Father of our Lord Jesus Christ, who has blessed us in Christ with every spiritual blessing in the <u>heavenly places</u>.*

Ephesians 2:6 *(God the Father) raised us up with Him and seated us with Him in the <u>heavenly places</u> in Christ Jesus.*

Ephesians 1:20-21 *… that He worked in Christ when He raised Him from the dead and seated Him at His right hand in the <u>heavenly places</u>, far above all rule and authority and power and dominion, and above every name that is named, not only in this age but also in the one to come.*

Ephesians 3:8-10 *To me, who am less than the least of all the saints, this grace was given, that I should preach among the Gentiles the unsearchable riches of Christ, and to make all see what is the fellowship of the mystery, which from the beginning of the ages has been hidden in God who created all things through Jesus Christ; to the intent that now the manifold wisdom of God might be made known by the church to the principalities and powers in the <u>heavenly places</u>.*

Ephesians 6:12 *For we do not wrestle against flesh and blood, but against the rulers, against the authorities, against* *the cosmic powers over this present darkness, against the spiritual forces of evil in the <u>heavenly places</u>.*

What do we learn? We see that Father has blessed all who are *"in Christ"* with every spiritual blessing in the heavenly places. Next, we see that Jesus Christ was raised from the dead and *ascended into heavenly places* at the right hand of the Father (Eph 1:20). In Ephesians 3:10, we see that the current Satanic rulers and authorities are also in the heavenly places. This is also the place where spiritual battle occurs, as we see in Ephesians 6:12, where Paul says *"we wrestle … against the spiritual forces of evil in the heavenly places."*

"The heavenly places encompass the entire supernatural realm of God, His complete domain, the full extent of His divine operation." [45] Where is heaven? I personally don't think that heaven is up in space somewhere far, far away. I don't think that we could send a space shuttle off into space and reach heaven somewhere out there in space. Therefore, it seems most likely that heaven is not another "galaxy" or "planet" somewhere in space. Instead, it seems most realistic in my mind to understand heaven as other dimensions "or levels" of realities within the multi-verse we live. Heaven is just as real and tangible as our own reality we live in. My speculation, though it cannot be proven, is that heaven is all around us, above us, paralleled with our own universe, except the light and energy is vibrating at a much higher frequency. John MacArthur states in his commentary on Ephesians: *"Christians have a paradoxical, two-level existence – a dual citizenship. While we remain on earth we are citizens of the earth … our true life is in the supernatural …. Our Father is there, our Savior is there, our family and loved ones are there, our name is there, and our eternal dwelling place and throne are there."* [46]

---

[45] John MacArthur, *Ephesians*, (Chicago, Moody Press: 1986), p. 9.
[46] Ibid.

Do We Really Believe?

Take a look at the passage below from the book of Hebrews:

Hebrews 12:22-24 *But you have come to Mount Zion and to the city of the living God, the heavenly Jerusalem, to an innumerable company of angels, to the general assembly and church of the firstborn who are registered in heaven, to God the Judge of all, to the spirits of just men made perfect, to Jesus the Mediator of the new covenant, and to the blood of sprinkling that speaks better things than that of Abel.*

Is this the truth? Yes of course it is! But the more important question is, *"Do you actually believe that?"* If you actually believe it, then how has this reality affected your life?

It is my firm belief that we see and understand Scripture and reality the way we do in America, not because of truth, but because of post-enlightenment, modernistic thought patterns which really contradict our own theology. We are too scared of mystical and spiritual experience as if there is something evil or dangerous about it.

I've often been told by teachers, professors, and other pastors that we must be extremely careful of being too interested or curious about angels, demons, spiritual gifts, heaven, or the spiritual realm in general. Those topics are often treated as taboo subjects, even in Bible-believing churches. Why? Good-intentioned and sincere brothers in Christ have said that the main reason is because the supernatural and other related topics is a subject *abused* and *over-exaggerated* by Biblically illiterate and confused Christians who don't really know what they're talking about. If you're like me, and you have actually taken the time to study the supernatural realm, angelology, demonology, heaven, and have an intimate relationship with God through His Spirit, you will nonetheless encounter blank stares, snickers, and sometimes even back-handed and sarcastic comments from Bible-believing Christians if you actually believe such truths. Even worse, to actually say you "talk to God and He talks directly to you" will sometimes cause you to be marginalized and possibly demonized by the "religious elite" and evangelical academia, who have a fairly tight control over the current psychological construct and paradigm of Protestant-flavored-Christianity on most main-line Christians in the western world.

What's the solution? We must become more balanced in our pursuit of godliness. We need to be grounded in the truth of God's word, but we must also spend just as much personal alone time with God, in stillness speaking to Him and waiting on him, to listen for him.

Questions for Reflection and Response:

- Do you really believe? What difference does it make in your life?

- Your body is now where God lives. Have you ever really thought about the fact that **you** are now the Holy of Holies?

Chapter Nine

The Marriage of Christ and the Church

I have found most people in America are interested in *"doing things."* Instead of thinking about the meaning of things, we want to just *do*. I think that can be a good thing … but it also can be a bad thing. It can be good, because all truth and wisdom should spur us to action, and our faith should be expressed and lived out in our everyday life as we go from place to place. But it also can be bad. A preoccupation with *doing* causes many people to never really stop and think about the deeper causes, effects, or purposes of life itself. Therefore, before moving onto more practical aspects of the Kingdom life and values, I want to look just a little bit deeper at this idea of being *"in Christ"* and Christ being *"in us"* because, according to Paul, it is pretty important. In fact, he tells us that *"Christ in us"* is the hope of glory. But what does that even mean? What does it feel like to have *"Christ in us?"* Is anyone out there actually experiencing that or is it just all talk?

Marriage: A Picture of Our Spiritual Union with Jesus

In Ephesians 5:21-33 Paul exhorts the Ephesian believers to have godly marriage relationships. In this passage Paul instructs his readers that:
- Wives are to submit to their husbands.

- Each husband is head of his wife.
- Likewise, Christ is the head of the Church.
- Christ is the Savior of the body.
- Therefore, just as the Church is subject to Christ, so each wife should be subject to her husband.
- A husband is to love his wife just as Christ has loved the Church (and has given Himself for her).
- Christ gave Himself for the church, so that He might:
    - *Sanctify and cleanse her* with the washing of water by the word.
    - *Present her to Himself a glorious Church*, not having spot, wrinkle, or any such thing; holy and without blemish.

Before moving ahead, a few points should be made that I seldom hear regarding this passage. Obviously, in the beginning of this section, Paul is offering *practical instructions* to husband and wives. Paul is making the point that God created man and woman differently; He created men and women to function differently in the family unit. *This is not about **value or worth**, but about **function**.* Equal value, different roles. But there is something more profound here.

After telling wives and husbands how they are to function in their own marital relationships, Paul says they are to *pattern their relationship according to Christ and the Church*. According to Paul, the implication here seems to be that the *basis* and *divine institution* of marriage really stems from the relationship of Christ and His church from eternity past. Why? Because in arguing for a biblical blueprint for marriage, it seems that Paul was talking about something even deeper than the function of husband and wife. Paul could have simply told wives to submit to their husbands, and for husbands to love their wives. He could have then stated the facts in Genesis 2-3, how God created Adam first and Eve second, and that God created the man to function as the head of the family relationship. But Paul does not do that. Instead, he pictures the marriage relationship as a symbolic representation of Christ and the Church.

Obviously, Christ loves His Church and the Church loves Christ. Christ protects us and nourishes us. Obviously, the Church should submit to His leadership as their Lord. But why didn't Paul use the analogy of father and child? Why not the analogies of shepherd and flock – or loving King and willing servants? Why not brother and sister of Christ? Would those same analogies not fit with the same principle, of Jesus Christ loving His followers – protecting, nourishing, and leading them – and His disciples willingly submitting to Him?

In the next few pages, I want to answer those questions – and present a strong case for why the marriage analogy is the best one to describe the relationship of Christ and the Church. In other words, we're going to focus on a passage that is typically used to teach about marriage and, instead, learn what it has to say about the spiritual union relationship between Jesus and the Church. Marriage makes an abstract spiritual reality understandable to people who are severed from a firm grasp of their own spirits, much less the inner working and reality of the spiritual realm itself.

It is in this context of the *relationship between a husband and wife* that Paul writes:

Ephesians 5:28-32 *So husbands ought to love their own wives as their own bodies; he who loves his wife loves himself. For no one ever hated his own flesh, but nourishes and cherishes it, just as the Lord does the church. For we are members of His body, of His flesh and of His bones. "FOR THIS REASON A MAN SHALL LEAVE HIS FATHER AND MOTHER AND BE JOINED TO HIS WIFE, AND THE TWO*

SHALL BECOME ONE FLESH." *This is a great mystery, but I speak concerning Christ and the church.*

In the twenty eighth verse, the apostle says that a man should love his wife the way he loves himself. I think this could be simply a figure of speech, though there is more to this, as will be seen later. Paul teaches in verse twenty nine that *"No one hates his own body or himself."* We take care of our bodies, we nourish them, protect them, and feed them in order to stay comfortable and alive. Just as we take care of our own physical bodies, the Lord also cares for His body, His Church. In verse thirty, Paul notes that we are members of Christ's body. In fact, the passage tells us that we (the Church) are actually *"His flesh and bones."* We are Christ in the world.

Verse thirty is especially interesting in the context of this larger section. In many passages the Church is called the body of Christ and we are *"partakers of Christ."* Each believer is a *"member"* of the body of Christ. However, when do we ever consider ourselves an actual part of His flesh and of His bones?

1 Corinthians 10:15-17 *I speak as to wise men; judge for yourselves what I say. The cup of blessing which we bless, is it not the communion of the blood of Christ? The bread which we break, is it not the communion of the body of Christ? For we, though many, are one bread and one body; for we all partake of that one bread.*

Jesus said He is the *"Bread of Life"* (John 6:35). Just as physical bread sustains us and keeps us alive, He is our spiritual life, nourishing and sustaining us spiritually. His Spirit has made our spirits alive in the spiritual realm. He Himself is life. All life was made in and through Him (John 1:3-4). In fact, Paul makes it clear in his letter to Colossae that Christ actually *is our life:*

Colossians 3:1-4 *If then you were raised with Christ, seek* *those things which are above, where Christ is, sitting at the right hand of God. Set your mind on things above, not on things on the earth. For you died, and your life is hidden with Christ in God. When Christ who is our life appears, then you also will appear with Him in glory.*

In Ephesians 5:30-31, there is a clear allusion to the creation of Eve coming out of Adam. Let's refresh your memory by reading Genesis 2:21-23.

And the LORD God caused a deep sleep to fall on Adam, and he slept; and He took one of his ribs, and closed up the flesh in its place. Then the rib which the LORD God had taken from man He made into a woman, and He brought her to the man. And Adam said: **"This is now bone of my bones and flesh of my flesh; she shall be called Woman, because she was taken out of Man."**

Paul says in Ephesians 5:31 *"For this reason a man shall leave his father and mother and be joined to his wife, and the two shall become one flesh."* Paul quotes directly from Genesis 2:24! In regards to Genesis 2:24, commentators argue as to whether this is what Adam said prophetically or is an excerpt that Moses wrote in this text for his audience. Regardless, this was inspired by the Holy Spirit to be remembered by Moses' audience as an important truth in regards to marriage and its origin. *It is also clear from Paul, here in Ephesians 5:31, that the union between husband and wife was, from eternity past, used by the Lord as a type of the mystical union that one day would take place between Christ and His Church.* How so? Paul was talking about husband and wife, but there is a clear break in Paul's thought from v.29-32. Paul takes a detour to reflect on Christ and the Church. Then, in verse 33 Paul comes back to his thought and closes this section by saying *"Nevertheless let each one of you in particular so love his own wife as himself, and let the wife see that she respects her husband."*

Hold that thought for a moment and let's go back to the Genesis account. The first part of verse 2:24 reads *"For this reason...."* Apparently Adam and Eve were joined together in marital union *because the woman was brought forth out of man* (the Hebrew word is *adam*) as a partner and help-mate for Adam. Genesis 2:18 says, *"And the LORD God said, It is not good that man should be alone; I will make him a helper comparable to him."* Eve actually came directly from Adam's own flesh and his own rib bone. She was biologically "one" with Adam in flesh and bone. In other words, she originated from Adam, at least in her material composition. Also, it seems that one can conclude or presuppose that the spirit (or "life") that was in Eve was also from the "breath" of God Himself (cf. Gen 1:27, 2:7). Genesis 1:27 states that God created man "both male and female He created them **in His own image**." **Therefore, Adam and Eve were both biologically and spiritually equal.** [47] They were both one in body, soul, and spirit - equal in both "material" and "immaterial" aspects of their beings. [48]

The Two Shall Become One Flesh

There are several interpretations to the meaning of *"the two shall become one flesh"* in Genesis 2:24. The word translated *"one"* [49] is the Hebrew word *'echad,* which is an adjective meaning *one, first, once,* and *the same.* Deuteronomy 6:4 says

---

[47] This is not to imply that they were functionally equal. It is clear from looking at scripture as a whole, particularly in Ephesians 5, that God created man to be the functional head of his wife and family; the domestic and spiritual leader of the household.

[48] See James Montgomery Boice. *Ephesians* (Grand Rapids: Baker Books, 1997), p. 207. Also see pages 204-209 for a further reference to this passage. Boice provides a wonderful commentary to Paul's passage and thought process. You will be blessed by Boice's work on Ephesians and many of his other writings.

[49] Spiros Zodhiates, *The Complete Word Study Dictionary Old Testament*, Chattanooga: AMG Publishers, 2003, p. 33. See Zodhiates' note of H259 ('echad): "a person from among many (Gen. 3:22; 42:19; 1 Sam. 26:15). **It has the idea of unity or integrity as when it designates one justice for all (Num. 15:16) or actual physical unity (Exodus 36:12). The Lord is one (Deut. 6:4). It expresses agreement or unity among persons (Exo. 24:3) or physical unity (Zephaniah 3:9)**. It may serve as an indefinite article, one man (1 Sam. 1:1), or to indicate the first of something, e.g., the first day of the month (Gen. 8:5). The word is pluralized to mean several, few, or a while (Gen. 11:1; 27:44)."

"Hear, O Israel! The Lord is our God, the Lord is One." The word "one" in Deut. 6:4 is the same Hebrew word 'echad. However, 'echad can also imply the idea of unity or integrity, agreement among persons, and sometimes also used in a plural way (Gen. 11:1; 27:44).

Let's take a brief look at what some commentators from times past wrote about man and woman joining together to become "one flesh." Adam Clark writes,

> **These two shall be one flesh, shall be considered as one body**, having no separate or independent rights, privileges, cares, concerns, etc., each being equally interested in all things that concern the marriage state. **These two shall be for the production of one flesh; from their union a posterity shall spring**, as exactly resembling themselves as they do each other. [50]

John Gill stated,

> **The union between them is so close, as if they were but one person, one soul, one body;** and which is to be observed against polygamy, unlawful divorces, and all uncleanness, fornication, and adultery: only one man and one woman, being joined in lawful wedlock, have a right of copulation with each other, **in order to produce a legitimate offspring, partaking of the same one flesh, as children do of their parents**, without being able to distinguish the flesh of the one from the other, they partake of." [51]

Keil and Delitzsch were two great German theologians of a previous generation. They give great insight to this idea of marriage and the spiritual union of Christ and the Church.

---

[50] Adam Clark, *Clark's Commentary on the Bible*, (E-Sword, electronic edition), Genesis 2:24.
[51] John Gill, *John Gill's Exposition of the Entire Bible*, (E-Sword, electronic edition), Genesis 2:24.

The Marriage of Christ and the Church

They are the words of Moses, written to bring out the truth embodied in the fact recorded as a divinely appointed result, to exhibit marriage as the deepest corporeal and spiritual unity of man and woman, and to hold up monogamy before the eyes of the people of Israel as the form of marriage ordained by God .... By the leaving of father and mother, which applies to the woman as well as to the man, the conjugal union is shown to be a spiritual oneness, a vital communion of heart as well as of body, in which it finds its consummation. This union is of a totally different nature from that of parents and children; hence marriage between parents and children is entirely opposed to the ordinance of God. [52]

Finally, David Guzik writes that the idea of one flesh is taken by many *"to be mainly a way of expressing sexual union. While sexual union is certainly related to the idea of **one flesh**, it is only one part of what it means to be **one flesh**. **There are also important spiritual dimensions to one flesh.**"* [53]

It seems clear from a quick view at these various commentaries on Gen. 2:24 that marriage was a divine institution by God which involved a male and a female. God's plan was for a man and woman to be physically and spiritually united, joined together as one entity, in both physical and spiritual union, resulting in flesh and blood offspring of the same race. One man and one woman becoming one flesh through sexual union and ultimately resulting in a new offspring (one from two).

Paul directly alludes to this account back in Ephesians 5:30-31. Just like Eve came directly from the physical body of Adam, Paul states that we (those *"in Christ"*) are members of Christ's body; from His very flesh and bones. Paul clearly lets his readers know that this is what he has in mind by referring back to Genesis 2:22-24. Paul, as a learned Hebrew Pharisee and theologian, surely had

---

[52] Keil and Delitzsch, *Commentary on the Old Testament*, (E-Sword, electronic edition), Genesis 2:24.
[53] David Guzik, *Commentary on the Bible*, (E-Sword, electronic edition), Genesis 2:24.

a deep understanding of the meaning of that passage.

Paul takes this a step further when he says that the relationship of Adam and Eve coming together in physical and spiritual union as *"one flesh"* was a type of the relationship of Christ and His Church. It was in the mind of God from eternity past to use the physical and spiritual union of husband and wife to illustrate the union that would one day be accomplished in the mystical union between Jesus and His followers.

This, indeed, is a deep mystery, which is exactly what Paul states in verse 32: *"This is a great mystery, but I speak concerning Christ and the church."*

Understanding the Mystery

First, it is a *great* mystery. In Paul's mind, this revelation about Christ and the Church was of enormous magnitude, intensity, and value. The word *"mystery"* (*musterion*) is significant. Paul uses this word several times in Ephesians and other epistles. The word itself is derived from the Greek word *mustes* which referred to a person initiated into sacred mysteries by learning special rituals or secrets. [54] In general, the word *musterion* denotes something hidden or not fully manifest. It is some sacred truth or a principle unknown to human reason and known only by the revelation of God. [55]

The Apostle speaks in 1 Corinthians 13:2 of a man understanding all mysteries, that is all the revealed truths of the Christian religion stemming out of, or off-shooting from that which is elsewhere called *"the mystery of the faith"* (1 Timothy 3:9).[56] In Matthew 13:10-11, we read that *"the disciples came*

---

[54] Zodhiates, Spiros, *Complete Word Study Dictionary of the New Testament*, (E-Sword, electronic edition), Ephesians 5:31-32, p. 1000.

[55] See Rom. 11:25; 1 Cor. 4:1; 14:2; 15:51; Col. 2:2; 1 Tim. 3:16; 1 Cor. 2:7.

[56] My personal study of Paul's usage of "the faith" or "the doctrine," particularly in the Pastoral

and said to Him, 'Why do You speak to them in parables?' He answered and said to them, 'Because it has been given to you to know the mysteries of the kingdom of heaven, but to them it has not been given.'" The emphasis in the New Testament is that we who have believed in Jesus Christ as our Lord and Savior have been given the understanding of the mysteries.

The respected Greek and New Testament scholar, A.T. Robertson, expounded upon the word *"mystery."* He comments that the mystery-religions of the ancient Near East had all sorts of secrets and signs and mysteries just as secret societies still do to this day. But only those initiated into the secret society knew them. In the same way, the disciples have been initiated into the secrets of the kingdom of heaven by Jesus Christ. Paul uses the term freely to describe the mystery once hidden, but now revealed, now made known in Christ (Rom. 16:25; 1 Cor. 2:7). In Philippians 4:12, Paul says: *"I have learned the secret or been initiated."* [57]

According to Zodhiates, *musterion* refers to a spiritual truth couched under an external representation or similarity but will remain concealed or hidden unless some explanation is given.[58] In the writings of Paul, the word *musterion* is sometimes applied in a peculiar sense to the calling of the Gentiles. In Ephesians 3:3-6, the fact that Gentiles could be fellow-heirs and of the same body and partakers of Christ by the Gospel is called *"the mystery"* and *"the mystery of Christ."* In other generations, such a thing was not made known to men as it has been revealed to the Apostles of Christ Jesus and to the prophets by the Spirit.[59]

Both A.T. Robertson and Marvin Vincent confirm that here in

Epistles revealed that the faith itself refers to God's redemptive plan for mankind through the man Christ Jesus who was the One and only mediator between God and Man.

57 Robertson's' Word Pictures, (E-Sword, electronic edition), Philippians 4:12.

58 Zodhiates, p. 1000. See also Mark 4:11; Luke 8:10; Revelation 1:20, 10:7, 17:5, 17:7, in their respective contexts.

59 Romans 16:25; Ephesians 1:9, 3:9, 6:19; Colossians 1:26-27, 4:3.

Eph. 5:31, *"great mystery"* is directly related to the *"marriage"* of Christ to His Church: *"Clearly, Paul means to say that the comparison of marriage to the union of Christ and the church is the mystery."*[60] Vincent notes that:

> Great is predicative, not attributive; correctly, this mystery is great. The reference in this mystery is to the preceding statement of the conjugal relation of the Church with Christ, typified by the human marriage relation. Not calling your attention to the mere human relationship, but to the mysterious relation between Christ and His Church, of which that is a mere semblance. [61]

Why Is This Mystery So Great?

Now finally, the question becomes, *Why is this mystery so great?* Paul does not really expound upon this mystery that he has just made known to his Ephesian audience. Rather, he kind of builds up in this passage to a climax then stops, leaving the inquisitive mind left wanting more. According to Paul, this idea of the marriage-like union between Christ and the Church is a great mystery. Thus, there are two ideas that were possibly in Paul's mind as he wrote here.

First, Paul may be saying that the mysterious union between Christ and His Church is such that the unregenerate mind is unable to fathom or understand. It was even hidden from the evil principalities, powers, and spiritual forces from eons past. However, to Paul this secret mystery is able to be understood by (what we would call) Spirit filled followers of Christ. Maybe, like many other "spiritual realities," Paul simply means that this teaching is too hard for an unregenerate person to understand or come up with. Clearly, Paul teaches in other passages that the

---

[60] Archibald Thomas Robinson, *Word Pictures in the New Testament*, note on Eph 5:31,(E-Sword, electronic edition), Ephesians 5:31, p. 547.

[61] Marvin Vincent, *Word Studies*, (E-Sword, electronic edition), Ephesians 5:32.

mysteries surrounding the Gospel are difficult to understand.

Ephesians 3:1-12 *For this reason I, Paul, the prisoner of Christ Jesus for you Gentiles— if indeed you have heard of the dispensation of the grace of God which was given to me for you, how that by revelation He made known to me the mystery (as I have briefly written already, by which, when you read, you may understand my knowledge in the mystery of Christ), which in other ages was not made known to the sons of men, as it has now been revealed by the Spirit to His holy apostles and prophets: that the Gentiles should be fellow heirs, of the same body, and partakers of His promise in Christ through the gospel, of which I became a minister according to the gift of the grace of God given to me by the effective working of His power. To me, who am less than the least of all the saints, this grace was given, that I should preach among the Gentiles the unsearchable riches of Christ,* **and to make all see what is the fellowship of the mystery**, *which from the beginning of the ages has been hidden in God who created all things through Jesus Christ; to the intent* **that now the manifold wisdom of God might be made known by the church to the principalities and powers in the heavenly places, according to the eternal purpose which He accomplished in Christ Jesus our Lord,** *in whom we have boldness and access with confidence through faith in Him.*

Colossians 1:24-27 *I now rejoice in my sufferings for you, and fill up in my flesh what is lacking in the afflictions of Christ, for the sake of His body, which is the church, of which I became a minister according to the stewardship from God which was given to me for you, to fulfill the word of God, the mystery which has been hidden from ages and from generations, but now has been revealed to His saints.* **To them** *God willed to* **make known what are the riches of the glory of this mystery among the Gentiles**: *which is Christ in you, the hope of glory.*

Ephesians 1:7-14 *In Him we have redemption through His blood, the forgiveness of sins, according to the riches of His grace which He made to abound toward us in all wisdom and prudence,* **having made known to us the mystery of His will**, *according to His good pleasure which He purposed in Himself, that in the dispensation of the fullness of the times He might gather together in one all things in Christ, both which are in heaven and which are on earth—in Him. In Him also we have obtained* **an inheritance**, *being predestined according to the purpose of Him who works all things according to the counsel of His will, that we who first trusted in Christ should be to the praise of His glory. In Him you also trusted, after you heard the word of truth, the gospel of your salvation; in whom also, having believed, you were sealed with the Holy Spirit of promise,* **who is the guarantee of our inheritance until the redemption of the purchased possession**, *to the praise of His glory.*

If so, this is the typical and normal understanding of Ephesians 5:28-31. In nearly every commentary I have read, this relationship (union) between Christ and His church is not even expounded upon. It is a seemingly simple concept to understand for all believers who believe the Word of God to be true and inspired: **Jesus is the "head" of the Church, as in He is the Lord and King and ruler of His body. His "body" is symbolic for a large mass of "called out" people who are filled with the Holy Spirit of God.** The marriage of Christ to His church is merely symbolic of Christ loving His Church and His Church loving Him intimately – for all of eternity. It is an intimate bond and eternal relationship between the two. Likewise, Christ as the "head" protects, nourishes, and tends to his bride while His bride submits to His Lordship – for all eternity. But what is so hard or mysterious to understand and comprehend about that? I'm positive that any person, saved or un-saved, could grasp such a simple concept. More difficult is to actually believe such a concept, in faith.

The Marriage of Christ and the Church

A Possible Alternative Explanation of this Relationship

The second possible interpretation is that Paul is implying that this spiritual union between Christ and His Church is such a great mystery that illumination from the Holy Spirit is required for even the regenerate believer and student of the Word to understand this great *"spiritual truth couched under an external representation or similitude and concealed or hidden thereby unless some explanation is given."*[62]

Let's now look at the Ephesians passage and make several comparisons. Moving forward, it should be known that I fully understand the danger in allegorizing Scripture and finding "types" in every passage. Therefore, I stay away from allegorizing. However, the types I will now discuss seem to come not from me, but from Paul under direction and inspiration of the Holy Spirit. We are on solid ground when we acknowledge the typology that is inherently in Scripture. Here, Paul alludes back to Adam and Eve and the passage in Gen. 2:24. Thus, it may be possible to draw a spiritual analogy or type which may have been in Paul's thinking as he wrote this passage: **It is possible that Adam is symbolic or typological of Christ.**

We already know Paul often considered Adam to be a type of Christ. Many times he talked about Adam being *"the first man."* For example, 1 Corinthians 15:45-47 says, *"The first man Adam became a living being; the last Adam became a life-giving spirit. But it is not the spiritual that is first but the natural, and then the spiritual. The first man was from the earth, a man of dust; the second man is from heaven."*

Since this is so, can we also see in Ephesians 5 that Eve is symbolic or typical of the Church?

It was Adam who said of Eve *"This is now bone of my bones*

---

[62] Spiros Zodhiates, (E-Sword, electronic edition), Ephesians 5:31-32, p. 1000.

And flesh of my flesh; she shall be called Woman, because she was taken out of Man." Likewise, Paul states in Ephesians 5:30, *"For we are members of His body, of His flesh and of His bones."* Eve originated from the same biological and spiritual essence of Adam; Eve was an extension of Adam's body. In a similar way, we too share in the same humanity of Jesus Christ. [63] We are baptized by the spirit "into the body of Christ" and become a spiritual extension of the body of Christ. The Spirit of Christ dwells inside each believer. In fact, there are dozens of verses in the New Testament which explicitly state that Christ lives inside the bodies of believers. These statements are spoken as a literal truth, not as symbolism or a figure of speech. The mystery of the ages is "Christ in me, the hope of glory."

Romans 8:9-11 *But you are not in the flesh but in the Spirit, if indeed the Spirit of God dwells in you. Now if anyone does not have the Spirit of Christ, he is not His. And if Christ is in you, the body is dead because of sin, but the Spirit is life because of righteousness. But if the Spirit of Him who raised Jesus from the dead dwells in you, He who raised Christ from the dead will also give life to your mortal bodies through His Spirit who dwells in you.*

1 Corinthians 6:13-20 *Foods for the stomach and the stomach for foods, but God will destroy both it and them. Now the body is not for sexual immorality but for the Lord, and the Lord for the body. And God both raised up the Lord and will also raise us up by His power. Do you not know that your bodies are members of Christ? Shall I then take the members of Christ and make them members of a harlot? Certainly not! Or do you not know that he who is joined to a harlot is one body with her? For "THE TWO," He says, "SHALL BECOME ONE FLESH." But he who is joined to the*

---

[63] Philippians 2:6-8 tells us that He took on human flesh just like us. His humanity was different than ours in that He had no sin nature, nor did He sin. Hebrews 4:15 says that He was tempted in all ways like we are, yet was without sin.

Lord is one spirit with Him. Flee sexual immorality. Every sin that a man does is outside the body, but he who commits sexual immorality sins against his own body. Or do you not know that your body is the temple of the Holy Spirit who is in you, whom you have from God, and you are not your own? For you were bought at a price; therefore glorify God in your body and in your spirit, which are God's.

2 Corinthians 13:5 *Examine yourselves as to whether you are in the faith. Test yourselves. Do you not know yourselves, that Jesus Christ is in you?—unless indeed you are disqualified.*

Galatians 2:20-21 *I have been crucified with Christ; it is no longer I who live, but Christ lives in me; and the life which I now live in the flesh I live by faith in the Son of God, who loved me and gave Himself for me. I do not set aside the grace of God; for if righteousness comes through the law, then Christ died in vain.*

Colossians 3:9-11 *Do not lie to one another, since you have put off the old man with his deeds, and have put on the new man who is renewed in knowledge according to the image of Him who created him, where there is neither Greek nor Jew, circumcised nor uncircumcised, barbarian, Scythian, slave nor free, but Christ is all and in all.*

Hebrews 3:14 *For we have become partakers of Christ if we hold the beginning of our confidence steadfast to the end.*
Galatians 3:24-29 *Therefore the law was our tutor to bring us to Christ, that we might be justified by faith. But after faith has come, we are no longer under a tutor. For you are all sons of God through faith in Christ Jesus. For as many of you as were baptized into Christ have put on Christ. There is neither Jew nor Greek, there is neither slave nor free, there is neither male nor female; for you are all one in Christ Jesus. And if you are Christ's, then you are Abraham's seed, and heirs according to*

the promise.

Philippians 1:21 *For to me, to live is Christ, and to die is gain.*

Romans 12:4-5 *For as we have many members in one body, but all the members do not have the same function, so we, being many, are one body in Christ, and individually members of one another.*

1 Corinthians 12:12-14 *For as the body is one and has many members, but all the members of that one body, being many, are one body, so also is Christ. For by one Spirit we were all baptized into one body—whether Jews or Greeks, whether slaves or free—and have all been made to drink into one Spirit. For in fact the body is not one member but many.*

As noted above, we (the church) like Eve are **spiritually born from Christ**, out of or from His actual Spirit. As Jesus said, "*Most assuredly, I say to you, unless one is born of water and the Spirit, he cannot enter the kingdom of God.* **That which is born of the flesh is flesh, and that which is born of the Spirit is spirit**" (John 3:5-6).

We are members of His Spiritual Body. Each believer is a partaker and an extension of Christ's body. In other passages, the Church is referred to as a house which Christ lives in (Heb. 3:6), a temple, branches connected to One True Vine (John 15:1-8), spiritual stones of a living house (1 Pet. 2:4-5), partakers of Christ, and members of Christ's body. See what Paul already told the Ephesians earlier in his letter …

Ephesians 2:4-7 *But God, who is rich in mercy, because of His great love with which He loved us, even when we were dead in trespasses, made us alive* **together** *with Christ (by grace you have been saved), and raised* **us** *up* **together**, *and made* **us** *sit together in the heavenly places* **in Christ Jesus**, *that in* the ages to come He might show the exceeding riches of His grace in His kindness toward us in Christ Jesus.

Ephesians 2:19-22 Now, therefore, you are no longer strangers and foreigners, but fellow citizens with the saints and members of the household of God, having been built on the foundation of the apostles and prophets, Jesus Christ Himself being the chief cornerstone, in whom the whole building, being fitted together, grows into a holy temple in the Lord, in whom you also are being built together for a dwelling place of God in the Spirit.

Look what Peter and the writer of Hebrews also had to say:

1 Peter 2:4-5 Coming to Him as to a living stone, rejected indeed by men, but chosen by God and precious, **you also, as living stones, are being built up a spiritual house**, a holy priesthood, to offer up spiritual sacrifices acceptable to God through Jesus Christ.

Hebrews 3:4-6 For every house is built by someone, but He who built all things is God. And Moses indeed was faithful in all His house as a servant, for a testimony of those things which would be spoken afterward, **but Christ as a Son over His own house, whose house we are** if we hold fast the confidence and the rejoicing of the hope firm to the end.

In the Genesis passage, we saw that Eve came from Adam and thus the two individuals were not two separate races or types of creatures, but both of the same kind – they were comparable (See Genesis 1:27, 2:18). Then, the *iysh* and *iyshah* (man and woman), the two joined together and *became one flesh*, which at that time was a sexual union. The man left his father, took his wife and they became one. Likewise, at the final marriage banquet of the Lamb, Jesus Christ (the Bridegroom) will bring His beautiful, spotless, clean, sanctified Body of believers (His Bride) and be "married" to Her. <u>Obviously, this is not a sexual union</u>. That would be irrational and repugnant. However, in the Genesis passage, the physical and spiritual union was consummated through a sexual union. It was physical and spiritual beings <u>of the same "kind"</u> coming together to become one body (joined and glued together), one soul and Spirit, which ultimately resulted in a new offspring of the same kind.

Is it possible that Paul is teaching something similar in relation to Christ and the Church? Could it be that Paul is teaching that at the completion of the eschatological marriage supper, Christ will be spiritually joined to His bride and the two shall become one new collective body and organism? As some would say, *"one new man"* or one new collective type of glorified humanity?

Revelation 19:6-7 *And I heard, as it were, the voice of a great multitude, as the sound of many waters and as the sound of mighty thunderings, saying, 'Alleluia! For the Lord God Omnipotent reigns! Let us be glad and rejoice and give Him glory,* **for the marriage of the Lamb has come, and His wife has made herself ready**.'

Paul implies that at the marriage of the Lamb we will all be changed. In the twinkling of an eye, each member of the body of Christ will be transformed into a new glorified resurrected body, while also simultaneously being fully indwelt with the Spirit of Christ. We have already been immersed into the body of Christ by the Holy Spirit – but the final marriage/consummation of our future glory (*"inheritance"* in Eph 1:13 seen above) is not yet fulfilled. The glorified bodies of the Church will actually become the physical dwelling place of Christ. As Eve was born out of Adam, so the Church has been spiritually born out of Christ, becoming individual extensions of Christ's spiritual body. As Adam and Eve joined to become one flesh through physical and sexual union (while remaining distinct and separate), will Christ's Spirit then be united inside of each believer (and all other believers at the same time) to become a new living, breathing organism – Christ in His Church – while at the same time, the two entities (Christ and the Church) remaining distinct and separate?

I am not suggesting that each one of us become divine or become God. That is what many pagan, new age heretics have taught for centuries. Rather, I am proposing that the divine Christ, the eternal *Logos* permanently and fully dwells in each glorified believer simultaneously at the same time, making the entire "household of God" separate and yet one at the same time. Each member of the body becomes unified with Christ as the two become one.

Though this seems like a hard concept to me, what is Paul (and John) really teaching in these passages?

> **1 Corinthians 15:45-54** *And so it is written, "The first man Adam became a living being." The last Adam became a life-giving spirit. However, the spiritual is not first, but the natural, and afterward the spiritual. The first man was of the earth, made of dust; the second Man is the Lord from heaven. As was the man of dust, so also are those who are made of dust; and as is the heavenly Man, so also are those who are heavenly. And as we have borne the image of the man of dust, we shall also bear the image of the heavenly Man. Now this I say, brethren, that flesh and blood cannot inherit the kingdom of God; nor does corruption inherit incorruption. Behold, I tell you a mystery: We shall not all sleep, but we shall all be changed— in a moment, in the twinkling of an eye, at the last trumpet. For the trumpet will sound, and the dead will be raised incorruptible, and we shall be changed. For this corruptible must put on incorruption, and this mortal must put on immortality. So when this corruptible has put on incorruption, and this mortal has put on immortality, then shall be brought to pass the saying that is written: "Death is swallowed up in victory."*

2 Corinthians 3:15-18 *But even to this day, when Moses is read, a veil lies on their heart. Nevertheless when one turns to the Lord, the veil is taken away. Now the Lord is the Spirit; and where the Spirit of the Lord is, there is liberty. But we all, with unveiled face, beholding as in a mirror the glory of the Lord, are being transformed into the same image from glory to glory, just as by the Spirit of the Lord.*

Philippians 3:20-21 *For our citizenship is in heaven, from which we also eagerly wait for the Savior, the Lord Jesus Christ, who will transform our lowly body that it may be conformed to His glorious body, according to the working by which He is able even to subdue all things to Himself.*

1 John 3:1-2 *Behold what manner of love the Father has bestowed on us, that we should be called children of God! Therefore the world does not know us, because it did not know Him. Beloved, now we are children of God; and* **it has not yet been revealed what we shall be**, *but we know that when He is revealed, we shall be like Him, for we shall see Him as He is.*

2 Corinthians 11:2-3 *For I am jealous for you with godly jealousy. For I have betrothed you to one husband, that I may present you as a chaste virgin to Christ. But I fear, lest somehow, as the serpent deceived Eve by his craftiness, so your minds may be corrupted from the simplicity that is in Christ.*

Questions for Reflection and Response:

- What are the implications of Christ eternally inhabiting and filling His body of people?

- What difference does the marriage of Christ and His Church make in your life today?

Chapter Ten

Kingdom Life vs. Religious Life: It's a Relationship, Not a Religion!

Jeremiah 2:1-13 *Moreover the word of the LORD came to me, saying, "Go and cry in the hearing of Jerusalem, saying, 'Thus says the LORD: "I remember you, the kindness of your youth, the love of your betrothal, when you went after Me in the wilderness, in a land not sown. Israel was holiness to the LORD, the firstfruits of His increase. All that devour him will offend; disaster will come upon them," says the LORD.' " Hear the word of the LORD, O house of Jacob and all the families of the house of Israel. Thus says the LORD: "What injustice have your fathers found in Me, that they have gone far from Me, have followed idols, and have become idolaters? Neither did they say, 'Where is the LORD, Who brought us up out of the land of Egypt, Who led us through the wilderness, through a land of deserts and pits, through a land of drought and the shadow of death, through a land that no one crossed and where no one dwelt?' I brought you into a bountiful country, to eat its fruit and its goodness. But when you entered, you defiled My land and made My heritage an abomination. The priests did not say, 'Where is the LORD?' those who handle the law did not know Me; the rulers also transgressed against Me; the prophets prophesied by Baal, and walked after things that do not profit. Therefore I will yet* bring charges against you," says the LORD, "And against your children's children I will bring charges. For pass beyond the coasts of Cyprus and see, send to Kedar and consider diligently, and see if there has been such a thing. Has a nation changed its gods, which are not gods? But My people have changed their Glory for what does not profit. Be astonished, O heavens, at this, and be horribly afraid; be very desolate," says the LORD. "For My people have committed two evils: They have forsaken Me, the fountain of living waters, and hewn themselves cisterns—broken cisterns that can hold no water.

An Old Message that Still Rings True Today: Jeremiah's Cry Against Empty Religion

Six and a half centuries before Christ, a young man named Jeremiah was commissioned by God to be a prophet to God's people as well as to the other nations. We pick up his story in Jeremiah 1 where God gives him his marching orders. Jeremiah was a lonely, weeping prophet who lived in a time of spiritual darkness, spiritual idolatry, spiritual apathy, and outright rebellion against God (Jeremiah 2-3). For forty plus years Jeremiah prophesied and ministered to his people, speaking truth as a direct spokesman for the Lord God. But very few people listened to anything he said. He went against the establishment and against the status quo. He was a lone ranger, like a fish swimming against the current of the political, social, and religious cultural paradigm of virtually everyone in his day.

When Jeremiah spoke the truth directly from Almighty God, he experienced harassment, rejection, and rage from the very people who claimed to know God, to know God's Word, and to be following God the right way. Jeremiah's message to his people was to REPENT because God was angry. God had promised to bring destruction on them from the Babylonian powerhouse coming from the north. The Jews would be sent into exile as punishment ... but in the end, God would bring back His people and restore the nation once again after His anger was appeased.

Needless to say, His message was scoffed at, mocked, and fell on deaf ears. All the other priests and prophets were preaching, peace and prosperity – it's what the people wanted to hear. But like a true prophet, Jeremiah lived to see his horrifying prophecies come true. Essentially, Jeremiah was preaching God's word to a people who had forgotten who and what God is. [64] Jeremiah nurtured and nourished the people with God's Word, but they refused to accept it.

The Context

Chapter two opens up with Jeremiah preaching to the people in Jerusalem as God commissioned him. The whole chapter is a passionate, powerful, and graphic indictment of the nation's rebellion.

In verses 2-3, God reminisces of Israel's early years in which they were so devoted to Him. They were faithful, loyal, devoted, dependent, and in love with Him. Worship was only given to Him. That is the way God intended it to be. Israel was like God's wife and He was their husband. They were in an intimate covenant relationship. He led them out of bondage into freedom, into their promised land of rest where God provided for them. Israel was holy and set apart to the Lord, plucked out of the rest of the world as His own. He established them, chose them, and desired from the very beginning to use them as an object of blessing to the rest of the world.

In verses 4-5, God turns and poses a question, like a judge

---

[64] F.B. Huey Jr., *New American Commentary: Jeremiah and Lamentations*, (Nashville: Broadman Press, 1993), p. 33. For a good study of the theology in the book of Jeremiah, see also Walter Brueggemann, *The Theology of the Book of Jeremiah*, Cambridge University Press, 2007.

sitting on his throne of judgment. He asks *"What fault could your ancestors have possibly found in me that they strayed so far from me?"* God then declares that their fathers chased after worthless idols and gods. The word *"worthless"* means *"meaningless, nothing, empty, and total vanity."* Essentially, worshipping other gods was by default a total rejection of the one true God, Yahweh. Yahweh, the God of Israel, is the name of the Most High God Who created all the angels and all heavenly beings and creatures (which were considered "gods" by the people of the world and worshipped just as Hindus and other religions still do to this day). Idols are simply objects of wood, metal, stone, and other materials that represent real, live demons and fallen beings of other dimensions. They are spirit-beings created by the One True God who followed after Lucifer (Satan, the Devil) in his proud and arrogant rebellion against God. Godless people degenerated to the point of worshipping those fallen, wicked, evil, worthless, disgusting beings who rebelled against Yahweh.

Adding to the guilt of such despicable apostasy, the people had no gratitude for God's deliverance. Verses 6-8 tell us that God delivered and protected His people miraculously from a land of darkness (Egypt), but they had spiritual amnesia. They forgot about God's miraculous deliverance and provision. (Lest we think that we are immune to such ingratitude and forgetfulness, let me ask this question: *how many of us so quickly forget the blessings and deliverance that God has provided for us?* It's a common human malady – and we are guilty as charged … just like the Israelites in Jeremiah's day.)

God continues His indictment of the nation by addressing their spiritual leaders. He declares that the priests don't seek Him, and the scribes and teachers of God's Word don't have a true personal and intimate knowledge of Him. They know *about* God, but they don't *know Him personally*. The government and political leaders totally disregard His ways and authority. They act like their father, the devil, and have rebelled against God. The prophets speak lies, demonic messages, fables, and imaginations, which don't come from God. *All the leaders – political and religious – are worshipping and chasing after worthless, meaningless, empty, vain idols.*

Jeremiah lived within a culture and among people who were extremely religious. They still had the shell of Judaism, the law, and the commandments. God's temple was still there. They still had their priests, teachers, scribes, and prophets. People were still going to the temple, celebrating festivals and the whole nine yards. It was *"a way of life"* for them … but it was devoid of real love and fire for their God. Most of their worship was devoted to false, meaningless gods. In short, Jeremiah was living among a people who were totally alienated from God. Their religion was a sham. They had no real, intimate knowledge and relationship with their God.

Everyone stop! Look! Listen! By the time we get to verse 12, God is outraged and appalled. He calls to all of the heavenly beings and creatures – millions and possibly billions of beings – to look in shock and disbelief at the depravity and insanity of Judah. Are they mad? He calls them to be his witnesses about the guilt of Judah. Nothing like this has ever occurred. Nothing like this has ever been thought of by the angels.

The height of God's condemnation comes in verse 13 where Yahweh says, *"For My people have committed two evils: they have forsaken Me, the fountain of living waters, hewed out cisterns for themselves, broken cisterns that can hold no water."* They had committed a double-wrong. It wasn't that they had committed just these two sins … if you read the entire book of Jeremiah, you will find they committed numerous sins. Rather, God is saying that His people had committed two principle and foundational sins … two evils which upset Him to the point of wrath.

To Jeremiah's audience, the symbolism here is very clear. Every landowner would greatly desire to have a piece of land with a flowing spring on the property, which would be a tremendous help to him in meeting his daily needs for water and survival. He wouldn't have to labor and work hard to go and bring water.

Several years ago I was in Ethiopia, south of Addis Ababa in an area called Langano. As we drove down the road and through the wilderness, we kept seeing people walking along the road carrying blue and white plastic containers that looked like gas cans we use in America to fill our lawnmowers. They were really 3 and 5 gallon plastic water jugs that the people carried to a nearby river several miles away every day to fill up and carry back home in order to have water for the day for cooking, cleaning and drinking. Water was such a precious commodity and needed resource to these people. It hit me there how beneficial it would be if they could just dig a well right where they lived. There is a parallel to our lives: we don't have to work and struggle to find fulfillment. God Himself is our source of life-giving waters. He provides an endless, eternal, flowing, source of blessing, nourishment, life and love. Jesus said, *"If anyone thirsts, let him come to Me and drink. He who believes in Me, as the Scripture has said, out of his heart will flow rivers of living water." But this He spoke concerning the Spirit, whom those believing in Him would receive; for the Holy Spirit was not yet given, because Jesus was not yet glorified"* (John 7:37-39).

Living inside of us, the Spirit of God provides endless power to each child of God. Are we tapping into that power? Are we relying on God's Spirit to fill, control and empower us on a daily basis?

Anyone in Judah who did not have a natural source of flowing, clean water would dig a cistern – a pit dug in the ground to collect water. Then the people would dig canals to direct rain water into the cistern when the rain came to store up as much water as possible. Usually these cisterns were built into limestone rock in the ground. But before water was stored they had to be covered and sealed with plaster to prevent water from leaking out. Regardless, cisterns often became corroded, damaged and cracked, which allowed the collected rainwater to seep out and empty the cistern, leaving the farmer or landowner without the precious life-giving commodity. [65]

Sin # 1 – They Rejected God

> God said, *"They [My people] have rejected Me."* The word *"rejected"* or *"forsaken"* means *"to leave or to abandon, to turn your back on something or someone."* One commentator wrote,
> In the context of Jeremiah 2 this word implies that Israel and Judah *"walked out on the marriage."* The people said in v. 20, *"I will not serve"*; v.23, *"I have not gone after Baal,"* when they did; v.31,
> *"We are free, we will come to you no more;"* v.35, *"I am innocent; surely His anger is turned from me. I have not sinned."* Such infidelity, abandonment, and unfaithfulness evoked the heated anger of God like a husband who just found out his wife was cheating on him with his dreaded enemies, bringing him to the point of going berserk in rage. [66]

Who is it they had rejected? *"The Fountain of Life-Giving Waters."* God declares that He is the fountain of life-giving waters. The word fountain could also be translated *"source."* God is the source of life-giving water. He provides an unending flow and stock of water that does not run out, a natural flowing spring, bubbling up from the ground. The word *"fountain"* is used to describe the source of flowing rivers. As the fountain of life-giving

---
[65] J.A. Thompson (General Editors: R.K. Harrison, Robert L. Hubbard) *New International Commentary of the Old Testament, Jeremiah* (William B. Eerdmans Publishing Company, Grand Rapids: 1980) p. 171.
[66] Walter Brueggeman, *The Theology of Jeremiah* (Cambridge University Press, New York: 2007), p. 82.

waters, God is the source of refreshment. He is the Source which quenches our deep-seated spiritual needs. HE IS LIFE! God is everything that Judah needed for spiritual and physical blessings, for protection, and every other need. *But they turned their backs on Him and walked away.* They forsook God. They rejected Him and His provision.

How did they reject God? If you go back to chapter 1:16, you will read, *"I will pass sentence on the people of Jerusalem and Judah because of their wickedness. For they have rejected Me and offered sacrifices to other gods, worshipping what they made with their own hands."* Judah committed the "sin-trifecta": they forsook their God; they pledged allegiance to and worshipped false gods; and they crafted idols with their own hands. In chapter 2:19, God also says, *"Your evil will chastise you and your apostasy will reprove you. Know and see that it is evil and bitter for you to forsake the Lord your God; the fear of Me is not in you, declares the Lord of Hosts."* Their series of poor choices brought about the judgment of God. All these bad things happened to them because they walked away from God and sought idols.

Sin # 2 – Devotion to Empty, Meaningless Religion

What did the people do to fill the void in their lives when they rejected the One True God? They *"dug cisterns for themselves … broken cisterns which can hold no water."* The people rejected God – the source of all blessing – and chased after worthless gods, idols. Basically, they pursued empty, worthless, meaningless religion.

> *"They had forsaken Yahweh who, like a fountain, had provided for their deepest needs (cf. Ps. 36:9; John 4:10-14; Rev. 21:6). And they had pursued idols who, like broken cisterns, could not even hold water – much less provide it. The most reliable source of water in Israel was a natural spring, and the least*

reliable was a cistern." [67]

They devoted themselves to idols that could not really fulfill their needs, quench their spiritual thirst, and bless them or protect them at all. Judah had given up everything and had gone after nothing. She cheated herself.

Fast-forward to the 21st Century

If you really begin to think about this particular passage we have examined, you will see some unsettling similarities between Judah's culture and ours. Just as Israel and Judah represented the people of God, today we, as followers of Jesus Christ, are the people of God. In Jeremiah's day God's people had rejected God and chosen empty formal and meaningless, shallow religion and idol worship. Today we settle for the same thing. Oh, our idols may look different – but the truth is, we have traded in a vibrant, intimate, love-relationship with God for a shell of religiousness. *Christianity is simply a religion for most people today.* Pollsters and social commentators tell us that over 70% of Americans claim to be Christians today. Church buildings are full of people who claim to be the people of God, who have no business making that claim. There is but a small remnant of God's Kingdom-citizens, genuine Christ-followers. We Christians are the *"people of God."* Jesus said *"Narrow is the way to life and few find it"* (Matthew 7:13-14).

Though we understand this passage in its own historical context as applying to the people of Jeremiah's day, we can see some scary parallels between then and now. Are we not guilty of the same thing: rejecting the fountain or source of life-giving waters? Chasing after meaningless religion was the great sin that so angered God. It was spiritual adultery. And just like the rest of humanity since the beginning of time, we have desired religion

---

[67] Tom Constable, *Expository Bible Study Notes: Jeremiah 2:13*, (Electronic edition).

and rejected God.

Can I take a moment to share my heart with you? Some of you are pastors, Bible teachers, or professors and are ready to criticize some of my theological points. Others of you may be worship leaders, small group leaders, elders, or deacons ready to do the same. When I preached this message, the people in my audience could feel both my passion and compassion ... and I want you to do the same. I am not angry ... in fact, I am a bit sorrowful requesting that we – both you and me, in truth and love – face the facts and be real with God, ourselves, and each other. Friends, I'm afraid that what we have here, what we're doing, if we're not careful, is NOT about God. It is empty, shallow, meaningless, vain, self-gratifying religion. You say, "Jesse, what do you mean? How can you say that?"

Religion is and always has been a system of control. Religion is and always has tended to be a system of manipulation. Religion usually winds up being a system man uses to manipulate others and, in the end, God Himself. How so? Religion teaches us that by doing, saying, giving, attending, and striving, we fulfill our duties and thus earn favor with God. God therefore must fulfill certain obligations to us as a result. We basically place ourselves in the driver seat and have the ability to control our relationship with God. It is coming to God on our terms. The truth is that God HATES religion. He never desired to create a religious system as we know it. There would have been no need. As James tells us, God's idea of religion is simply helping widows and orphans and keeping yourself unstained by the sin of the world and the flesh (James 1:27).

God never intended to have temples and church buildings built. It was never God's purpose to have hymnals, creeds, dogmas, theology text books, rituals, and everything else. God created human beings in His own image and likeness. His desire was to have a close relationship with His creatures. He wants the most intimate spiritual union and physical relationship we can imagine. He walked and talked in Paradise with the first man Adam and the first woman Eve. That is what God desired. Personal – face to face – spirit to spirit connection and loving, mutual relationship with His creatures…in which His creatures found all of their pleasure, joy, and fulfillment in Him and with Him. *That was all lost when man fell. He rebelled against God and desired to be his own god and do things his own way.* In doing so, Adam and all of his progeny (the entire human race) joined Satan in his rebellion, placing themselves under Satan's dominion, authority, and control.

He is Still Seeking People Today

But do you know what? Jesus Christ came to seek and save THAT WHICH WAS LOST. He came, as my friend Rick Amato says so often, "to restore the possibility for man to have conscious contact restored to his Creator." The fullness of who and what God is dwelt in Jesus' body (Colossians 2:9). Jesus was the total and complete revelation and manifestation of God in human form. God has come to us. He became one of us. He came to deal with the one thing which separated us from knowing and connecting with our God: the deep-seated disease in the innermost parts of our beings called *sin*.

But Jesus destroyed and defeated sin on cross. He destroyed the power and work of Satan and judged all sins of all time by His sacrificial death for us. Our God and Savior placed our sins on His back, shed His blood, and let His body be broken and bruised for us. He died in our place. He defeated death by the power of God's Spirit at work in Him. The Father raised Him from the dead and seated Him at His right hand of power and authority.

Do you know what Jesus proclaimed? He said in the Gospel of John, *"If anyone thirsts, let him come to Me and drink. He who* believes in Me, as the Scripture has said, out of his heart will flow rivers of living water. But this He spoke concerning the Spirit, whom those believing in Him would receive; for the Holy Spirit was not yet given, because Jesus was not yet glorified" (John 7:37-39).

Every day we wake up, brush our teeth, grab a quick breakfast, read the newspaper, go to work, go home, go to sleep. Then on Sundays, we get dressed up and look nice, drive to a big building called a "church" and sit in a theater, listen to a concert, listen to a man speak from a holy book, and then we go home and wait to come back in another seven days. That is the typical lifestyle of a "Christian" in the Western World. For those of us who are more "committed" to Christ, we read the Bible. We may actually get in a prayer or two while driving to work. We might say short prayers throughout the day. If you're like me, you might even set aside thirty minutes or an hour to pray. *"Dear Lord, thank You for this day. Lord, please give me strength. Please help me against my struggles. Please help so and so, please do this, please do that."* Babbling out loud to ourselves, we really don't know if God is even listening.

We love listening to praise and worship music. It makes us feel so happy inside. Sometimes we even come in the church and hear the music and it gives us goose bumps and chills up and down our spine (like when we watch American Idol!), and if the emotional level is high enough we raise our hands, shout out loud to God, dance, sway, and close our eyes.

We have small groups for those who are even more committed, where we can meet together and talk *ABOUT* God. We can read *ABOUT* Jesus. We can dialogue and discuss *ABOUT* Bible verses. Sometimes, if we're honest, we share our problems with one another. We have every kind of class and every kind of topic under the sun. We have self-help classes. We can come to our place of "worship" and get help on money matters, raising children, dealing with depression and addictions, missions, apologetics, doctrine, and the list goes on and on and on. For many of us, this weekend encounter on Saturday/Sunday is "our battery charge" that keeps us going. By the way, there is nothing wrong with any of these things in and of themselves. In fact, many of these activities and programs are very essential and beneficial to Christ-followers and can contribute to our growth and discipleship.

But during the week, if we are honest with ourselves, who do we really worship? What god or gods do we chase after? We chase after the gods of sex, materialism, power and success. How many of us can honestly say we spend more time with the God who created us, the God of life-giving waters, than we do watching TV? What about Facebook? What about video games? What about doing yard work? Do we ever change?

I'm not trying to put you on a guilt trip or make you feel bad. I'm just trying to wake you up from being spiritually numb. *We are living and breathing Jeremiah 2 right now. In all of this religious stuff we are doing, where is God? How much time do you actually have "conscious contact" and intimate spiritual union with God? I'm not asking how much you read your Bible or how long you prayed. I'm not asking how many worship songs you listened to or how many pages in a theological book you read.* The question I am asking is this: *Are you experiencing God?* Psalm 91:1 says, *"He who dwells in the shelter of the Most High will abide in the shadow of the Almighty."* Do you have that type of intimate, day-to-day, moment-by-moment relationship with Him?

In Revelation 3:20, Jesus spoke to "the lukewarm church" of Laodicea, *"Behold, I stand at the door and knock. If anyone hears My voice and opens the door, I will come in to him and dine with him, and he with Me."* Today, we are the church of Laodicea. We are following in the footsteps of the Laodiceans. *Jesus was actually outside of the church, in the cold, and in the dark, knocking on the door, asking to come in. They kicked Jesus out of His own church.* You won't find Jesus in a building. You won't find Jesus by doing a bunch of religious works. He's not there. He is in heaven. You can't invite Jesus in your heart because He won't fit in there. Jesus is in Heaven, *but He has invited you into His Heavenly Kingdom to participate in His heavenly community of people.* It is His Spirit who is knocking on your door and asking you to let Him in. If you do, if you will listen and wait and hear His soft, gentle voice, speaking to you in your spirit, and you invite Him into your innermost being, the Spirit of Christ will live inside of you. In the last part of Revelation 3:20, Jesus promises, *"I will come in to him and eat with him, and he with Me."* In the culture of that day, that was a picture of intimate friendship – a one-on-one, real-life relationship, like two best friends.

The people of Jeremiah's day had the same problem we do. They chased after idols ... meaningless, worthless, vain idols. But idols can never satisfy our deepest needs. They can't fill that void in the most sensitive parts of our inner selves. This world is dark, perverted, and twisted, like a hot dry desert. Our God has come to us, saved us, and offered an oasis to quench our thirst. But many of us have rejected the oasis and settled for a broken, cracked, cistern – a religious system that can never satisfy.

IS CHURCH NOT SATISFYING YOUR NEEDS? Do you feel like you sit in the pew but don't really even know God? Is He real to you? Be honest. Do you feel like God is distant? Many of you are weary, tired, struggling, or tempted to give up and throw in the towel to all of this "stuff" because it's just not "working for you." I don't blame you. I felt the same way.

So what is the answer? Do we reject church and all the "religious stuff" we have filled our lives with? NO WAY! But if all that you know and experience is the religious trappings, then you have nothing – just an empty cracked cistern. Let me give you a simple illustration: If you took the engine out of a car, then got in the driver seat and tried to drive, would you be surprised that you are not able to get where you want to go? Religion without God's manifest power is no different. You will never get what you're seeking and experience God in the way you so desire by simply going through the motions. It is a relationship that must be developed.

Jesus said, *"Seek first the kingdom of God and His righteousness, and all these things will be added to you"* (Matthew 6:33). We are to seek God first – not His power or His blessing, but seek Him alone. He is our inheritance. He is our reward! We are to seek Him every day, every morning, every waking moment of the day, every evening. For it is through experiencing God and His manifest presence that you obtain everything you need in this life. *When His glory surrounds you, His refining fire and presence will change you from within. He will give you the strength and power you need to make it in this world and to minister the way He has called you to minister. He will speak through you; He will love others through you; He will allow you to be Christ in this world as an extension of His body. He will reveal to you who you are, the job He has for you, and what gifts He has given you to accomplish the mission He has given you.*

How Do You Experience God Every Day?

Ephesians 1:3 tells us that God has blessed us *"with every spiritual blessing."* As He reveals Himself to you and makes Himself known to you through prayer and His written Word, then you can reveal Him to others. Those two disciplines, prayer and Bible study, are critical in connecting with God every day.

Prayer isn't a public display of religious superiority. It's a love-conversation between a child of God and his/her Father. Jesus told us to get alone and pray in secret (Matthew 6:5-8). It's just you and God … together. Be still before the Lord. Stop the daily rush and grind. Imagine yourself in His throne room … if you ask him a question, be still and listen. Pray with your entire being. It is not a religious duty or chore. It is an unspeakable and unfathomable privilege to speak and be heard. Prayer takes time, practice, concentration, and work! Rick Amato has said, *"The secret to God's presence is God's presence when you're in secret."* Enjoy that time of sweet fellowship. David said, *"The Lord is my portion"* (Psalm 119:57). A *"portion"* is an allotment, a *"*share.*"* When a waiter delivers your food at a restaurant, he/she will often say, *"Enjoy!"* God has given Himself fully to us. Enjoy His presence. Enjoy your relationship with Him.

Learn to listen to His voice in His Word. The Bible was not given simply to inform us of correct theology. It is God's Word to direct us, to sustain us, to equip us, and to encourage us. The truest thing about you is what God says about you, so therefore read His Word. Study it. Listen to others who teach it well. Memorize it and meditate on it. Allow it to penetrate deeply into your life; obey what you hear; respond to its correction in your life.

One of the best things that you can do in your relationship with God is simply to be still. Be quiet. That's hard to do in our world today. In Psalm 46:10, God encourages us to *"Be still, and know that I am God."* The implication is that we cannot experience Him without being still. While you are still, read His Word; claim His promises; and listen carefully to His still small voice.

Involvement in a Kingdom-minded community of believers will also draw you deeper into fellowship with Him. I find that when I am with others whose hearts burn deeply for God, I am more motivated and sensitive to God's involvement in my life. It is a great thing when God's kids gather together to exalt their Father and express their love for Him.

My wife, who formerly had overseen our preschool ministry, had a volunteer tell her about a unique experience. She was adopted as a child and had always wondered what her biological mother was like. Recently her biological mother found her and they actually connected and have begun to get to know each other. I was thinking about that and our relationship with God. Many people have a similar relationship with God. They know they are His child and have been told that He loves them and they even know a lot of stuff about Him, but they've never actually crossed into the heavenly realm by faith and prayer and actually started meeting with God one-on-one in an intimate way. This is available to all of us if we simply believe. We don't have to wait to meet God one day. We can start knowing Him personally and intimately NOW! I want to know what makes my God happy, and sad; I want to know what makes Him laugh; I want to know how to really make Him smile; and I want to tell him about myself, too. We all need to strive to have a real, experiential, relationship with our Creator and maker. We can know God intimately today and experience a slice of heaven right now (Ephesians 1:13-14)!

Some people don't really want to experience God. They just want a system of religion, a system of control that keeps God at a safe distance. That way, there is not pressure or undue expectations that come with experiencing God. But if you want something more, His promise has always been that "if you seek Me, you will find Me when you search for Me with all your heart" (Jeremiah 29:14). If you don't know God yet, the only way to God is through Jesus Christ. He is the door. He is the gateway. Come to Him. He is all you have ever been looking for.

If you would like to begin a relationship with God through Jesus Christ and come into His Kingdom, or if you would like practical help in having a real, experiential relationship with God, please refer to the Appendix. You will find helpful tips and hints regarding effective prayer, Bible study, meditation, journaling, and other essential spiritual disciplines.

Questions for Reflection and Response:

- In what ways do you slip back into "religion" in your Christian walk? Why?

- What do you find the most difficult in passionately pursuing intimacy with Jesus Christ?

Chapter Eleven

Kingdom Life: Living Like Jesus Christ – A Life of Faith

Every day we are faced with a series of choices – some are large and significant, others are mundane and ordinary. But over the course of a lifetime, those choices define us and direct us. Every one of our lives are the result of the choices we have made up until that point. In his book, *A Pocket full of Pennies*, Rick Amato coined the phrase *"you can choose your choices, but you cannot chose the consequences of the choices you make."* We are all faced each day of our lives with the power to make choices for better or worse.

In this chapter, I want to challenge us to make the ultimate choice, the ultimate resolution, to live like Jesus every day of our lives. King David wrote in Psalm 16:8, *"I have set the Lord always before me; because He is at my right hand, I shall not be shaken."* Ultimately, living like Jesus is impossible. We lack the spiritual strength in our own lives to pull it off. Jesus said, *"Apart from Me, you can do nothing"* (John 15:5). But that statement must be balanced out by Paul's declaration, *"I can do all things through Christ who strengthens me"* (Philippians 4:13) and Jesus' words *"with God all things are possible"* (Matthew 19:26). I would like us to focus for a few minutes on *how to live like Jesus*. Really, it's fairly simple. It only requires one step … which we will study in

Psalm 16:8. But before getting into that verse, I would like us to read all eleven verses of that psalm so we can get a good context for verse eight.

Psalm 16:1-11 *Preserve me, O God, for in You I put my trust. O my soul, you have said to the LORD, "You are my Lord, my goodness is nothing apart from You." As for the saints who are on the earth, "They are the excellent ones, in whom is all my delight." Their sorrows shall be multiplied who hasten after another god; their drink offerings of blood I will not offer, nor take up their names on my lips.*

O LORD, You are the portion of my inheritance and my cup; You maintain my lot. The lines have fallen to me in pleasant places; yes, I have a good inheritance.

I will bless the LORD who has given me counsel; my heart also instructs me in the night seasons. I have set the LORD always before me; because He is at my right hand I shall not be moved.

Therefore my heart is glad, and my glory rejoices; my flesh also will rest in hope. For You will not leave my soul in Sheol, nor will You allow Your Holy One to see corruption. You will show me the path of life; in Your presence is fullness of joy; at Your right hand are pleasures forevermore.

This psalm expresses the joy David experienced in his life because he trusted in God. One Bible commentator has called it a psalm of confidence. [68] What gave David confidence? It was because God had proven faithful in the past. There is only one actual prayer request in this Psalm, and it comes in the first line: *"Preserve me, O God, for in You I take refuge."* The remaining verses weave David's testimony about how God has sustained him and provided for him.

---
68 Merrill, *Psalms*, p. 414.

I Have Set The Lord Always Before Me

David wrote in verse 8, *"I have set the Lord always before me."* This was a choice … a conscious choice David made every day. *"Because the Lord Himself was the main focus of David's attention and satisfaction, he knew no one would shake him in any major way from his stability in life."* [69] The NET Bible translates this as he was *"constantly aware of God's presence with me and around me."*

Picture David sitting face to face before the Lord God all day long. The one true God was his conscious and constant focus. How do we set the Lord before us? Two words: *faith* and *prayer*. Prayer is essential to your life … but I'm not talking about the "religious duty" of prayer that we so often think of. I am talking about practicing the presence of God in our lives each day … carrying on a day-long conversation with Him. That involves being still, meditation, contemplation, and silence … speaking to Him but also allowing Him to speak to us.

In another Psalm, David wrote, *"As the deer pants for the water so my soul longs after you …"* (Psalm 42:1-2). Picture a deer being chased by a predator. It is running for its life through the dry, desert climate of that area. Adrenaline is pumping through its body, its throat is parched, and its lungs are gasping for air. It has no conscious thought other than escaping with its life. Just as much as that deer longs for the cool comfort of a water spring, David says *"That's how much I want God!"* Is that your prayer? God desires spiritual union, connection, and conversation with you all day every day. That is possible and attainable – but few ever even experience a glimpse of that reality. Seek God, find God, and then make Him known to others. Never forget who our Lord is! Let me say it again: *never forget who our Lord is*. We must *"set the Lord before us."* We need to keep a proper image and belief about who exactly our Lord is, who exactly it is we

---

[69] Tom Constable, *Expository Bible Study Notes: Psalms*, (Electronic edition, Psalm 16:8).

are "setting before" our eyes of faith every day. In the next few chapters, I want to give you a tiny glimpse of the power, holiness, and majesty of our King and Savior Almighty God Himself.

Once Israel was freed from the grips of Egypt, God led them through the desert to teach them to depend on Him. One of their chief lessons was *"Remember the God of Israel."* Over and over, in Exodus chapters 19-33, God said, *"Remember Me!"*

In Exodus 19:9-14, God declared He would visit the people in a thick cloud of darkness. But before He would even come to the people in such a manifest way, He demanded that all the people wash their clothing. Furthermore, God commanded barriers to be set up all around the base of the mountain. No one could even touch the base of the mountain. It was holy ... separate ... and if anyone touched the mountain that God descended upon, God would kill them.

In verses 16-24, when God did come and descend on the mountain, His arrival came with loud thunder and lightning bolts. God's glory manifested itself in a thick cloud with ear-piercing blasts of noise, which sounded like trumpets and terrified the people to the point that they actually shook and trembled in fear (v.16). Then, *God's presence began to manifest in the appearance of smoke and fire blazing on the top of the mountain, causing the entire mountain to shake and vibrate "greatly"* (v.18). The noise of this blasting sound of God's presence grew louder and louder. ALL OF THIS WAS JUST HIS INTRODUCTION! The Lord then arrived and descended on the mountain and spoke out to Moses and the people in a voice that sounded like loud thunder. *God warned and reminded Moses to tell the people if they came near the base of this now HOLY SET APART MOUNTAIN, they would be killed.*

Needless to say, this whole divine encounter with the Almighty God of the universe was not well received by the people. They were not waving hands in the air, laughing and rejoicing. They were very scared of their God. They pleaded with Moses and said *"you speak to us, and we will listen; but do not let God speak to us, lest we die."* Then the people moved back further and further away from the mountain. Ironically, in church today, we often sing songs like "fire fall down" and "In the Presence of Jehovah." But what would we *actually do* in our worship services if the actual manifest presence of the Almighty actually broke into real time and real space of our gathering and appeared in all power, glory, righteousness, and majesty? Would everyone laugh, shout, and worship God or cry out in absolute terror and fear as the Israelites did?

Most likely, we would do what Isaiah did. This prophet, a man of God, trembled and said *"Woe is me! I am a man of unclean lips in the midst of unclean people!"* (Isaiah 6:5). We would fall on our faces in bone-rattling fear and tremble, exposed in unclean garments (like Joshua the High Priest of Israel in Zechariah 3). Yes, we are covered by the blood of the Lamb. Therefore, we are able to approach the throne of God, justified and free from wrath and condemnation, but we as the body of Christ have seemingly lost sight of the power, might, majesty, and power of God's presence. Sadly, very few people have actually encountered God's manifest presence in such a way.

Exodus 24:17 says, *"The sight of the glory of the LORD was like a consuming fire on the top of the mountain in the eyes of the children of Israel."* Later, in 33:18, Moses asked the Lord *"Please show me Your glory."* God granted his request but said, *"You cannot see My face, for man shall not see Me and live … I will put you in a cleft of the rock, and I will cover you with My hand until I have passed by. Then I will take away my hand, and you shall see my back, but my face shall not be seen"* (Exodus 33:20-23). EVEN MOSES WASN'T WORTHY TO LOOK DIRECTLY UPON THE GLORY OF THE LORD. IF HE DID, HE WOULD DIE.

Exodus 34:28-35 records what happened when Moses came down from the mountain. After being in the presence of God, his face and skin were shining bright, reflecting the manifest presence and glory of the real living true God. Verse 31 says, *"Aaron and all the people of Israel saw Moses and they were afraid to come near him."* As a result of the radiant reflection, Moses had to cover his face with a veil.

This section in Exodus has shown us a glimpse of God's holiness and severity. But we must also talk about His majesty, splendor, power, and prestige. There is no human way to comprehend His splendor and the riches of His dwelling place. Our omnipotent God is the preeminent ruler of the entire cosmic system and reality that we live in, whether it be this universe, this dimension, or other universes and dimensions that we know nothing about. He is over everything.

His Throne Room

The Bible gives us short glimpses of what God's throne room in heaven looks like. As you read through these verses, look for the majesty, power, splendor and awesomeness that surround the place from which our God rules the entire creation.

1 Kings 22:19 *I saw the LORD sitting on His throne, and all the host of heaven standing by, on His right hand and on His left.*

Psalms 11:4 *The LORD is in His holy temple, the LORD's throne is in heaven;*

Psalms 97:1-5 *The LORD reigns; let the earth rejoice; let the multitude of isles be glad! Clouds and darkness surround Him; righteousness and justice are the foundation of His throne. A fire goes before Him, and burns up His enemies round about.*

His lightnings light the world; the earth sees and trembles. The mountains melt like wax at the presence of the LORD.

Isaiah 6:1-5 *In the year that King Uzziah died, I saw the Lord sitting on a throne, high and lifted up, and the train of His robe filled the temple. Above it stood seraphim; each one had six wings: with two he covered his face, with two he covered his feet, and with two he flew. And one cried to another and said: "Holy, holy, holy is the LORD of hosts; The whole earth is full of His glory!" And the posts of the door were shaken by the voice of him who cried out, and the house was filled with smoke. So I said: "Woe is me, for I am undone! Because I am a man of unclean lips, And I dwell in the midst of a people of unclean lips; For my eyes have seen the King, The LORD of hosts."*

Daniel 7:9-10 *And the Ancient of Days was seated; His garment was white as snow, and the hair of His head was like pure wool. His throne was a fiery flame, its wheels a burning fire; a fiery stream issued and came forth from before Him. A thousand thousands ministered to Him; ten thousand times ten thousand stood before Him. The court was seated, and the books were opened.*

Revelation 4:2-11 *Immediately I was in the Spirit; and behold, a throne set in heaven, and One sat on the throne. And He who sat there was like a jasper and a sardius stone in appearance; and there was a rainbow around the throne, in appearance like an emerald. Around the throne were twenty-four thrones, and on the thrones I saw twenty-four elders sitting, clothed in white robes; and they had crowns of gold on their heads. And from the throne proceeded lightnings, thunderings, and voices. Seven lamps of fire were burning before the throne, which are the seven Spirits of God. Before the throne there was a sea of glass, like crystal. And in the midst of the throne, and around the throne, were* *four living creatures full of eyes in front and in back. The first living creature was like a lion, the second living creature like a calf, the third living creature had a face like a man, and the fourth living creature was like a flying eagle. The four living creatures, each having six wings, were full of eyes around and within. And they do not rest day or night, saying: "Holy, holy, holy, Lord God Almighty, Who was and is and is to come!" Whenever the living creatures give glory and honor and thanks to Him who sits on the throne, who lives forever and ever, the twenty-four elders fall down before Him who sits on the throne and worship Him who lives forever and ever, and cast their crowns before the throne, saying: "You are worthy, O Lord, To receive glory and honor and power; For You created all things, And by Your will they exist and were created."*

Did you catch the greatness of God's dwelling place? What these verses have just described represent the heavenly Holy of Holies! Earlier we read from Matthew 27:50-51 about what happened as Jesus was crucified: *"Jesus, when He had cried again with a loud voice, yielded up the ghost. And, behold, the veil of the temple was rent in twain from the top to the bottom."* The tearing of the veil meant that the way into the Holy of Holies, which was NOT available or open before was now wide open for entrance to all believers.

Our Invitation to Pray

By the way, if we believe that God can hear us when we pray, then is it not already as if we are actually in the real throne room of God, speaking to God? What is the difference? We just don't believe we are really talking to God. What if you had the opportunity to meet with the President of the United States in the Oval Office. How would you approach that event? What would you say as you talked with such an important person?

If I speak to someone on the phone, is it any less real than if I were to speak with that person in the same room with me? While talking on the phone takes away the ability for me to see that person, our communication is nonetheless real. What is the difference? If you speak out loud right now, can God hear you? When you close your eyes, bow your head, and pray to God, does He listen to you? Of course He does. How does He hear you? Think about it. Ponder that. Reflect for a moment. Where is God? Do you really believe you're talking to THE GOD OF THE UNIVERSE? My point is this: *If God is that near to us, if He is that close to us, and in fact if He has put His own Spirit in us and we all say we believe that – then why am I the "weird guy" by saying that God speaks to me directly and I speak to Him directly? It baffles me. Isn't it realistic to think that God would speak to us if His actual Spirit was living in us?*

The problem with saying we're talking to directly to God and hearing directly from God is not a matter of logic and reason. It's a faith issue. For example, many people say that God was silent between the days of the prophet Malachi to the time of John the Baptists' birth (when He spoke with angelic interaction to John's mother and father, and Mary and Joseph). This is true in the sense that no new revelation was given to Israel during that period. However, it is also clear from the Gospels that two different Jewish figures (Simeon and Anna) had heard from God and were expecting the arrival of the Messiah to be born. [70] How did they hear from God if God was silent from communicating to all people during those days? If He spoke to Simeon and Anna, isn't it reasonable to suppose He spoke to many others over the period of four hundred or more years?

God still speaks today. But please remember that God "speaking" to us is not a black and white thing to be written out on a note card … at least not all the time. Don't take each thing I say and box me in on every single point – hear

---

[70] Among others, God spoke to Elizabeth and Zacharias (Luke 1:5-25), Mary (Luke 1:26-33), Joseph (Matthew 1:20-21; 2:13-14, 19-20), Simeon (2:25-26) and Anna (2:36-38).

me out. Communication is not only about "hearing words." Communication occurs in many different ways. Sign language, body language, facial expressions all communicate certain things to the observer. Art and music can evoke or communicate certain emotions or feelings to a person without using words. God is spirit and we have a spirit. We communicate at a spiritual level.

I think what most Christians fear is saying, *"God told me this or that,"* and then being wrong and thus becoming a false prophet. That is valid, and we as believers should be extremely careful to not put words in God's mouth that He never said. However, I go back to my point that God's very own Spirit is in us! He can communicate directly and intimately with me in my spirit. We are always connected. He can bring thoughts into my mind; He can give me ideas; He can instruct me on what to do; He can give me a *jolt* and wake me up in the middle of the night to pray and be with Him; He can let me feel his love, joy, peace, kindness, holiness, peace, serenity, beauty, or truth, as He pleases. And He does so often. Not one audible sound is needed for us to "hear" God, because our spirits do not require sound waves to communicate with God. I don't think our "spirit man" has physical ears to receive the sound waves we call *words*. God can hear the thoughts in our heads and sometimes doesn't even speak to us … He simply shows us a vision or a memory or a beautiful image in our mind or imagination to communicate his divine thought to us.

This is most likely what you're thinking now: well, how do I know when it's God and when it's not? First of all, stop pushing God away. He wants you to draw near to Him! Second, you must practice and learn to hear His voice. It takes time. You do this by reading God's Word. You need to know God's Word and be dedicated to it. He who knows God's written Word will have no problem hearing God's living word which speaks to the heart like a cool morning breeze, crisp and clear, perfect and true, pure wisdom and love. You have the most wonderful counselor, mathematician, architect, inventor, scientist, artist, leader, general, lover, king, and God living inside of you and He desires to give you an abundant life of faith, hope, love, and joy. There is no problem too big and no question too hard to ask. Ask Him and wait. Listen to Him ... believe. Have faith. Wait upon the Lord. Is that not what our Scriptures teach us? Call out to Him and He will answer you, if you wait, remain still, and listen with "ears of faith!" Just beware that He is not a *fast-food style, drive-thru, quick and easy type of a God*. He deserves to be your top priority and most valued, respected, loved, cherished, prized, miracle, which has been freely given to you. Treat Him right and have faith and you will be blessed!

God still speaks today. We have the opportunity in prayer each day to converse Spirit-to-spirit with the Ruler of Creation. That is an immense thought! The following verses talk about our attitude in approaching God in prayer:

Hebrews 10:19-22 *Therefore, brethren, having boldness to enter the Holiest by the blood of Jesus, by a new and living way which He consecrated for us, through the veil, that is, His flesh, and having a High Priest over the house of God, let us* **draw near** *with a true heart in full assurance of faith, having our hearts sprinkled from an evil conscience and our bodies washed with pure water.*

Ephesians 2:6 *(He) raised us up together, and made us sit together in the heavenly places in Christ Jesus.*

Hebrews 4:16 *Let us therefore come boldly to the throne of grace, that we may obtain mercy and find grace to help in time of need.*

All of these Scriptures have talked about the throne room of God in heaven. By the blood of Jesus Christ, we now have direct access into this throne room. I am not speaking symbolically or using a metaphor. Right now, today, we can dwell in His presence and glory at the foot of His mighty throne. Do we actually believe that with full faith? I wonder how many of us really do. I don't think the majority of us believe it is possible to enter directly into God's presence. If we did , our lives would be radically different. We would never leave God's presence.

How we act reflects what we believe about God. If we really believed how big God is, and how small we are in comparison to His entire creation; if we truly understood the invitation to approach His throne room; if we were able to see the millions of angels (any one of whom could strike down an entire army of men); and then have the audacity to come into His presence – in front of entire armies of angels and men from old; then how could we pray self-absorbed, nonchalant, arrogant, near-sighted prayers – sometimes treating God like a genie in a bottle? Is it possible to truly believe the right things about God … and then pray meaningless, flesh-driven, and sometimes even "shallow" prayers to the Lord of the universe with cold hearts of dead-faith?

I assure you, if you simply by FAITH believe that the very fabric of time and space is being ripped open into the scene of God's throne room and see into the heavenly realms and the reality of what is going on when we pray, I honestly don't think anyone could utter an empty or shallow word. After getting past the shock, awe, and terror of such a holy God, the only thing coming from our mouths would be pure praise, worship, and thanksgiving … in fear and trembling because of the awesome power and holiness of our Creator.

I Have Set the Lord Before Me

Why am I saying all this? When we *"set the Lord before us,"* we understand that it is all about prayer – constant prayer. Prayer is a privilege; it is an honor; it is a precious gift given to each one of us. Prayer is more than just speaking words. Prayer is spiritual communion, connection, and conversation with the Father. It is walking into His actual throne room chambers, humbly, and silently, and having a direct conversation with the Most High God of the entire universe. Most of us would be unable to gain access to the mayor of our city … yet we have direct access to the Lord. If we really believed this one small truth, it would transform our lives from inside out.

I have been at fault many times in the past with treating prayer as *religious duty* (praying with empty meaningless words), *a wish list* (praying arrogant, self-absorbed prayers), and as an *excessive burden* (not praying at all because it's too much effort).

Here is the biggest kicker: God has placed His own Spirit inside of us! Can you imagine: the fullness of His glory, His presence, His light, His consciousness and mind inside us! This was something the ancients could only have dreamed of. Yes, great and mighty works were done in the power of the Spirit in the Old Testament. He was WITH THEM … but in the New Testament, He has put His Spirit IN US. Our job is to soak and bask in the presence of the Lord … as Moses did … and by doing so, the light and glory of God will shine inside of us. The sin and filth in our hearts, minds, and souls will begin to melt like wax. God's manifest power and presence will then begin to shine through our lives. We can *"let our lights shine before men"* so they will see the presence of God in our lives. When that happens, you don't have to tell people *"I've been in the presence of God;"* or *"I was so near to God today;"* or *"I am so spiritual and have so many spiritual gifts."* People will just be able to look at you and see your light and they will know that you have been in the presence of the Lord.

He Is At My Right Hand

David said, *"I have set the Lord always before me; because He is at my right hand, I shall not be shaken."* The term *"right hand"* is often used symbolically to signify a place of dignity, honor, and counsel. More specifically, especially in this context, the *"right hand"* was symbolic of a king's military strength. We read in Isaiah 62:8, *"The Lord swears by His right hand."* Exodus 15:6 says, *"Your right hand, O LORD, glorious in power, your right hand, O LORD, shatters the enemy."* Essentially, David was saying, *"God is always right next to me. His sword is in His hand, and there is fire in His eyes. He is alert, steadfast, watching over me, going before me. God is my protector. The Most High God is my shield, my strong tower, my army. He'll fight my fights for me; He is my wisdom, guide, protector, savior, king, counselor, and comforter."*

David was a military man. He was both a king and a commander in a legitimate army. He needed actual physical protection more times that we can count. God went before him and brought him great military success and victory. You and I are not in a physical confrontation with enemies. But do you realize we are in a serious, all out, spiritual war every single day? I think many of us have wrong ways of thinking (at least I do) about what this battle is. No, we're not fighting Muslims, Hindus, Buddhists, atheists, Republicans, Democrats, or any other human agency. We are fighting spiritual hand-to-hand combat against the kingdom of Satan. We fight against demons – against fallen angelic beings – on a daily basis. Does that sound strange? Paul says in Ephesians 6:10-20 that we don't fight against flesh and blood, but against spiritual forces of darkness. People are not our enemy. God loves all people and Jesus died for all people. We are in a fight against a spiritual enemy working in and through people, and working in and around our personal lives, families, churches, states, countries, and world.

But are you even in the fight?

The New Testament often uses a military and soldier motif to describe Christians. We are an army of human beings indwelt by God's Spirit. We represent a new way of life to the world. We are part of a new kingdom and have a new government – God's government – and Satan's army is not happy about that. We have all the resources that we need through the power and authority of Christ Jesus. We have God "at our right hand" … representing authority, power and our ultimate guarantee of victory.

But who is winning? Why are Christians so often "on the run"? Why do so many live lives of constant defeat, wallowing in sorrow and shame?

Our enemy is watching us. What do they see? Are they shaking and trembling and full of fear? Or do they even recognize us? There is an intriguing section in the book of Acts where some Jewish exorcists tried to duplicate the miracles Paul was doing. Acts 17:15 quotes the evil spirit as saying to them, *I recognize Jesus, and I know about Paul, but who are you?* Do the evil spirits even have an awareness of you? Is your name known in hell? Jesus said, "I will build my church and the gates of hell will not prevail against it" (Matthew 16:18). In Jesus' words, the actual gates of Hell would not be able to withstand the attacks and advances that the army of God's Kingdom people would wage against his actual throne and fortress. Let us stop being deceived by our enemy. His tactic in the supreme art of war is to win the fight through fear, intimidation and lies without ever having to even fight us. It's the old school military tactic called psychological warfare and it is effective!

Our weapons are not physical but spiritual. Paul talks about the sword of the Spirit (the Word of God), the breastplate of righteousness (right ways of living and thinking), the helmet of salvation (knowing who you are in Jesus Christ, what salvation means, understanding the Gospel and His Kingdom), and the list goes on and on. At the end of that list in Ephesians 6, he says we should pray at all times in the Spirit. Real prayer, prayed in faith, is the most untapped resource and asset in the body of Christ today. Our enemy, Satan, and his team assigned to our geographical location and church body cannot stand up to a *Holy Spirit, united, like-minded group of Jesus followers. They cannot prevail against Kingdom people who take the offensive and pray in faith against their evil tactics.*

Unshaken

David's conclusion in Psalm 16:8 is a great statement of confident faith: *"I shall not be shaken."* The term *"shaken"* gives the images of stumbling, wobbling around, and instability. It often referred to someone who was walking on a path but then slipped off. It indicates failure and has the nuance of suddenness and surprise. The fact that David said he would not be moved meant that God would keep him safe, secure, and moving directly in line with the will and purpose He had for David's life. *In order to live a life set apart for the Lord, the answer is to set the Lord always before you, to remember and believe moment by moment that He is at your right hand.* If we really believed that – and walked in full-faith of that promise – nothing in this life or world would shake us. Nothing would give us anxiety – nothing would cause fear. We would not be shaken.

Let me call your attention to one final point: Psalm 16:8 is not about David. It's about Jesus Christ. Jesus Christ embodied Psalm 16, especially verse 8. On the day of Pentecost, Peter stood up and preached about Jesus. He quoted from Psalm 16 saying, *"For David says **concerning Him**, 'I saw the Lord always before me, for He is at my right hand that I may not be shaken.'"* This verse is **not** about what you do. It's about what you believe. It's about setting the Lord in front of you AT ALL TIMES. It is really about living a life of 'spiritual poverty,' knowing that we are powerless in ourselves. It is living a life totally dependent upon God's presence, power, providence, and protection: *"Oh my soul, you have said to the Lord, You are my Lord, my goodness is nothing apart from you,"* (16:2). As Peter said, Psalm 16 was fulfilled through the life of Jesus Christ.

Jesus said only what the Father told Him to say. He went only where the Father told him to go. He did only what He saw the Father doing. Jesus could truly say with all of his heart, soul, and mind that He always set the Lord before Him and the Lord God of Israel truly was at Jesus' right hand. Jesus showed us the way to live … and it is very simple. It is a way of life that can solve all of your problems, all of your fears, all of your pain and the sources of that pain (whether emotional, spiritual, or relational). All it takes is faith. *"And the righteous shall live by faith." "Not by might, nor by power, but by my Spirit, says the Lord."* And Jesus lived this way His entire life. At the end, on the cross, Jesus yelled the words, *"It is finished"* (John 19:3). By walking in a "Psalm 16:8 way of life," He completed the work God gave Him to do – and He was fully prepared and ready to meet His Father. He didn't fix everyone, heal everyone, or teach everyone – but He did everything the Father gave Him to do.

After His death, He commissioned us to complete what He had begun. Jesus has given each one of us a job to do. Whether you are a mechanic, school teacher, scientist, or pastor, as a believer in Jesus Christ, you have been commissioned into His service. We have a job to do. You will find His promises and commitments to us are always true! Let us consecrate ourselves to live just like Jesus did (Psalm 16:8) and prepare for the arrival and appearance of our Lord. Just like God told Moses and the Israelites, get your clothes ready; clean yourselves up and prepare to meet the Lord.

What is shaking you? What is causing you instability,

failure, or keeping you off track? For some, it might be sexual temptations; for others, materialism or greed. Anxiety, fear and the uncertainty of the future can derail others. And for some, it is physical suffering, emotional suffering, relational breakdowns, and the pain of broken relationships, broken hearts, and broken families. All of us face hardships of many kinds. Maybe you have legal problems looming over your head. For many, it is the daily pressure to pay your bills and put food on the table for your family.

The answer to all of these sins, trials, and difficulties is the power and presence of the Holy Spirit in your life, working in you, around you and through you. He will take care of everything if you simply take the time to connect with Him. I urge you today, seek His presence. Seek His glory with all your heart.

I began this chapter by talking about how life is a series of choices. Psalm 16:8 contains the necessary ingredients to help make those right choices: Stay in the Lord's presence through prayer, study and memorization of Scripture and fellowship with other believers in Church and small groups where you can grow and develop as His disciple. Walking with Him is a great adventure. Are you ready?

Questions for Reflection and Response:

- What keeps you from seeking God wholeheartedly? What gets you "off course"?

- How do you respond when things "shake" you? What do you need to do differently in the future?

Chapter Twelve

Kingdom Citizenship: What Kingdom Citizens Are Not

The Pharisees: A Case Study of What Kingdom Citizens Are Not!

To the average Christian, the word Pharisee evokes an image of an evil, conspiring, and hypocritical religious leader who is responsible for the death of Jesus. However, most Christians have a distorted understanding of who the Pharisees and other religious leaders were. W.E. Phipps noted that *"The caricature of the Pharisees by Christians is as absurd as that of Jesus in the Talmud. There he is alluded to as [an illegitimate son] and a sorcerer."*[71] Israel's history, as seen in the Old Testament, is filled with examples of prophets who used harsh words for the corrupt prophets and priests of their day. Jesus' condemnation of the religious leaders of His day was no different.[72] The Pharisees were sincerely religious men who believed they were devoted to God. They were the most "righteous" followers of Almighty God in their culture. One writer stated that *"The Pharisees received such 'harsh' treatment from Jesus, not because they were so far from*

---

[71] Tom Hovestol, *Extreme Righteousness* (Moody Press: Chicago, 1997), p. 24. (quotation taken from: William E. Phipps, "Jesus, the Prophetic Pharisee," *Journal of Ecumenical Studies* 14 (winter 1977): p. 29).

[72] Michael L. Brown. *Answering Jewish Objections to Jesus.* Vol. 4 (Baker Books: Grand Rapids, 2007), p. 148.

the truth, but because they were so close." [73]

To better understand Jesus and the Gospels, it is important to understand the culture in which Jesus lived. More importantly, it is essential to have an understanding of the religious and political opposition which Jesus faced in Israel. There were five identifiable religious and political groups in first century Palestine. The five groups included the Herodians, Sadducees, Pharisees, Zealots, and Essenes.[74] The Pharisees, Sadducees, and Essenes were the most prevalent groups while Jesus lived in Palestine. Josephus, the Jewish historian, considered the Sadducees, Pharisees, and Essenes to be different "philosophical schools" inside a larger national philosophy of Judaism.[75]

Most scribes belonged to the Pharisaic party. Scribes were responsible for the copying of the law and were responsible for developing the legal traditions the Pharisees followed so strictly.[76] Finally, there were the Herodian and Zealot groups. These were two completely opposite groups. The Herodians were the most accommodating to the Roman rule in Palestine. The Zealots were completely anti-Roman. The Herodians were also supporters of Herod and many were tax collectors. In contrast, Zealots were extremely nationalistic, despised Herod and the Romans, and advocated the use of force to try and change the political system.[77]

Although there were five distinct political/religious parties in Jesus' day, the Gospels focus mostly upon the Pharisees and Sadducees. However, the Pharisees were usually the primary focus. In the NIV, the Pharisees are mentioned ninety-eight

---

[73] Hovestol, p. 34.
[74] Ibid., 36.
[75] Steve Mason. *Josephus and The New Testament* (Hendrickson Publishers: Peabody, Massachusetts, 1992), p. 132.
[76] Dick France. *"Jewish Religion in New Testament Times,"* in *Zondervan Handbook to the Bible.* Revised edition. (Zondervan Publishing House: Grand Rapids, 1999), p. 528.
[77] Hovestol, p. 36.

times.[78] Interestingly, the Essenes are not even mentioned once in the New Testament. [79] Therefore, we will focus on the relationship between Jesus and the Pharisees.

The Pharisees first appeared as a distinct party in the latter half of the second century B.C. The term *"Pharisee"* originally comes from the Aramaic word *"pera."* The word literally means *"to separate,"* and has the idea of separating for a manner of life that is separate from the general public. [80] The Pharisees were direct descendants of the Jews, who in exile, refused to conform and compromise religion and worship in the midst of paganism. The Pharisees were first called "Pharisees" during the reign of John Hyrcanus, who reigned from one hundred thirty-five to one hundred and four B.C.[81]

The Pharisees were not a united group. They were divided theologically into two distinct groups. One group devoted themselves to the more moderate teachings of Rabbi Hillel, while others held fast to the very strict teachings and interpretations of Rabbi Shammai.[82] Nevertheless, the Pharisees were united together in their dislike of the Sadducees. The Pharisees and Sadducees had been political competitors for the control of the temple and priesthood for nearly two centuries before Christ. At the time Jesus lived, it was the Sadducees who had favor with the Romans and were in control of the temple and the priesthood.[83] Regardless, the Pharisees were much more popular with the people of Israel. The Pharisees controlled the synagogues, were devoted to studying Scripture, and provided doctrinal and

---

[78] John R. Kohlenberger III, Edward W. Goodrick, and James A. Swanson. *The Greek-English Concordance To The New Testament* (Zondervan: Grand Rapids, 1997), p. 942

[79] Steve Mason, *Josephus and The New Testament*, (Peabody, Massachusetts: Hendrickson Publishers, 1992), p. 131.

[80] W.E. Vine. *Vine's Complete Expository Dictionary* (Thomas Nelson Publishers: Nashville,1984), p. 470.

[81] Merrill C. Tenney. *Exploring New Testament Culture* (World Bible Publishers, Inc.: Iowa Falls, IA, 2000).

[82] Hovestol, *Extreme Righteousness*, p. 37.

[83] Joseph L. Gift. *Life and Customs in Jesus' Time* (Standard Publishing: Cincinnati, 1957), p. 93.

practical guidance for the people.[84] Josephus claimed that the Pharisees were the most influential among the people and they held the beliefs of the general population.[85] In addition, the Pharisees could be considered the "middle class" of the Jews and were really the "backbone of the Jewish life," unlike the wealthy aristocratic Sadducees.[86]

During the life of Jesus several Pharisees accepted Jesus' teachings. For example, Nicodemus became a follower of Jesus, and in John 9:16 the Pharisees were divided over the question of Jesus' authority to perform a miracle on the Sabbath day. It seems that some of the Pharisees may have sided with Jesus. In fact the Apostle Paul was a Pharisee and the book of Acts records many Pharisees becoming followers of Christ.[87] Regardless, the overwhelming majority of Pharisees despised Jesus. In fact, the Pharisees hated Jesus so much that they were willing to join forces with the Herodians and the other political groups in order to stop Jesus! Bock notes, *"Ironically, he had brought the leaders of the nation together, but in rejection, not acceptance of his message."*[88] The Pharisees had numerous problems with Jesus. They viewed Jesus as blasphemous, a friend of sinners and drunkards, a Sabbath breaker, demonic, defiant of tradition, and a false Messiah.[89]

The Pharisees and other religious leaders felt threatened by Jesus. Their biggest problem with Jesus was His authoritative teachings which astonished the crowds. Jesus was becoming popular with the people! The leaders felt extremely endangered by Jesus because His teachings were so radical. The Pharisees feared that their authoritative teachings and traditions would be challenged and scrutinized by the people if Jesus was not

---

[84] Ibid., p. 94.
[85] Mason, p. 133.
[86] Tenney, *Exploring New Testament Culture*, p. 93.
[87] Hovestol, pp. 32-33.
[88] Darrell L. Bock. *Jesus According to Scripture* (Baker Academic: Grand Rapids, 2002), p. 321.
[89] A.T. Robertson. *The Pharisees and Jesus* (Charles Scribner's Sons: New York, 1920), pp. 66-109.

stopped.[90] It is no wonder that the Pharisees despised Jesus the way they did. In the book of Matthew the hostility between Jesus and the Pharisees is extremely severe. In Matthew 23 Jesus warns the people about the Pharisees and scribes. One commentator noted that *"This is the most biting, pointed, and severe pronouncement of judgment in the Bible. It came directly from the Savior's lips and was directed at self-centered spiritual hypocrisy."*[91]

In the Gospels, Jesus warned about the leaven of the Pharisees five times. Charles C. Ryrie explains that the leaven of Pharisees that Jesus warned about was externalism. The Pharisees were outwardly righteous and well educated about Scripture but they were unrighteous on the inside. Jesus despised the hypocrisy of the Pharisees.[92] In Matthew 23, Jesus declared woes upon the Pharisees and Scribes. Interestingly, Jesus urged His disciples and the people to listen to and obey what the Pharisees say, but not to live as they do (Matt 23:3). Jesus' biggest problem with the Pharisees was that they *"added to the law, applied it without compassion, and were hypocritical about how they worked with the law."* [93] Jesus even called the scribes and Pharisees whitewashed tombs! In Jesus' day, tombs were whitewashed to make them look clean and stand out. The whitewashed tombs were brilliantly white. However, inside, the tombs were filled with decay and corruption.[94] In other words, the Pharisees were clean on the outside but dirty on the inside.

Jesus' condemnation of the Pharisees and scribes in Matthew 23 is mostly targeted at the hypocrisy and pride of the religious leaders. Ultimately, Jesus was declaring judgment on the leadership. In doing so, Jesus was claiming His own authority over

---

[90] Bock, pp. 321-322.

[91] Stuart K. Weber. *Holman New Testament Commentary. Matthew* (Broadman & Holman Publishers: Nashville, 2000), p. 370.

[92] Charles C. Ryrie. *Basic Theology* (Moody Press: Chicago, 1986), p. 245.

[93] Bock, p. 334.

[94] John MacArthur, *The MacArthur Bible Commentary* (Thomas Nelson, Inc.: Nashville, 2005), p. 1170

the leadership, just as He did in the cleansing of the temple.[95]

> It is like a judge pronouncing a national sentence over the leadership. It represents how he bears the right to call the nation to reform. The setting is particularly appropriate. It leaves beyond any doubt that Jesus is forcing a choice of who will direct the nation and, more importantly, represents both the people of God and the way to God.[96]

It is possible that *"the Pharisees received such 'harsh' treatment from Jesus not because they were so far from the truth but because they were so close."*[97] Jesus' main condemnation of the Pharisees was their hypocrisy. It seems Jesus was not so much opposed to their interpretation of the law as He was angered by their lack of inner righteousness. The Pharisees refused to accept Jesus' authority. Even worse, they failed to recognize their Messiah and rejected the notion that Jesus' ministry was somehow connected to the long awaited kingdom that they had hoped for.[98] The Pharisees believed that they were the closest to the kingdom because of their *"righteousness."* Sadly, they were really the farthest away. [99]

Modern Day Pharisees ... We're Not That Much Different

The problem with the Pharisees wasn't their theology. They were orthodox, Biblical; they believed the right things. But there were four problems that kept them from the Kingdom of God. These are four of the same problems that can keep people from God's Kingdom today.

---

[95] Bock, p. 336.
[96] Ibid.
[97] Hovestol, p. 34.
[98] Bock, pp. 646-647.
[99] Hovestol, p. 34.

First, they failed to recognize Jesus as their Messiah.
Though He fulfilled all the prophecies and came preaching the Gospel of the Kingdom, He didn't fit the Pharisees' notion of who and what the Messiah should be. Instead of submitting to His Lordship and Kingship, they attacked Him. They attributed His works to the power of Satan. And they were the ones who led the charge to ultimately crucify Him. What do we do when Jesus doesn't fit our paradigm? Do we change the paradigm – or do we become His enemy?

Second, the Pharisees misunderstood sin. They felt that if they could keep the law outwardly, they would become acceptable in God's sight and therefore *earn eternal life*. But the Law was not given to save us, but to condemn us. Paul writes that *"through the Law comes the knowledge of sin"* (Romans 3:20). The law is our *"tutor to lead us to Christ"* (Galatians 3:24) because Christ is our only hope for righteousness…not our own works (Ephesians 2:8-9). The English Standard version uses the word *"guardian."* The King James translates it *"schoolmaster."*

The law had no power to save us; its purpose was not to save us. It was simply to point us to Christ, who has the power to save us. Legalism is the philosophy that says I can become acceptable to God through my good works; that if my good works outweigh my bad works, I will earn eternal life. God says a resounding "NO" to legalism. Salvation is a gift – it is purely by grace alone through faith alone in Christ alone that we are saved. The Pharisees never understood that … and neither do many today. We must passionately defend grace as the only way men and women can be saved. The Gospel never starts with what we need to do; it always begins with what God has already done; to get it backwards is to miss the Gospel.

Most Christians already know that we're saved by God's grace through faith in Jesus Christ and His shed blood, death, and resurrection. However, it is simply an intellectual idea that is agreed upon, as opposed to a life changing, revolutionary, spirit-freeing, soul-healing burst of life, energy, and joy in our everyday lives. Beyond salvation itself, legalism and externalism also insult the power of the blood of Jesus Christ and His righteousness that has been given to us freely.

One of the most challenging truths I've had to actually learn and accept (over and over, almost daily) is the simple truth that God really does love me and He really does want to be in relationship with me. There is nothing that I can do to earn or win God's love. He already loves me and by the blood of Jesus Christ I'm free, I'm saved, I have the righteousness of Jesus Christ, and I can't personally do anything to earn or attain those things from God. That is very humbling to me. It causes me to be stirred with the deepest humility and love in my gut. I am totally thankful to my Lord – and He fills me with such perfect serenity, peace, and joy in Christ Jesus. In contrast, Pharisees (like myself for most of my life) actually believe that they please God and make Him happy by doing "good things" and by "obeying a law" outwardly (i.e., going to church, giving money, studying theology and doctrine, not having sex outside of marriage, abstaining from drugs and alcohol, abstaining from pornography or R-rated movies, and all the other "do's and don'ts" associated with religion.

Meanwhile, things such as gossip, anger, resentment, pride, impatience, greed, anxiety, covetousness, lust, and many other internal (invisible) sins are overlooked. The truth is that even our most righteous acts are like filthy rags to God.

Some may ask me, *"So, Jesse are you saying that what we do on the outside doesn't matter as long as we're good on the inside?"* My answer would be *"Absolutely not!"* Many people will take what I've just said as a license to live any old way they want to. No! In James 4:8, Christ-followers are instructed to have both *"clean hands"* and a *"pure heart."* We should have a clean *outward* lifestyle which is the true manifestation of a pure and godly *inside*, not just one or the other.

The bottom line is this: God hates sin because sin is detrimental to His children, whom He loves dearly. Sin is destructive and it corrupts what God created. Sin hurts us and other people and God wants us to have an abundant life. Pharisees see it the opposite way and actually feel they're doing God a favor and are "good" because they obey a law. When one judges himself as "good" because he obeys some or even "most" of God's laws (as a Pharisee typically does), he begins to see himself as righteous and those who do not observe God's laws *as well as he does* as "bad," "dirty," and "unfit for love and mercy." This way of thinking is legalism, a parasitic and sickening mind disease, which has plagued God's people (young and old people) from the beginning of time until now. The truth is that "*all have sinned and fall short of the glory of God*" and "*there is none righteous, no not even one*" (Romans 3:10-12; 3:19-23). The only true righteousness anyone can ever find is the righteousness of Jesus Christ which is freely given to us through His shed blood on the cross.

Third, the Pharisees were guilty of judgmentalism and spiritual pride. They paraded their religiosity in front of the crowds and looked down on those who were not like them. One of the most compelling stories Jesus ever told involved a Pharisee and a *"sinner,"* (translate that as "a person just like you and me").

Luke 18:9-14 *Also He spoke this parable to some who trusted in themselves that they were righteous, and despised others: "Two men went up to the temple to pray, one a Pharisee and the other a tax collector. The Pharisee stood and prayed thus with himself, 'God, I thank You that I am not like other men—extortioners, unjust, adulterers, or even as this tax collector. I fast twice a week; I give tithes of all that I possess.' And the tax collector, standing afar off, would not so much as* *raise his eyes to heaven, but beat his breast, saying, 'God, be merciful to me a sinner!' I tell you, this man went down to his house justified rather than the other; for everyone who exalts himself will be humbled, and he who humbles himself will be exalted."*

Notice what Jesus said: (1) This was a man who *"trusted in themselves that they were righteous."* That's legalism. (2) He *"treated others with contempt."* That's being judgmental. (3) The Pharisee told God about his spiritual pedigree: *"I'm not like other men; I do all these religious activities."* That's pride. In contrast, the tax collector simply begged for mercy. He knew he was a sinner. He knew what he deserved. But he cried out for grace, forgiveness and acceptance, not based on what *he* had done, but based on God's merciful character. He was the one who *"went home justified,"* spiritually right with God. Those who have tasted of God's grace know the depth of their sin; they know what they deserved ... and therefore they can never look down on anyone else. We're all in the same boat. We all deserve judgment and are only saved by God's gracious mercy. The Gospel frees us to realize that, while we matter, we're not the point. Jesus is the point!

Fourth, the Pharisees were hypocrites, because they never really kept the Law properly. Jesus spent all of Matthew chapter 23 exposing the hypocrisy of the Pharisees. Two verses will suffice here: *"Woe to you, scribes and Pharisees, hypocrites! For you cleanse the outside of the cup and dish, but inside they are full of extortion and self-indulgence. Blind Pharisee, first cleanse the inside of the cup and dish, that the outside of them may be clean also."* (Matthew 23:25-26). Ouch! That stings! It stings because we all know how hypocritical we really are. *None of us lives up to the truth we know.* We all *"believe better"* than we live. We need to acknowledge that "obedience gap" and humbly admit where we fall short. Christianity isn't a "religious show." It's a father-child relationship where we know how much we really fail ... but we also know how much He loves us anyway. Mt. Sinai says, *"You must do."* Mt. Calvary says, *"Because you couldn't, Jesus did."* Don't run to the wrong mountain for your hiding place.

How to Keep Focus

Many people think that the Gospel is just for non-Christians: it's the message they need to hear to get them into the Kingdom. I want to suggest that the Gospel is *also* for Christians: it's the message we need to hear to know how to *act like Kingdom Citizens,* to keep focus and perspective. The vertical truths of what God has done for us always precede horizontal imperatives of how we are to live in light of what God has done for us in Christ.

The Gospel doesn't simply ignite the Christian life; it's the fuel that keeps Christian's going and growing every day. Our identity and security are in Christ alone. That frees us to give everything we have for the sake of the Kingdom because in Christ we have everything we need.

We become more mature when we focus less on what we need to do for God and more on all God has already done for us. Slipping into "Pharisee-ism" puts us back on that performance treadmill where we are defined by "what we do," not by "who we are in Christ." Christian growth doesn't happen by working hard to get something you don't have. It happens by working hard to live in light of what you do have. The only antidote there has ever been to sin is the Gospel of Jesus Christ. Since we never cease sinning, we can never leave the Gospel.

Questions for Reflection and Response:

- Identify what Pharisee-tendencies there are in your life. What are you going to do about them?

- How can you help others who are caught in the web of legalism and performance-centered Christianity? What do they need to hear? How can you help them understand?

Chapter Thirteen

Kingdom Citizenship: What Kingdom Citizens Are

Life and Death

Israel had wandered in the wilderness for forty years. As they were about to go into the promised land, Moses preached a series of sermons that we know as the book of Deuteronomy in our Bible. He concludes his last sermon with these words: *"I call heaven and earth as witnesses today against you, that I have set before you life and death, blessing and cursing; therefore choose life, that both you and your descendants may live"* (Deuteronomy 30:19).

Life and death. Nothing could be more *opposite*. The choice seems clear. It was never more clear than in the first century. There were the Pharisees, with their strict code of laws and lifestyle, and there was Jesus. He taught with authority and clarity; He loved people relentlessly; He demonstrated compassion to those who had never tasted of its fruits; and He preached the Gospel of the Kingdom that gave people hope, joy and a future expectation of the grace of God in their lives. Jesus manifested this Kingdom power and authority by signs, wonders, and healings.

In the Gospel of Matthew (chapter four), there is a story about Jesus' face-to-face encounter with Satan. In the re-telling of the story, Matthew recalled that during the conversation, Satan took Jesus to a high mountain and showed Him all the kingdoms of the world. Then he said to Jesus, *"I will give You all this domain and its glory; for it has been handed over to me, and I give it to whomever I wish."* Jesus didn't argue with Satan about who was really in control of the world. Ultimately God has sovereign control and power. But Jesus knew that God gave man the free will to disobey God. Man had, by default, placed himself under the dominion of Satan and Satan's empire of fallen ones.

Satan's original goal seems to have been to create his own kingdom or system that rivals God's Kingdom but leaves God out of the equation. Therefore, this world is a counterfeit in which Satan attempts to be God. In this false and dark Kingdom, Satan has twisted the laws and principles of God's moral law – and has made it attractive to men. In God's kingdom, love and righteousness are the foundation – but in the world system of darkness, pride is the core foundation of each citizen. Pride was the original sin in the garden. It is the notion that we can be like God and be our own God. Thus, it appears that one of Satan's main goals is to make people give top priority to self; to buy into the philosophy that what happens here and now is what's most important. Satan wants you to focus all of your attention on the present rather than on eternity. That is why John reminds us in 1 John 2:17 that *"the world passes away but the one that does the will of God abides forever."*

The Beatitudes ... The Kingdom Citizens' Code of Ethics

In Luke 6 we find a passage in which Jesus teaches His followers several Kingdom principles. Essentially, I see this teaching section as perfect instructions about how to live as citizens of God's Kingdom. Jesus tells us the way we are expected to live now – and the way we will live for all eternity with God and with each other in the new heaven and on the new earth.

Jesus' message reveals a new way of life completely foreign and contrary to this present world system or "kingdom of darkness" that we live in. Regardless of our current geographical location, our culture and identity should be based upon Kingdom principles as described by Jesus Christ and His teachings as opposed to our own world-culture into which we were born. We were born into one kingdom system with a particular culture, worldview, and way of doing life. But once we experience the spiritual re-birth, we must begin the daily process of readjusting our mind and way of thinking to the way Jesus thinks and the way He did life.

We live in a completely different context, but we can still take the principles of what He taught and how He lived and adjust our lives accordingly. When we adjust our lives to emulate Jesus Christ and obey His teachings, we begin to find a joy and fulfillment never before experienced. We come into a new form of reality called the "abundant life," a life with meaning and purpose, not based upon temporal gain or pleasure in this lifetime. Our life becomes about loving God, loving other people, and doing Kingdom work which will last forever. We invest our time, energy, and resources in this life and this world in order to reap and have a foundation to build upon in the next life and the next world system – the eternal life and Kingdom promised to all Kingdom citizens. As citizens of God's Kingdom, how are we supposed to live?

Blessed Are the Poor ... Cursed Are the Rich

In Luke 6:20, 24, Jesus said *"Blessed are you who are poor, for yours is the Kingdom of God ... Woe to you who are rich, for you have received your consolation."* In this passage, the word "poor" can be defined as poverty-stricken; someone crouched or bent over begging for food.

A parallel passage to Luke 6 is Matthew 5:3, where Jesus says *"Blessed are you who are poor in spirit."* The idea here is not so much financial poverty as it is spiritual poverty, recognizing our total inadequacy to do anything that would gain favor with God. In this sense, we are utterly dependent on Jesus and His grace. In John 3:3, Jesus said, *"Truly, truly, I say to you, unless one is born again he cannot see the kingdom of God."* There must be a spiritual re-birth.

In the first-century culture and historical context, the word *"blessed"* would be understood to describe a long life, wealth, a large healthy family, a full barn, and no enemies. But according to Jesus, to be blessed is not really about what you get or what you have. It is not even necessarily about what you own or the circumstances of your life. Blessedness is a state of favor with Almighty God. Rather than a happiness based on external circumstances, it is an inner happiness and deep-seated joy that results from being favored by the God of heaven and earth.

"You're blessed if you're poor, because the Kingdom of God is yours." The idea seems to be that you are in possession of or entitled to be in God's Kingdom. You are a Kingdom citizen. You have something that money could never buy. Jesus said if you're poor, then you're blessed. Being poor, when it gets down to it, is about being humble. Humility is a quality that every Kingdom citizen must pursue because Jesus Christ Himself was humble (see Philippians 2:5-11). However, humility is not being a door-mat or beating yourself up. In fact, many people are guilty of false humility and seem to get stuck in a cycle of depressive thoughts and self-pity. Humility is really about understanding who God is and who you are in relation to God and God's creation. Being "poor" is about **spiritual** poverty … it is an attitude of the heart. There is nothing more holy or godly about not having money or resources. Rich people are not evil because they have money. A poor person is not good because He is poor. Poverty is a state of being, experienced by rich, poor, or middle class. We are all poor

because we are all in need of our Master and Creator God.

Revelation 4 pictures God on His throne in heaven, encompassed by an emerald-colored rainbow. There are flashes of lightning, rolls of thunder, torches of fire all surrounding God. He is so holy and powerful –not poor or inadequate. Spiritual poverty turns into humility when we realize that we are but a speck of dust on a little tiny planet who have knowingly and willingly sinned against the Creator of the entire universe. It's at that point when we fall on our face and cry out for mercy, for help, for grace. That is when spiritual poverty begins. Then we do not forget that place – the place of poverty and submission and dependence upon God who has all power, resources, and control. Spiritual poverty could also be likened to being childlike in our relationship with our God. In Matthew 18:3-4, Jesus said *"Truly, I say to you, unless you turn and become like children, you will never enter the kingdom of heaven. Whoever humbles himself like this child is the greatest in the kingdom of heaven."*

Spiritual poverty is not only the starting point to come into God's Kingdom. Real, true humility is a mindset that we should keep forever. If you *are "poor in spirit"* you are highly favored by God. The amount of money in your wallet has nothing to do with your spiritual poverty and humility.

But Jesus said, "*Woe to you who are rich, for you have received your consolation.*" *Woe* is a very harsh word. It was almost a curse –misfortune waiting ahead, nearness of judgment. BUT IT IS NOT JUST A WARNING – it is really a declaration judgment. We love to assume Jesus is talking about the evil bankers, CEO's of insurance companies, and politicians. But I'd be careful with that interpretation.

I read once that if the world was a village of one hundred people, twenty of those people live on one dollar a day, and sixty would be poor children who rarely have access to clean water or more than one meal a day. If we interpret this to mean people with money or wealth are evil, then the average "Joe plumber" in America is the evil, rich person. But Jesus had followers who were wealthy. For example, Joseph of Arimathea, Zacchaeus, and possibly Nicodemus seemed to be men of wealth. In addition, many of the great men of faith in the Old Testament were extremely wealthy: Job, Abraham, David, Solomon, and many others.

In this passage, Jesus is speaking of those who think they are spiritually rich; but they are independent, arrogant people. They are the ones who just don't believe they need God; they are not really concerned about God or eternity; and they are not willing to humble themselves (like a poor person) and submit to God's authority as ruler. This is the very reason why Jesus says they are cursed: they have already received their consolation.

"Consolation" refers to comfort or happiness or payment for what you've earned. The person who thinks he or she is something special or is successful based upon material wealth or financial prosperity is deceived. The best they are going to get is a short temporary span of several years on this planet until they die and then they lose everything. Is that true wealth? Jesus is talking about the folly and deception of a lifestyle of pride, greed, and materialism as a way of life. Those things are worldly and they are not beneficial to us. They hurt us rather than help us, but more importantly, they do not reflect God's character. As Kingdom citizens we must re-adjust our minds to align with God's plan for being human and God's code of ethics.

Blessed are the Hungry ... Cursed are the Well-Fed

Jesus said, *"Blessed are those who hunger and thirst for righteousness, for they shall be filled"* (Matthew 5:6). We all know what it feels like to be hungry ... desperate, craving, tired, weak, dizzy, etc. But what are we to hunger for? Food? No, not in this context. Jesus is referring to righteousness …. hunger and craving for God, or an intimate, fulfilling fellowship with Him. In Luke's version of this statement, he quotes, *"Blessed are you who are hungry now, for you shall be filled"* (Luke 6:21). Blessed are you who hunger *"now."* This hunger is only temporal; it is not forever. God's going to bring relief to the hungry Kingdom citizens on earth one day. We will soon be filled up beyond our wildest dreams, be completely satisfied for all of eternity. This blessing is for those of us who want to experience the full benefits of our salvation now! Those who hunger and thirst after righteousness and seek after God with a fervent passion can begin to experience victory over sin now, we can know God today.

ARE YOU HUNGRY TODAY? ARE YOU HUNGRY RIGHT NOW FOR RIGHTEOUSNESS? If so, then according to Jesus, YOU ARE BLESSED AND FAVORED BY GOD. REJOICE BECAUSE ONE DAY YOU WILL FIND REST FROM THAT LONGING IN YOUR SOUL! But for now, it is good because it keeps you anchored into the place you need to be while on earth. We can never "arrive" in our relationship with God or be totally perfect. We always long for more of God and more of His Word. We must keep that hunger and thirst our entire lives.

In verse 25, Jesus said, *"Woe to you who are full now, for you shall be hungry"* (Luke 6:25). You know what it means to be full? Happy, content, no worries, feet propped up in the air. You feel like you need to loosen your belt, you are sleepy, lethargic – but you have no worries. You are both bloated and happy! Sounds like the after-math of the typical Thanksgiving meal in America.

That is the spiritual condition Jesus is talking about. You who are rich – you who are proud and think you have no need for God – you're living in perpetual sin – but you don't care! In fact you're content with it. The more you sin, the more and more filled up you get on the sin. So you go ahead and gorge yourself. Fill up your stomach with food and wine now, because you're going to spend eternity realizing what you missed out on. You are trading eternal riches for temporary pleasures. You could be experiencing the joy of God's Kingdom right now, but eventually it will be too late and you will be hungry and thirsty for God's presence. As C. S. Lewis said in his essay *The Weight of Glory*, *"We are half-hearted creatures, fooling about with drink and sex and ambition when infinite joy is offered us, like an ignorant child who wants to go on making mud pies in a slum because he cannot imagine what is meant by the offer of a holiday at the sea. We are far too easily pleased."* If you reject God's presence now, it is something that you cannot chose to have later – it will be too late.

Blessed are the Mourners ... Cursed are the Partiers

Again, Jesus gave a contrast: *"Blessed are you who weep now, for you shall laugh; Woe to you who laugh now, for you shall mourn and weep"* Luke 6:21, 25). To *mourn* literally means to weep out loud. I think we are to mourn over the things that break God's heart. What breaks God's heart? The earthquake in Haiti; little girls being sold into slavery all around the world; children abandoned by parents; sin and corruption in society; divorce and the break-up of families; single mothers having to make life work all on their own; disease, injustice and oppression of the poor; death, and those who wail and cry out to God for help, in total dependence on Him to fix everything.

They were also mourning because of their own personal sins they had committed against God. I once heard that there is no reference in the Gospels of Jesus ever smiling or laughing. This is not to say that Jesus did not have fun or have joy, but it is still interesting to see that Jesus was not remembered as a "funny guy." Sincere and wholesome laughter is a gift from God, but Jesus is speaking to the inner state of our hearts. Are we truly broken over sin and suffering in the world and our own participation in sin and corruption? Though we may not murder, steal, or commit adultery we still have anger, greed, jealousy, lust and other sinful attitudes which often cause the very sin and suffering and injustice that makes the world a nasty place! Are we really broken over our sin – or are we numb to it and its effect on our lives?

"But woe to you who are laughing right now." I think the laughter Jesus is talking about here is symbolic of worldly ease, this idea that *"Sin is fun … I'm going to live my life the way I want to live it. I make my own rules. Who cares what's right or wrong?"*

When I think of this laughter, I think of my mindset when I was in high school and college, a time in my life when all that really mattered was partying and just having fun. I was living my life for myself and to have fun and laugh. Many of us get our thrills and joy from money, our big houses, and the toys that we buy. Basically, Jesus was saying *"enjoy it and laugh it up now, because everything is going to be taken away …. and when eternity really begins for you, you're going to be mourning and weeping."* In accordance with this mindset, James 4:9 instructs the readers to let your laughing be turned to mourning and weeping.

Blessed are the Persecuted … Cursed are the Respected and Loved.

In verse 21, Jesus said you are blessed when people *"hate you."* They detest and abhor you and what you stand for. This implies persecution because of your faith-convictions. You are blessed when people *"exclude or ostracize you,"* separating you from or casting you out of society. You are shunned, ignored, excommunicated. He goes on to say that you are blessed when people *"revile or insult you."* Here the idea is to defame, disparage or cause reproach, using abusive words against someone. Finally, Jesus says you are blessed when they *"spurn or scorn you."* The picture here is one of hissing an actor off the stage. There is shame and rejection. Have you ever experienced any of those actions? Many around the world have.

"According to the World Evangelical Alliance, over 200 million Christians in at least 60 countries are denied fundamental human rights solely because of their faith. In their 2009 report in the International Bulletin of Missionary Research (Vol. 33, No. 1: 32), they estimate that approximately 176,000 Christians will have been martyred from mid-2008 to mid-2009. This, according to the authors, compares to 160,000 martyrs in mid-2000 and 34,400 at the beginning of the 20th century. If current trends continue, Barrett, Johnson and Crossing estimate that by 2025, an average of 210,000 Christians will be martyred annually." [100] Now notice something. None of this happened because someone did not like the political party they belonged to. It wasn't their ideology or their view of the healthcare bill. This is not about a personality difference – it's about being hated and ostracized, reviled, and scorned – simply because you love Jesus and follow Him. If you are looked down upon, oppressed, hated, reviled, scorned, or mistreated and hurt because of doing what is right and loving God and His Kingdom, His truth, living according to His Spirit, and loving other people, than you are truly going to be rich in eternity. Jesus calls you a blessed person. You have a gift and a wealth and a status in heaven! You are loved in God's Kingdom! In God's Kingdom, the heroes are the ones who serve, who love, who give, who promote unity, who promote peace, and who go the extra mile to help out their fellow man who is in need. That is Kingdom work and Kingdom ethics and values.

The bottom line is that this "Blessing and Woe" stuff is about your attitude. It's an internal, heart thing. Jesus cursed those who are only concerned about what other people think: *"Woe to you when men speak well of you."* If the world, which is controlled by sin, corruption, and Satan, speaks well of you and loves you

---

[100] http://www.m-b-t.org/2010/03/25/how-many-christians-are-killed-for-their-faith-every-year.

and props you up, it's probably not a good thing from a Kingdom perspective (though there are exceptions to that rule). But more specifically, it seems Jesus is saying *"woe"* to you if your desire is to make other people happy instead of making God happy. Why are we so concerned about impressing people and not God? That's what the false prophets did. They tickled people's ears; they told them what the people wanted to hear, not the truth that was hard to hear. The question for us is: who are we trying to please? Who are we seeking glory from – man or God?

Now this is a hard pill to swallow, but Jesus told His followers that they are to respond to persecution with joy! Jesus said, when someone insults you, reviles you, hates you, spits on you, kicks you when you're down, or tries to take away your rights and freedoms on account of His Name, then leap for joy. For truly your reward is great in heaven. From what I've seen and experienced here in America, if we feel the slightest bit of discomfort or perceived persecution or injustice, we call a lawyer and sue. We form a big mob and go down to the courthouse and protest with signs and megaphones demanding that the slightest bit of persecution be stopped immediately. When we get "slapped in the face," we try to find a way that we can slap our opponent back harder. This is not the way of Christ or His followers. This is not the way of His Kingdom. Don't get me wrong here. I'm not saying don't protect your family from danger. I'm simply saying we are to love our enemies, and to pray for them, and do whatever we can to be at peace with everyone and help all who are in need … even if they don't like us!

The Future of the Blessed

Early on in the book of Acts some of the Apostles were arrested and beaten on account of this testimony of Jesus Christ. *"They left the presence of the council, rejoicing that they were counted worthy to suffer dishonor for His Name"* (Acts 5:41).

Leap for joy if you are counted worthy to suffer with Him just as He suffered for us. This is exactly what the prophets of old had to experience, but I promise you that today, they are rejoicing in heaven – dancing, and singing, and laughing! They counted it an immense privilege that they were considered worthy to suffer for Jesus Christ.

While all of that is true, I must also add some other words of advice in order to keep the balance here. I do not think that God wants us all to walk around with a "martyr complex." God does not get some type of special joy or thrill if we get "hurt" for His sake. We should not seek or pursue such a danger or persecution in order to be labeled as especially holy or righteous. When Paul was under threat on one of his missionary journeys, he escaped in the night through a window in the back of a building! He got out of town and fled for his life! Kingdom citizens should avoid violence; we should avoid any type of physical conflict or confrontation if at all possible; we should also be careful to be prepared and have a well-thought out plan to avoid injury or death.

Now I am not claiming to be a prophet, but I believe there is coming a day in this country, whether tomorrow or in a generation yet to come, when followers of Jesus Christ will be forced to suffer for their faith. There is coming a world system and a world dictator who will make us choose between Christ and him. And if we make the "wrong decision," it will not be pretty for us. Are you willing to lay down your life for Christ? Are you willing to lose your family, your children, your wife, or your husband to follow Christ? Jesus said *"If anyone would come after me, let him deny himself and take up his cross daily and follow me. For whoever would save his life will lose it, but whoever loses his life for my sake will save it. For what does it profit a man if he gains the whole world and loses or forfeits himself?"* (Luke 9:23-25).

But if we are the blessed people of God, then let us stop

trying to live like the world and stop acting like the world! We have been called to live like Jesus. Jesus is the embodiment of this message and of this Sermon on the Mount (Matthew 5-7; Luke 6:20-49). He lived out these attitudes and ways of thinking while on the earth. They show us how to live as Kingdom citizens. Jesus was poor. He was not only poor in material needs, but was also completely dependent upon God. With every step or direction Jesus took, He was depending completely on the Father. Jesus was not hungry for righteousness – for He embodied complete righteousness … He was hungry for the Word of God and deep communion with the Father. He went forty days without food in the wilderness and said that His food was God's Word alone. Jesus didn't weep and mourn over His own sins – He had none; but He did weep over the lost sheep who didn't have a shepherd. He wept over the sins of His people. He wept over the oppression, disease, and death that they experienced. Jesus was willing to suffer for His Father. He was mocked, reviled, scorned, spit upon, threatened, beaten, unpopular, and ultimately murdered. Jesus' concern was completely focused on God and the Kingdom of God – not this world or Himself. If our Master and King was willing to live like that, then we must, too.

I see two polar opposites running through the middle of this passage: there is the Kingdom of God and there is the kingdom of this world; there are blessed people, and there are cursed people; there are the poor and there are the rich. *To be blessed is to be favored by God, and blessed people are those who live for eternity with eternal values.* There are also people on earth living today who are "cursed" and "worldly," because they live for themselves, for temporal gain. They reject God's free gift of salvation through Jesus Christ. If we truly are concerned about eternity, and truly believe we are citizens of the Kingdom, then we are to live our lives with a sense of spiritual brokenness and humility before the Lord. We must keep hungering and thirsting for righteousness; we must be broken-hearted over our sin and the sin of others; and we must to be willing to suffer for the sake of Christ.

Where is our faith? What are we trusting in? Is our faith in God – or in Wall Street and the economy? Is our faith and hope in Jesus Christ – or in a political party? Are we truly hungry and thirsty for righteousness? If we are so hungry and thirsty, why do we persist in the same habitual sins over and over and over again until we get numb and calloused to our sinful way of living? If we are hungry and thirsty for righteousness, then why do we listen to what we do on the radio and watch what we do on television? The very things that we believe are wrong and frown upon are the same garbage that we watch on TV and soak our minds on nearly every day of our weekly existence. Are we really hungry for close fellowship with Christ? We say we don't have time to have a close relationship with Christ, but we spend between one and two hours watching TV and at least half of that amount of time on Facebook, Twitter, and the internet every day. Our schedule reveals our priorities. What does our schedule say about us and our priorities? Are we truly heartbroken over our sins and submitted to His Lordship?

Eternal Perspective

What is our focus on? What are we really living our lives for? Why are we wasting our time? Why, if we are citizens of a different realm are we still longing and desiring to be part of this world? Jesus is calling us today to live our lives as Kingdom citizens, focused on things that will matter for eternity. We must repent and change our way of thinking. We must start thinking rightly – God's way of thinking. The only way we can get "God's way of thinking" into our mind is to soak in His Word and in His presence every day!

I'm reminded of what Paul said in 2 Timothy 4:7-8, *"I have fought the good fight, I have finished the race, I have kept the faith. Finally, there is laid up for me the crown of righteousness, which the Lord, the righteous Judge, will give to me on that Day, and not to me only but also to all who have loved His appearing."* Paul's motivation was not to get rich here or get a mansion on a hill or to be famous. His motivation was to be crowned with a crown of righteousness for the King of Kings and Lord of Lords, Jesus Christ.

You know what I want? I want to make it to the other side, to the heavenly Kingdom, with as few regrets as possible. I want to fight this fight. I want to run this race. I want to finish strong. It's not a sprint – it's a marathon. And it's not about how fast you start, but about whether or not you finish. Today many of you are terribly hurt. You've got problems: you've lost your house; you can't pay your bills; you've got medical problems; your marriage is going down in the dumps; you're addicted to drugs; you're having panic attacks; or maybe you just feel depressed.

JUST REMEMBER THIS: all of these problems and pain, all of this suffering and heartache is temporary. It comes along with the territory. Satan wants us to focus on the temporary. He wants us to only care about what we can see, hear, and touch right now. But friends, keep running, keep going, and keep trusting in God. Don't take your eyes off of Him. Trust in the Lord with all of your heart. Keep your eyes on the prize. For this life is but a shadow, a vapor in the wind. The world system and the success ladder is really just a rat race. You'll spin on a wheel like a hamster your whole life trying to make a name for yourself, only to wake up one day in eternity to find that it is all a waste.

Today, right now, make Christ your focal point. More than that, make His mission and His commission to you your life focus! That is really what living with an eternal mindset is all about. There are so many people in this world without a relationship with Jesus Christ, with no hope. We must show them love and meet their needs. Help the hurting, feed the hungry, lend a helping-hand to the mourning and the suffering. Just as Christ would do. Then tell them about Jesus Christ and His Glorious Kingdom that they, too, can join … if they believe! You don't need to be a professional theologian or a pastor. Just be yourself and tell anyone and everyone who will listen to the good news of Jesus Christ, His cross, His shed blood, His resurrection life, and His Kingdom!

It's Not about What you Do … It's about What You Are!

All kingdoms in the world have rules, laws, regulations, and procedures which govern the citizens living in them. In addition, the citizens of earthly kingdoms are expected to behave and live properly confined within the rules set forth by the ruler of each particular kingdom. The Kingdom of God is no different. However, the desired **behavior and nature** of all Kingdom citizens can be summed up in one word: **godliness**. In 1 Timothy 3:16, Paul wrote *"great indeed, we confess, is the mystery of godliness."* The two verses preceding that profound statement say, *"I am writing these things to you so that, if I delay, you may know how one ought to behave in the household of God, which is the church of the living God, a pillar and buttress of the truth"* (1 Timothy 3:14-15). Do you see it? First, Paul reminds Timothy that God Himself lives not in a temple made by hands but in the collective body of believers called the Church. The living God lives in His Church. This agrees with what Paul wrote:

Ephesians 2:19-22 *Now, therefore, you are no longer strangers and foreigners, but fellow citizens with the saints and members of the household of God, having been built on the foundation of the apostles and prophets, Jesus Christ Himself being the chief cornerstone, in whom the whole building, being fitted together, grows into a holy temple in the Lord, in whom you also are being built together for a dwelling place of God in the Spirit.*

Paul describes the church (the household of God) as a building being slowly built up. But this building of "people" is actually God's Temple. As we all know, a temple (whether in Judaism or all forms of paganism) is the place in which deity lives; it is the house of a god or gods. The Bible teaches us that we, the church (collectively), are God's house! If that does not make you scratch your head in bewilderment, than I don't know what will. According to our divinely inspired Holy Book, WE (the church) are the DWELLING place for God, through His Spirit, to live in! This brings us back to Paul's statement that **"great ... is the mystery of godliness."**

For most of my life I have understood godliness as an external attribute of Christians. All of my life I have heard the phrase, "He is such a godly man" or "She is such a godly woman." Normally, hearing such a phrase evoked in my mind images of a loving, gentle, gracious man or woman ... especially elderly with gray or white hair. Thinking of a "godly woman" brought to my mind an old praying lady who wouldn't hurt a fly. To me, godliness seemed to be an adjective describing someone who read his Bible every day for an hour, spent long periods of time on his knees praying, never missed church, and always dressed properly in a suit coat and tie. To be godly was to "not smoke, not drink, not chew, not watch questionable movies, or anything else that could get you into trouble." Essentially, godliness was more about one's lifestyle, morality, and outer appearance as opposed to an inner reality and state of being.

It is *now* my personal conviction (which I believe to be founded strongly upon Scripture) that **godliness is not about what you do but about what you are.** Godliness is not about DOING, but about BEING. Godliness is not about the works of your hands but about the condition and attitude of your heart. Godliness is the pursuit of every Kingdom citizen.

If godliness was just an adjective to describe someone

who lived a very religious and moral life, than what is the big mystery? Paul was a very competent theologian in his day. He was extremely well-versed in the Scriptures and philosophy. Why then would Paul call godliness such a mystery? The mystery of godliness (in Paul's mind) was related to the mystery of the incarnation of Christ Jesus. Look at the second part of 1 Timothy 3:16, *"Great indeed, we confess, is the mystery of godliness: He was manifested in the flesh, vindicated by the Spirit, seen by angels, proclaimed among the nations, believed on in the world, taken up in glory."*

As noted above (and evidenced in the rest of 1 Timothy 3:16), the mystery of godliness pertains to the incarnation of Jesus Christ: *"He was manifested in the flesh."* But taking it further, the mystery is really pertaining to Christ Himself. In Colossians, Paul prayed that the Christ followers in the city of Colossae would be *"knit together in love, to reach all the riches of* **full assurance of understanding and the knowledge of God's mystery, which is Christ**, *in whom are hidden all the treasures of wisdom and knowledge."* Earlier in the first chapter of Colossians, Paul wrote of Jesus Christ that *"in Him all the fullness of God was pleased to dwell, and through Him to reconcile to Himself all things, whether on earth or in heaven, making peace by the blood of His cross."* Look at what Jesus Himself said:

John 10:38 *But if I do, though you do not believe Me, believe the works, that you may know and believe that the Father is in Me, and I in Him.*

John 14:10-11 *Do you not believe that I am in the Father, and the Father in Me? The words that I speak to you I do not speak on My own authority; but the Father who dwells in Me does the works. Believe Me that I am in the Father and the Father in Me, or else believe Me for the sake of the works themselves.*

John 17:11 *Now I am no longer in the world, but these are in the world, and I come to You. Holy Father, keep through Your name those whom You have given Me, that they may be one as We are.*

The word godliness (Greek, *eusebeia*) is found in the New Testament fifteen times. Paul uses the word ten of those times. Interestingly, every one of those references are all in the Pastoral Epistles (instructions to Timothy and Titus in 1-2 Timothy and Titus). Do you know what that tells me? That godliness in the local church is of great importance to God. He wants His people to relate rightly with Him and with each other – in His body, the Church – in loving, wholesome relationships.

What is *godliness*? Godliness is the key which unlocks resurrection power. As each of us learns the mystery of godliness we will realize that self-denial and self-death precede true godliness. By putting our flesh to death, we allow Christ to live and shine out of our earthly lives. Godliness is purity in all areas of our lives and being: a pure mind, a pure heart and pure hands. Godliness is the absence of all things which would grieve, quench or hinder the Holy Spirit of God in our lives.

The mystery of godliness is learned through spiritual illumination of God's Word. If you know God, then you know what it means to be godly, because being godly is simply a reflection and manifestation of God's Spirit through our lives. Many people *fake* godliness and put on a false view which is only skin deep. True godliness comes from the inner man.

Paul called godliness a mystery. Is godliness wearing a suit coat and tie, having a strict diet, or being a good steward of my money? Maybe telling people about Christ? Going to church, leading a Bible study, praying every morning? No, it is not necessarily any of those things. GODLINESS IS NOT ABOUT WHAT YOU DO. **GODLINESS IS ABOUT WHAT YOU ARE.**

GODLINESS COMES, NOT FROM WHAT YOU DO, BUT IS SOMETHING THAT YOU ARE in and through Christ alone. As the Spirit of God takes over more and more control in our lives, He fills us and dwells in us, taking over more and more control in our lives. As He takes more and more control of our minds, wills, emotions, and bodies, we glorify Christ and increasingly take on characteristics of godliness.

Some day you ought to do a study in the New Testament about all the times the phrase *"one another"* is used. Here's a start: *loving one another, giving preference to one another in honor, not judging one another, accepting one another, caring for one another, serving one another, encouraging one another, building up one another, forgiving one another.* [101] After reading those statements, do you think godliness in God's family is important?

Questions for Reflection and Response:

- So much of Jesus' teaching is counter-intuitive to the wisdom of today's world. Why do you think that is?

- If that is true, how important is it to *"not be conformed to this world, but be transformed by the renewal of your mind"* (Romans 12:2)? How can we do that?

---

[101] For starters, see John 15:12; Romans 12:10; 14:13; 15:5, 7; 1 Cor. 12:25; Gal. 5:13; Eph. 4:32; Col. 3:13; 1 Thess. 5:11; Heb. 3:13; Heb. 10:24.

Section Three

Extending the Kingdom

Chapter Fourteen

Exercise Your Kingdom Calling

Road Signs

Sometimes signs are good. When you're traveling to an unfamiliar city, it's helpful when there are exit signs on the Interstate. It's good when there are street signs, stop signs, and even speed limit signs. But sometimes signs aren't so good.

Such was the case when Jesus was teaching and ministering to the sick, infirmed and demon-possessed people of His day. After casting out a demon, Luke 11:15-16 tells us *"But some of them said, 'He casts out demons by Beelzebub, the ruler of the demons. Others, testing Him, sought from Him a sign from heaven.'"* The crowd asked for a sign. But it seems their minds were already made up. It was as if they were predisposed to not believe anything He did was from God. They demanded a supernatural miracle of cosmic proportions. Luke tells us that they did this *"to test Him,"* not because they wanted to believe in Him.

A few minutes later, Jesus said *"This is an evil generation. It seeks a sign, and no sign will be given to it except the sign of Jonah the prophet. For as Jonah became a sign to the Ninevites, so also the Son of Man will be to this generation"* (Luke 11:29-30). In the parallel passage in Matthew 12:38-39, Jesus says that this is a *"wicked and adulterous generation."* What a shocking statement! At first glance, we might be prone to recommend Jesus read *"How to Win Friends and Influence People."* Let's examine His statement a little more closely.

Telling the Harsh Truth

First of all, *"this generation"* refers to the Jewish population of Jesus' day whom He interacted with directly. It is clear that Jesus is speaking to the people here listening to Him as if they are a perfect representation of all of Israel: the status quo, the mainstream, mainline, ideology, way of thinking, and attitude.

It is not politically correct or fair in our modern day to castigate an entire culture, race, or demographic of people. For example, it is unfair to say "all white people are like this," or "African Americans are like that." We are a very individualistic, diverse, and unique country in which everyone is encouraged to think for himself or herself. But the very words of God Himself in the flesh (John 1:1-18), with perfect judgment and indisputable wisdom and insight, viewed these people as the representation of the overwhelming majority of Israel and even more Judaism. The word *"evil" is a strong word.* Jesus said to the people, *"You are an evil, corrupt, and sinful collection of people."* Demons are often referred to as "evil, wicked, and unclean spirits." Jesus uses the same word that describes demons to describe the people of His day.

Matthew 12:39 also notes in the same story that Jesus also called this generation an *"adulterous"* one. Adulterous? Is Jesus talking to them literally, saying they're all running around on their husbands or wives, cheating and having affairs? I'm sure, according to statistics that some of them were. *But it is clear Jesus is speaking to them in spiritual terms … they were a spiritually adulterous people.*

In his commentary on Ezekiel, Peter Jeffrey noted that *"adultery is giving yourself to someone who has no right to you. It implies a deep relationship with a lover, and dissatisfaction with one's legitimate marriage partner. It is a denial of all past promises and allegiances, and will involve lies and cover up. How does this work out in spiritual terms? Adultery, however, is the rejection of a true and deep love. It is dissatisfaction with God and looks elsewhere for that which only God can legitimately supply. It is only possible when there is no enjoyment of God."* [102]

Throughout the book of Jeremiah, especially chapters 2-3, you see Jeremiah make a similar accusation. *"I remember the devotion of your youth, your love as a bride, how you followed Me in the wilderness, in a land not sown"* (2:2, ESV). In chapter 3:1, the Lord spoke to Israel and said, *"'If a man divorces his wife and she goes from him and becomes another man's wife, will he return to her? Would not that land be greatly polluted? You have played the whore with many lovers; and would you return to Me?' declares the LORD. 'Return, O backsliding children,' says the LORD; 'for I am married to you.'"*

In common Old Testament-style prophetic tradition, Jesus points out, just like most of the prophets, that the very people God called out and chose to be His figurative "wife" had rejected God and had looked elsewhere for spiritual satisfaction and fulfillment. But where did they turn? It is pretty well documented and noted that for the most part, after the Babylonian exile the Jewish people stayed very faithful to God and stamped out the worshipping of idols. They were strict, legalistic, and strongly monotheistic. When the Word of the Lord came to Jeremiah, he accused Judah of being unfaithful and playing the part of a whore, sleeping with other lovers and cheating on God. Now the Word had come to the people in the first century in bodily form and spoke to them directly and they didn't recognize Him. This time they were not cheating on God with idols and pagans as

---

[102] Peter Jeffery, *Opening up Ezekiel's Visions*, (Leominster: Day One Publications, 2004), p. 86.

much as they were married to an empty religion that shoved God out of the equation. Like Jeremiah 2:13 says, they had rejected God and His presence and embraced the empty, cracked, and broken cisterns of religion. *They placed their religion above the God their religion was supposed to represent.*

Jesus made this scathing indictment to the crowds of people who had come to see what He was all about. Jesus did not operate the way we do. In fact, I think it'd be safe to say He was quite the opposite in His way of thinking and doing ministry than most of us are. Rather than being thrilled that large crowds came to see Him, He was grieved. He didn't get pumped up and energized by big crowds of people. He didn't say, *"Hey, whatever it takes to gather a big crowd here, let's do it. After all, the more people who come, the more opportunity we have a better chance of leading more to the truth!"* He was wary of the crowds because He knew how fickle they were. They were interested in the "show," not in repentance and godliness.

Jesus called the people wicked and evil because they came looking to see a sign. But note, in Matthew's account of the story, he specifically states that it was the religious leaders and scribes present in the audience who challenged Jesus for a sign: *"Then some of the scribes and Pharisees answered, saying, 'Teacher, we want to see a sign from You'"* (Matthew 12:38).

According to Zodhiates, a sign is a visible manifestation of God's power. It is *"a supernatural event or act, a token, wonder, or miracle, by which the power and presence of God is manifested, either directly or through the agency of those whom He sends."* [103] Some believe they were asking for a sign from heaven (see Luke 11:16). They wanted to see something miraculous: the sun to turn black, or the moon appear, or Jesus to open up the heavens to look straight into God's throne room and see angels coming up and down in the clouds. In fact, it

---
[103] Spiros Zodhiates, *The Complete Word Study Dictionary: New Testament* (Electronic ed., Chattanooga, TN: AMG Publishers).

was not unheard of for people to request signs from rabbis to authenticate their message. [104]

Earlier in Luke (11:20), Jesus drove a demon out of a person's life. The critics said He was driving them out by using Satan's power. Jesus proved them wrong and then told them that He drove out demons by the *"finger of God,"* and that the Kingdom of God had come upon them. Make no mistake, these experts in theology and Scripture knew Jesus was calling them out BIG TIME. The finger of God referred back to Exodus 8:19. *"Then the magicians said to Pharaoh, "This is the finger of God." But Pharaoh's heart grew hard, and he did not heed them, just as the LORD had said."*

In that passage, Pharaoh's heart was hardened and he was unwilling to accept the clear sign that the plagues were a manifestation of the power of God over the gods of Egypt. Essentially, if Jesus drove out demons by the finger of God (the power of God), just as Moses did over a millennia earlier, it validated His message and Person. The religious leaders revered Moses, but they rejected Jesus. Jesus was calling them out and proving that He was casting out demons by the finger of God. Instead of seeing and believing, the Pharisees and religious leaders were acting just like the evil, pagan, unbelieving, idolatrous Pharaoh of Egypt who was destroyed and humiliated by God. That was a cut-down of all cut-downs, and they knew it. Jesus did not play games. He spoke the truth in love with authority and clarity and didn't beat around the bush or get sucked into their game.

The problem was not signs. Jesus performed many signs during His ministry: He raised the dead, He healed sickness, He cast out demons, and He taught with authority as no man has every taught. People were captivated by His teaching. But they were hypocrites. Those who requested "a sign from heaven"

---

[104] John MacArthur, *The MacArthur New Testament Commentary: Matthew 8-15*, (Chicago: Moody Press, 1987), p.327. MacArthur notes several interesting examples in his commentary.

had already made up their minds that He was evil, crazy and dangerous, despite the fact that He had performed many signs and miracles. They were skeptical and unbelieving. They were just like Pharaoh in Exodus whose heart was unwilling to budge. Instead of opening their eyes and recognizing the truth, they refused to hear what Jesus had to say.

Why Did The Pharisees React The Way They Did?

The Pharisees were married to their religious ideological system and way of life. They had authority: all the right doctrines, rules and regulations. They were God's spokesmen for the common people. If Jesus was really the Messiah – if He really was from God and represented God and His Word to the people of Israel, then that meant they were wrong. Their ideas were out of touch with truth and God's standard. Their lives were a charade: claiming to be clean and righteous in their religious attire, but they were unwilling to change. It meant that many of the *truths* and *teachings* and *social norms* they held tightly were not necessarily good and true. It meant giving up certain ways of thinking about God, man, and certain theological perspectives and religious traditions. Their values and worldview were twisted and perverted in God's eyes … and they were unwilling to budge when it came to who Jesus was. Instead of accepting the truth, which was authenticated right before their eyes, they stiffened their stance and began to attack Him.

They had a choice. They could humble themselves, repent, and change their entire way of thinking and understanding of God … or they could simply reject the message and kill the messenger. They chose to call the Messenger evil because He was a threat to their authority, their status, their place in society, and their perceived place in God's eyes. Pride hardened the hearts of the religious leaders and therefore, they were like Pharaoh – and Jesus was like Moses in this stand-off.

The Greatest of All

Luke 11:29-32 *And while the crowds were thickly gathered together, He began to say, "This is an evil generation. It seeks a sign, and no sign will be given to it except the sign of Jonah the prophet. For as Jonah became a sign to the Ninevites, so also the Son of Man will be to this generation. The queen of the South will rise up in the judgment with the men of this generation and condemn them, for she came from the ends of the earth to hear the wisdom of Solomon; and indeed a greater than Solomon is here. The men of Nineveh will rise up in the judgment with this generation and condemn it, for they repented at the preaching of Jonah; and indeed a greater than Jonah is here."*

We all know the story of Jonah. God called Jonah the prophet to go and preach to the hated enemies of Israel, the Assyrians who lived in Nineveh. Jonah eventually went to Nineveh, though quite reluctantly. At the heart of his struggle was the knowledge that if he preached the Gospel, the Ninevites would repent. And they did … and God spared that generation from judgment. I think the point that Jesus was making was that, when all was said and done, there were people from other nations – pagan Gentiles who had far less revelation than Jesus' listeners – but they believed the Word of the Lord.

The second story is the visit of the queen of the South (Sheba) who came to see for herself Solomon's wisdom. Of course, he made a believer out of her by answering all her questions. Here was a queen from another land, not an Israelite, who had very little information other than that the wisdom of God was in this king, and she came, she heard, and she was convinced. Her presence in the Kingdom will also condemn Israel, for if she could believe what she heard about God's wisdom in Solomon after a brief visit, they should have believed with all that they had seen and heard. For Christ is far greater than Solomon.

Jesus was, is, and always will be THE GREATEST AMONG THE GREAT. He is the greatest of all prophets and greatest of all kings. HE IS THE KING OF KINGS AND THE LORD OF LORDS, and yet they could not see with their spiritual eyes and understand with their spiritual hearts that Jesus was Who He claimed to be. So Jesus made this striking point that the stakes are now much higher. Pagans believed in the Lord at the preaching of Jonah ... *but Jesus is much greater than Jonah.* His words were words of life and truth ... and He did amazing miracles that authenticated His words. *They should have believed.* A pagan queen believed because she heard wise sayings from the king of Israel. But Jesus is far greater than Solomon. His wisdom and His knowledge surpass them all. *They should have believed.*

Now, two thousand years later, we hear those words and say, *"Of course that's true!"* But hindsight is 20-20. Imagine sitting in the crowd when Jesus spoke those words. What would you have thought? I like what Philip Yancey wrote in his book *The Jesus I Never Knew*. He said:

> *Jesus was a human being, a Jew in Galilee with a name and a family, a person who was in a way like everyone else. Yet in another way he was different than anyone who ever lived on earth before. It took the church five centuries of active debate to agree on some sort of doctrinal statement to balance between Jesus being "just like everyone else" and "something different.*

Was Jesus God in the flesh, fully God and fully man? Of course He was. John 1 says the eternal Word of God became flesh and walked and talked on the earth. Jesus was a man. There is an important word in theology called the *Kenosis*. It means Jesus emptied Himself of His visible deity and took the form of a servant, a human being. Though He never ceased to be God, He took the form of man and became fully human just like us. He was both fully God and fully man (Philippians 2:8-9).

The only difference between Him and the rest of us was that He did not sin or have an inherited sin nature like we do. But He walked, talked, ate, drank, and went through puberty just like everyone else. He had to learn how to read and write; He had to memorize Scriptures and prophecies that He read in the Word. He needed to sleep and rest. He often grew weary and tired and just needed some time alone and isolated Himself from everyone else. He got tired and frustrated sometimes, especially with His disciples. He got ticked off and enraged. One day, He became so agitated that He picked up a whip and began flipping tables in the temple courtyard and chasing people away! In fact, the Gospels show Jesus exhibiting just about every human emotion. When Jesus needed to get to the next town, He didn't hop on His magic carpet like Aladdin. He didn't go into the phone booth and put on His superhero cape. When He wanted to travel, He walked on foot, camping outside under the stars, sometime feeling hungry, thirsty, and alone. Most of us are guilty of divorcing Jesus from historical and cultural context. We look at him in Scriptures like he was Super-Jesus.

You want to know something? There was nothing special about Jesus' physical appearance or social status. Even more, Jesus was not from Jerusalem. He was from Galilee. Let me say it this way: Jesus was not from the city, He was from the country. He probably wouldn't have been a "Mac" person if they had iPads in those days. He was not up to date on the latest styles. I have traveled to Israel several times now and have seen the beautiful glistening waters of Galilee for myself. The first thing that shocked me was that it was not actually a "Sea" but a lake. Today, the locals call it *Lake Ga'lee* or something like that. You can drive around the entire lake in about thirty minutes. I've done it. Maybe that doesn't shock you but it did me. I had this larger than life idea about Jesus and the Holy Land but when I went there, I found out that it was a relatively insignificant and small place. In fact, other than Tiberias, it is still a fairly unpopulated place – beautiful and pristine, but rural.

Basically, Jesus lived in what we would consider third world conditions. You've seen those little huts when you look out the bus window on missions trips. Yeah, Jesus was the poor kid living in the hut with a dirt floor and fire cooking dinner on the ground. What is even crazier is I find myself actually having to remind myself Jesus is not American! Going to Israel, being a foreigner, an outsider of a different tongue, and culture, I was a little taken back when several people kept correcting me saying *"His name is not 'Jesus,' it is 'Yeshua.' Please pronounce it correctly!"* It hit me that Jesus spoke a different language than me! What a thought!

Suddenly, my world was flipped upside down and I realized that I had this fairy-tale image and idea about who and what Jesus was. It was based upon pure opinion but totally irrelevant to the true person of Jesus as He was in His context. Some see Jesus as a hippie, some see Him as a rebel, some see Him as a Baptist, some see Him as a Mother-Teresa, some see Him like Gandhi, and some don't even think He existed! From my experience and perspective, it's almost as if we have fought so hard to protect Jesus' divinity from heretics and cults that we have totally stripped Him of His humanity and "down-to-earth-ness." This new Jesus, created in our own image, borders on Gnosticism – the teaching that denies that Jesus came in the flesh and was actually human as well as divine. How ironic! Paul was very clear: "there is One God, and One mediator between God and man, the man Christ Jesus" (1 Timothy 2:5). He was both God and Man in perfect mysterious harmony.

In their cultural context, Galileans were looked at as outsiders, hillbillies, country-bumpkins from a little po-dunk town. They didn't have a great reputation around the rest of the country. The night Peter denied Christ, they knew he was from Galilee because of his accent. We experience the same thing today, recognizing the region of the country people are from by the way they talk.

But do you want to know what blew my mind? On my first

trip to Israel, I was driving in a car with a few friends and our tour guide, Gideon, "the best tour guide in Israel," in my opinion, of course! Gideon is literally a walking talking Biblical encyclopedia. As we were driving around Lake Galilee one day, Gideon was pointing out various places and monuments to us and in passing said, *"And up there on the hillside is the cave where many people and ancients say Jesus lived while in Galilee."* We all said, *"Stop the car!"* Gideon stopped and pulled over and we ran up the hill. There were no tourists, buses, or even stairs to climb the hill. It had been left as is. When we got to the cave, I couldn't believe my eyes. It was like a little "dug out" in the side of a hill looking directly over the entire sea of Galilee.

According to our tour guide, there is some evidence that people did in fact live and dwell within the cave as early as the first century during Jesus' lifetime, and Jesus could have very well stayed in the cave. Of course, there is no way to prove that Jesus slept in that exact cave. But it is a definite possibility, and according to tradition dating back to the Byzantine era, it is probable that He did. I sat there silently, in that tiny cave that smelled musty and dark and looked out at the water below. It was a breathtaking sight. I felt like Christopher Columbus who just discovered America. Then it hit me. Please don't take me as being disrespectful … but Jesus, for a short time, was what people in our world would call a "bum." Jesus didn't have His own place to stay. He was living off the land. In fact, that is what He said with His own mouth, "Foxes have holes, birds have nests, but the Son of Man has nowhere to lay his head" (Matthew 8:20). Am I wrong?

Jesus was for a time homeless and poor – that is, without His own place to lay His head. He didn't dress well. He walked around probably barefoot and people thought He was a little on the crazy side. If nothing else, He was "different." Though this doesn't fit perfectly, the only way I could describe it is that He was almost like a "hippie" in our culture. He was certainly countercultural.

As I flew home from Israel, I remember thinking of all the sites and places, seeing the historical ruins right in front of my own eyes. I was thinking, how was it possible? How did He do it? He was just a poor man from a rural third world country under the oppression of a powerful Roman Empire who never traveled outside of a 90 mile radius. How do I reflect Jesus? How do I even remotely represent Jesus in my own day? All I could see was a stunning vision. It was a vision of Jesus: a poor, homeless, unkempt man, standing on a hillside alone in the wilderness looking at a quiet lake in a remote place known as Galilee. He knew Who He was. Then, I saw a swirling vortex of cathedrals, wars, crusades, mega-churches, monasteries, huge Christian music concerts in football stadiums, huge conferences in big cities with celebrities and rock stars, and music labels, massive Christian conglomerates, corporations, and libraries full of books. I sat there wondering ... is this what Jesus intended? Did Jesus plan to create "Christianity" and everything that goes along with it as we know it and see it today? I challenge you to answer that question for yourself. Jesus came to destroy the work of the devil, destroy the power of death, seek and save that which was lost, to bring the Kingdom of God to the earth, and to build His church – a community of people indwelt by His own Spirit who are one collective body and temple for God to live in, who will one day be resurrected to live forever in the presence of God on a new earth with access to a new heaven.

Jesus didn't fit within the social norms of His society. He did not go with the flow of society, politics, or religion. For example, in John 4 Jesus spoke to the Samaritan woman at the well. He broke many societal norms: He, a Jew, spoke to her, a Samaritan. Jews of that day had no dealings with Samaritans. They considered them unclean and inferior. Jesus, a man, spoke to her, a woman. Jesus included women in His traveling band ... something that was scandalous and taboo in that day. Nowadays, in religion we would have accused Jesus of using poor judgment and bad discretion in the way He communicated and broke social norms. He certainly enjoyed Himself at parties … He was called a glutton, a drunkard, and a friend of tax collectors and prostitutes. The religious establishment viewed Jesus as irreligious, scandalous, and pushing the envelope.

I always hear people quoting the passage that Jesus ate and drank with sinners … but seriously, what would you think if you saw your senior pastor drinking a glass of beer with a group of sleazy businessmen and scantily dressed and buzzed prostitutes in the local sports bar on a Friday night? See my point? Don't get mad at me – I'm just the messenger. But that is pretty much exactly what the good, faithful, religious church people of Jesus' day saw Him doing. At least, that is how they perceived Him.

Now, please let me remind you, I did not say Jesus ever once *condoned* sin or immoral acts of the spiritually sick and poor people He ministered to. I also did not say that the senior pastor mentioned in the above paragraph condoned sleazy business practices, sexual immorality or drunkenness. However, based upon *the company he was seen with*, people would be tempted to judge him. Maybe he was ministering to them. Perhaps he had developed a relationship of trust with them after months of praying and fasting for them as led by the Holy Spirit. But most people, myself included, would self-righteously judge that man. I think I would be very suspicious if I saw some TV pastor sitting in a sports bar drinking beer, laughing with such a crowd. And based upon our culture and the history of scandal and immorality in our churches, we'd have good reason to think such a way. That is my point! Jesus was demonized by the good people of His day because of the false impression His peers had of Him. I know this, because that is exactly what the Gospels recorded. I'm not making it up! You've got to put yourself in their shoes.

The only thing different about Jesus was that He actually

could manifest miracles and He was a powerful exorcist. I've read secular, unbelieving historians who have studied the life of Jesus and from their perspective, the historical figure Jesus of Nazareth was a Jewish mystic and exorcist on the fringe of Judaism. You disagree with me? Read Geza Vermesh's *Jesus the Jew* and see for yourself. It is a fascinating book written by a brilliant Jewish scholar and historian who is an atheist. I was recently in Israel and had lunch with a world renowned archeologist and scholar ... and those were his thoughts as well. He said *"Jesus Himself was unsuccessful at garnering popular support and really launching a true religious movement .... He was executed for being a troublemaker and would've been a failure ... until Paul hijacked the movement and, with help from others, catalyzed and spread the movement."* Is that the truth? Let's look at the facts and see why a world-class historian would say such a thing.

According to Darrell Bock's book *"Studying the Historical Jesus,"* Jerusalem was a city most likely of around 100,000 people during Jesus' day. The entire population of Palestine/Israel was estimated to be between 700,000 to 2.5 million. The entire Galilean province where Jesus spent most of His time ministering was probably around 200,000 people. Prominent cities like Capernaum right on the sea ranged from five to ten thousand people. It wasn't a huge population. But if you take the total population of Jesus' country of Palestine and get a middle range average between estimates for the total population, you come up with around 1.6 million people. [105]

In the book of Acts, when Jesus ascended into heaven, and the dedicated followers of Jesus went back to the upper room to pray and wait for the coming of the Holy Spirit, do you know how many of them were there? One hundred and twenty. That's all ... and that is .0075% of Israel's total population and .12% of Jerusalem's population. [106] Paul records in 1 Corinthians 15

---

[105] Population estimates taken from Darrell L. Bock, *Studying the Historical Jesus*, (Grand Rapids: Baker Book House Company, 2002), p. 110.

[106] These figures come from using the estimated average population of 1.6 million noted in the para-

that Jesus appeared to 500 people at one point. Let's make a massive overestimation and say Jesus had 10,000 dedicated hardcore followers, it would still only come out to .63% of the nation's population. When Jesus died and resurrected from the dead, He had not created a major movement. He didn't shake the foundations of Israel. He didn't change the world. He didn't even come close to garnering a tiny percentage of the population. In the eyes of His people, He was a delirious, poor man from the country who managed to lead a fringe and extreme group of people astray from mainstream Judaism.

What am I trying to say? Why am I squashing all your warm fuzzy ideas about Jesus? That is not my intent. He is my Savior and Lord and my only goal is to glorify Him. But I do want you to see the setting when the crowd sat there and listened to Him. They didn't necessarily love Him or devote themselves to Him. They were fickle, shallow, skeptical, and unbelieving. There was nothing special about Jesus' social status, education level, or credentials. Jesus did have the power to cast out demons, heal the sick, mend the broken-hearted, and finally actually defeat the power of death itself and be transformed into a glorified and resurrected human being. He was showing people in real time that He was the long awaited Messiah promised to them in their Scriptures! *He was, is, and always will be Lord of Lords, King of Kings, the greatest of the great ones, the most glorious and honored among the righteous, and the pinnacle and cornerstone of God's heavenly kingdom.*

Jesus was saying *"I am the sign from God to your generation. My resurrection life will prove I am who I say I am."* He is the one sign everyone will ultimately have. They may have seen Him with their eyes while in resurrection form on the earth; they might have heard powerful preaching about Him years later from Jesus' followers; or ultimately they faced Him in the final judgment. One way or another, they had their "sign."

---

graph above.

Now let me say clearly: the resurrection life of Jesus Christ is still the sign for the world today. If you are looking for a sign to somehow prove God is real, to prove that the Bible is true, to prove that Jesus is the only way to God ... if you want to see a miracle or healing or exorcism, you're probably going to miss it. Miracles do happen ... they happen every day. I have seen demons cast out of people. I have met people who have been *miraculously healed*. I have personally spoken with many genuine and honest TTI church planters who have told legitimate stories of blind people receiving sight – and many other miraculous healings and events. But somehow that hasn't seemed to impact us. We're still searching for the ultimate sign from God. Signs and wonders will impact our generation no more than they did in the first century. There's only one sign you need: the empty tomb and the appearances of Jesus of Nazareth.

If you're wandering around looking for a wonder, you need to wander no more, because Christ in you is the greatest wonder that's ever happened before!!! The only sign that our generation is going to have is the *manifest display of the resurrection life and power of Jesus Christ* working through the lives of His followers. Satan doesn't want us to know, experience, or allow Christ, who lives in us to be manifest through us. Why? He doesn't want any of us to realize that the all-powerful, all-knowing, all-present Spirit of Christ who overcame death dwells inside of each of us. Jesus has delegated His power, authority, and Kingdom citizenship to represent Him in this world. Satan is fine and comfortable with us going to church on Sunday and doing our own thing the rest of the week.

Three Essentials: #1 - Resurrection Power

Let me conclude this chapter by talking about three issues that are absolutely relevant to exercising your Kingdom calling. The first is experiencing God's resurrection power in our lives.

What happened when Jesus was raised from the dead? Everything. The victory was won. He went from death to life. He conquered death and was enthroned as the Lord of Life, no longer to taste death again. When you put your faith in Jesus Christ to pay for the guilt and debt of your sin, you believe in the power of His cleansing blood, and His body which was broken for you, to break the curse of death. He was buried and was swallowed up into the dark bowels of this earth in death. And then like a military hero and victor, He punched death and Satan in the face, knocking them both down and said, *"Get outta My way … I'm not staying here. And I'm taking your captives with Me."* He's the only one with such power. The Bible teaches that we were born dead, under the curse of sin and destined to physical death and spiritual death (see Romans 3:9-19, 23-24; Ephesians 2:1-5). But when you put your faith in Jesus Christ, His resurrection becomes your resurrection. We are raised to life in the spiritual realm; we have a forever-relationship with God; and we have direct access to God's presence. Spiritual rebirth, resurrection and regeneration occurs in our lives – and brings us into the Kingdom of God.

This means that Jesus's life, authority, and power, now dwells within each one of us through the Spirit of Christ that now lives within us. We need His resurrection power daily … to live as Kingdom citizens and to extend His Kingdom in the world.

Three Essentials: #2 – Gifted Leaders in Kingdom Offices

The second essential to exercising our Kingdom calling is understanding the spiritual gifts God has given us and the leadership position to which He has called each believer. Ultimately, leadership determines the success and impact of any organization, including the local church. Kingdom leaders must be called, qualified, trained and equipped to oversee their local Kingdom communities. I believe this begins with identifying individuals who are called and gifted to lead.

Alan Hirsch has done an excellent job identifying the five roles of leadership in the local church. Taken from Ephesians 4:11-16, he refers to these gifted individuals as A-P-E-S-T: [107]

- **Apostles**, who are the missional leaders and movement directors who extend the Gospel to regions beyond.
- **Prophets**, who are truth proclaimers and cultural influencers who know God's will and are particularly attuned to God and His truth for today.
- **Evangelists**, who are Gospel presenters and Biblical catalysts who call others to personal response to God's redemption in Christ.
- **Shepherds**, who are pastoral influencers and caregivers who nurture and protect those in God's family.
- **Teachers**, who are communicators of systematic, Biblical truth and are able to explain God's truth and wisdom clearly, accurately. and relevantly.

If there is to be any type of impact for the Kingdom of God, it will require a team of gifted individuals who are functioning faithfully and fruitfully with the gifts God has given them. No one person has all the gifts. That's why on a macro level – as well as on a local, micro level – there must be teams of leaders. For there to be movement or growth in any context, a team should draw upon the supernatural energy and momentum inherent in each member.

---

[107] Alan Hirsch, *The Forgotten Ways: Reactivating the Missional Church*, (Zondervan Publishing Company, 2006), pp. 149-178.

Three Essentials: #3 - The Priesthood of the Believer

Finally, if we are going to exercise our Kingdom calling, it's critical for every Kingdom citizen to understand the "priesthood" of every Christ follower. In Old Testament times, believers in God had to go through a priest (a go-between) in order for their prayers and sacrifices to be acceptable to God. But when Jesus saved us, He made us *"a kingdom of priests to His God and Father"* (Revelation 1:6). No longer do we need to *find a priest* … we need to *exercise our office as priests to our God*. All believers are *"on mission"* and must be missional in their lives. Every Kingdom community must, at its heart, be a missional community, meeting spiritual, physical, emotional, and economic needs in their communities and contexts.

We represent Him to others. We intercede on their behalf, praying for their salvation, praying for the extension of God's Kingdom in this world, praying for His glory to come down through our ministries, and praying for His will to be done on earth as it is in heaven.

Questions for Reflection and Response:

- How has God's resurrection power been evidenced in your life?

- Describe how you have been involved in God's missional enterprise in your local Kingdom Community. What role do you think God has for you in the future?

Chapter Fifteen

Jesus Christ, Kingdom Divider

It Is In Your Best Interest to Choose Your Side Now!

It's easy to talk about my wife, Sara, and my baby daughter, Selah. They are gifts from God and have made my life so happy and fulfilling. They are the most wonderful and important things in my life. But what I want to talk about in this chapter is something much more important than Sara and Selah, something that takes priority and preference even over my own family. This is a message of Jesus Christ in Luke 12 where we find that Jesus is a divider!

> **Luke 12:49-53 (NET Bible)** *I have come to bring fire on the earth – and how I wish it were already kindled! I have a baptism to undergo and how distressed I am until it is finished! Do you think I have come to bring peace on the earth? No, I tell you, but rather division! For from now on there will be five in one household divided, three against two and two against three. They will be divided, father against son and son against father, mother against daughter and daughter against mother, mother-in-law against her daughter-in-law and daughter-in-law against mother-in-law.*

Shocking words, aren't they? In fact, they are really words that we don't expect out of the mouth of Jesus Christ. We assume we are going to hear words of love, encouragement, acceptance and hope. But division? C'mon, man! The main point Jesus wanted to leave with His audience when He spoke these words two thousand years ago was this: *Something huge is happening. A message is being proclaimed that is important for you to understand. A man the prophets only dreamed about is standing in front of you who must be taken seriously. He is saying that it is worth giving up everything (family, friends, ambitions, dreams, money, jobs, and hopes for the future). But it comes at a cost. If you are not willing to take up your own cross and follow Me, and give up everything for this one thing, then you're neither willing nor able to be My disciple.* Jesus was crying out that if you could only comprehend the magnitude of this man, His mission, and His message, it would be worth leaving even your entire biological family to follow.

The Gospel ultimately brings peace with God (see Romans 5:1). But the main point of this passage is that Jesus' message is so radical that it can result in conflict. Coming to faith in Christ can result in strained family relationships, persecution, and even martyrdom. Jesus' ultimate mission was to divide, save, destroy, and then restore the earth.

Context

Bible passages are best understood in their *context*. That involves what came *before* and what came *after* the passage you are studying. Jesus begins in verse 49 by talking about fire coming on the earth – a picture of judgment. One day God will reign down fire from heaven and consume the earth. That's a sure, certain event … and one that we must be prepared for. Following this passage, Jesus warns that we must discern the times and seasons of God's prophetic fulfillment (v. 54-59). Those who understand the coming judgment will live differently as a result. Reconciliation and conflict resolution should be sought eagerly and quickly. Jesus is saying that we should make relationships right so that it will not bring cause for the Gospel to be dishonored in our lives (see 1 Corinthians 6:1-7). With that in mind, let's work through this passage a phrase at a time.

What Is Jesus Saying?

It has been said that the personality conveyed through much of Christian culture is not the personality of Jesus but of the people in charge of that particular "franchise." In this passage, we're going to have to take the blinders off and ask God for a fresh, Biblical view of who Jesus is.

Jesus said in verse 49, *"I came to cast fire on the earth."* In the Old Testament, God rained down fire on Sodom (Genesis 19). Elijah called fire down on Mount Carmel in his battle with the gods of Baal (1 Kings 18). Daniel chapter seven describes God's throne as ablaze with glory. When we read about these images, we see pictures of God's wrath and judgment as well as His glory and overwhelming presence.

What is Jesus saying here? Though some say this reference predicts the events of Pentecost where tongues of fire came to rest on each believer, I believe based on the context, it refers to God's final judgment at the end of time. [108] In Revelation 19:7-16, Jesus is pictured as coming on a white horse with flaming eyes of fire to wage war against Satan and the Anti-Christ. When He returns, He will destroy all the armies of the world, all the weapons of men who are opposing Him, and anyone and everyone who stands against Him. Peter talked about Jesus' return by saying,

2 Peter 3:8-13 *But, beloved, do not forget this one thing, that with the Lord one day is as a thousand years, and a thousand years as one day. The Lord is not slack concerning*

---

[108] The people who interpret this as fulfilled by Pentecost have a valid argument and some evidence to back it up. But my personal opinion is that the context points towards judgment by fire. Either way, my interpretation is definitely not outside of the bounds of normal, logical, contextual interpretation.

His promise, as some count slackness, but is longsuffering toward us, not willing that any should perish but that all should come to repentance.

But the day of the Lord will come as a thief in the night, in which the heavens will pass away with a great noise, and the elements will melt with fervent heat; both the earth and the works that are in it will be burned up. Therefore, since all these things will be dissolved, what manner of persons ought you to be in holy conduct and godliness, looking for and hastening the coming of the day of God, because of which the heavens will be dissolved, being on fire, and the elements will melt with fervent heat? Nevertheless we, according to His promise, look for new heavens and a new earth in which righteousness dwells.

In verse 49, Jesus says, *"How I wish it (the fire – destruction and judgment) were already kindled."* Is Jesus saying that He can't wait for the judgment of the world to begin? Is He really looking forward to wrath and destruction being poured out on our world at the tribulation? I don't think so. If we knew the deepest things of God and understood God's holiness and what He felt about what was yet to come upon the world, we would see God's deep sorrow about the judgment to come.

Look at the terrible sin, disease, oppression and suffering around the world – many of you know first-hand what is happening all over the globe. I imagine Jesus looking at all of that wickedness and saying *"I can't wait until all this is over! Enough! I wish my fire were already kindled and this wicked evil kingdom of Satan were already destroyed!"* Jesus had the ability to look forward to a brighter day – the day of a new heaven and new earth – where the Kingdom of God will be perfectly manifested on earth just like it is in heaven – and He longed to see that day!

In verse 50, He said, *"I have a baptism to undergo, and how distressed I am until it is finished."* Baptism. There's a word we're familiar with. But not so fast. Jesus is not referring to water baptism here. He's referring to suffering and death. He had a "cup to drink" (Matthew 20:22). He knew His mission required severe suffering and hardship – even to the point of death on a cross!

He goes on to say, *"And how distressed I am until it is finished."* The word *distressed* means to be totally focused, burdened and almost obsessed, determined to do something because nothing else really matters. This is the most important thing. But this one thing that Jesus just had to do was going to be the hardest thing that any human could ever endure! *Jesus was in agony over this thing He had to do in His humanity – but it was the one thing that He was pushing for and determined to do more than any other thing.*

The climax and pinnacle of His distress came in the garden of Gethsemane on the night before He died. In Matthew 26:38-39, Jesus said *"My soul is very sorrowful, even to death,"* and then He walked away alone and isolated, falling on His face to pray. Mark's account (14:33) says that Jesus was greatly distressed and troubled. Jesus cried, *"Father, take this cup from Me. God, this is too much!"*

Hebrews 5:7-8 *says that "in the days of His flesh, Jesus offered up prayers and supplications, with loud cries and tears, to Him who was able to save Him from death, and He was heard because of His reverence. Although He was a son, He learned obedience through what He suffered."* From this passage, it seems clear that Jesus not only cried out and wailed in Gethsemane, but He also cried out in prayer during the "days" (plural) of His flesh (throughout His lifetime). Can you imagine? Jesus cried out to God with tears, moaning, and groaning because of the nature of what His life, ministry, and ultimately death required Him to experience as the unique God-man.

Do you think Jesus was faking it? It seems that Jesus lived an entire lifetime of severe sorrow and suffering. He had to get away and pray all the time because His cup and His burden and His baptism were so great. The one thing He wanted to accomplish so badly was the hardest thing to fulfill. He was tempted in every way, just as we are (Hebrews 4:15). What a Lord and Savior we serve. What a wonderful high priest we have.

The next phrase that Jesus says is *"Do you think I have come to bring peace on earth? No, I tell you, but rather division"* (12:51). Wait ... isn't Jesus the Prince of Peace? Isn't He loving, kind, and gentle? Isn't He the dear little baby Jesus in the manger? What happened to that Jesus? Well, yes, Jesus Himself is the "Prince of Peace" and His Kingdom is an eternal Kingdom of glory, love, peace, and righteousness. But right now, Jesus' Kingdom has not yet totally overtaken this world.

Good Guys and Bad Guys

Movies from the 1960s were famous for pitting the bad guys against the good guys. To make it easy for us to tell them apart, they even put white hats on the good guys and black hats on the bad guys. Well, there still are good guys and there still are bad guys. They are the armies of heaven and the armies of darkness. The difference is that when Jesus and His armies return, He will call out to the entire world to beware. He will offer total protection and salvation from death and eternal suffering before He starts pouring out His wrath. Today, He is pleading with all the prisoners soon to experience death and destruction to come to safety and eternal life through His shed blood. *Jesus came, not to bring peace on the earth but division. Herein lies the core element and another key to understanding why Jesus is a divider and not a "uniter."*

There are two kingdoms: the Kingdom of God and the kingdom of Satan. That's it. A Kingdom of light and a kingdom of darkness. The world we live in is the kingdom of Satan – and look what kind of kingdom it is: a kingdom of decay, sickness, disease, perversion, oppression and injustice. There is rampant rape, abuse, drugs, sexual immorality, pride, rebellion, and fear. And the list goes on and on. Satan disguises himself as an angel of light, but the proof is always in the pudding. Where Satan's kingdom is ruling, his fruit begins to sprout and it isn't good. It's wicked and evil, because he himself is wicked and evil. But like alcohol, Satan's ways are also intoxicating. His influence pulls at our flesh like gravity pulls on the earth. Satan has the whole world drunk on his lies. Even our churches have drunk the Cool-Aid! I want to pull over here for a moment and focus on this point.

Satan and his evil forces have infiltrated our entire world system, including government, commerce, education, media, and religion. Even professing Christianity has been affected. Now we're at a point in history where it's really beginning to become visible. This anti-god system is symbolically referred to as *Babylon* in the Bible. And in the book of Revelation, we see Babylon as it appears in the last days – *political, economic, and spiritual Babylon*. And the goal of Babylon from the very beginning (even back in Genesis) is to unite the entire world together against God. Satan gets the entire world to sing KUM-BAH-YAH together and hold hands and say *"Peace, peace, peace! Anything goes, because we call the shots, not God."* He and his system stand opposed to the legitimate rule and authority of the Lord God of Heaven! And now it is late in the game. We're in a world that is now coming together – *globalism* is the talk of the sophisticated elite. We're all citizens of the earth. There is a global economy; there is a push for syncretism of religions. You like this, I like that, it's all ok. There's even something called Chrislam now to bridge the gap between Christians and Muslims!

People, wake up!!! It's so easy to see what is happening.

The Bible says that the nations of the world would become drunken and stupid from the sins of Babylon, the great whore of the earth. *Even the church has become intoxicated from the wine of Babylon. Have we fallen asleep? Are we so blind? Can we not see before our very eyes that our churches are being assimilated and many have already given in totally to spiritual Babylon?* 2 Thessalonians 2:11-12 says that *"God sends them a strong delusion, so that they may believe what is false, in order that all may be condemned who did not believe the truth but had pleasure in unrighteousness!"* Jude saw it already happening in the first century. John saw it, too. Paul saw it and said it would surely happen (1 Timothy 4:1-2; 2 Timothy 3:1-9). Now, here were are, in 2011 and sure enough it has happened and it's only going to get deeper and deeper.

A Call for a New Way of Life

Jesus' message was not simply a collection of devotional thoughts. It was infused with religious, political, and cultural implications. It was absolutely revolutionary! A new community of people was forming. He said God was doing something new and glorious right in front of them. And He claimed to be the fulfillment of everything Israel had hoped for: their long-awaited King, Priest, Warrior, and Messiah who represented God's Kingdom on earth. But unlike other wanna-be-messiahs, false prophets and delusional men, Jesus was actually performing signs and wonders and exorcisms to authenticate and fulfill what the prophets said would happen when He came. But it all looked and felt totally different than the people expected.

That is why Jesus said, *"For from now on there will be five in one household divided, three against two and two against three. They will be divided, father against son and son against father, mother against daughter and daughter against mother, mother-in-law against her daughter-in-law and daughter-in-law against mother-in-law"* (Luke 12:52-53). His message was divisive.

Despite the signs, wonders and fulfillments of ancient prophecies, Jesus' ministry appeared to be a terrible failure. As we saw earlier, only as many as 120 followers (Acts 1) out of 1.5 million residents in Palestine (0.0075% of the population) were true, dedicated, and willing to die for their commitment to Jesus as Messiah.

Jesus' ultimate mission was to divide, save, destroy, and then restore the earth. This passage reveals that Jesus was – and still is, for the time being – a divider. And the one thing that divides all people (Jew and Gentile, rich and poor, slave and free, male and female, fat and skinny, ugly and pretty, athletic and non-athletic, is one simple thing: THE BLOOD OF JESUS CHRIST! Today there are two types of people: those who are washed by the blood of Jesus – and those who are not … those who are saved and those who are lost.

Wake Up!

My Kingdom brothers and sisters, it's time to open our eyes and our ears, to wake up from this drunken stupor so many of us are stuck in today. It's time to come out of Babylon and into Mount Zion, the New Jerusalem. It's time to get off the fence – either get in or get out! If your relationship to God is not setting you against other people, dividing relationships, and causing friction in some capacity, then there is most likely something terribly wrong! Do you really have a true relationship with God? Notice, I did not ask how well you knew the Bible or if you could win the theological debates you participate in, or do you know all the current Christian music hits on the radio … but do you actually know God in a real and relational, intimate way?

Most of my life, I would have told you verbatim that

Christianity is not a religion, but a relationship with God, through Jesus Christ. I agreed wholeheartedly with that statement and was adamant about that fact, that it was true. But, if you were to get me to be totally honest, I would have had to admit that I didn't actually know or really have faith that God could really speak to me directly or communicate with directly ... and I didn't feel that I was ever really getting through to God. Not much of a relationship, huh? I think many of us have bought into some big-time lies ... and those lies come straight from the pit of hell. While many pastors, teachers and Christian leaders have stressed the necessity of having a *relationship with God,* it is my opinion that few (and I would include myself in this group for most of my Christian life) actually have lived out what that really means. Have we bought the lie that we *have a relationship with God ... when it's really not that much of a relationship?*

I've fallen into that trap myself. You see, I would pray and read my Bible, but it was more of a religious chore or duty that I did every day. Most people have equated how much they know about the Bible and doctrine as their barometer or gauge of how close their relationship to God is. However, this is really way off track. I have spoken with and "probed" many elders, pastors, and Bible teachers about this very issue. You see, I do not believe in "fresh revelation from God" in regards to new doctrine or theology. The Bible is the once for all, Scriptural canon containing God's entire redemptive plan and foundation for all doctrine and theology, for all truth and wisdom and knowledge. However, that does not mean that God cannot or will not regularly speak to us directly through His Spirit on a moment by moment basis about things pertaining to our life, our daily walk, our relationships, our needs, and all other matters pertaining to our personal spiritual growth and sanctification for godliness.

But we must be careful and be balanced. God is not a "genie in a bottle," or a fortune teller for us either. He speaks to us through our prayers, His written word, our life circumstances, our family and friends, and a variety of other ways. Sometimes God speaks to us through dreams, visions, or simply "gut-feelings." We must seek God daily, learn to "practice His presence" and learn to hear and recognize His soft gentle voice. I fully believe that I speak to God every single day directly and He speaks directly to me every day. I try to get my chores from God each day. I ask God for very specific directives, and I wait in the dark, sitting in silence on my face, being still in His presence often for up to three or four hours at a time. You know what? He speaks to me, and I journal my prayers with Him. It is our intimate relationship together. Have I ever heard his audible voice? No, but that makes it no more or less God's real voice. It is God's tangible, actual voice communicating to me at a spiritual level. We westerners – and really Christians in general – have become disconnected from true spirituality. Instead of being careful, we have become so far out of balance that most people really don't feel that God can actually communicate to us. Instead, we are just stuck on earth – with the Bible as a "road map" that we use to try and make the best decisions possible with our own minds and intellect and then pray some words out loud and hope that somehow God makes good use out of the decision we make.

Pastors and teachers who are leading Kingdom Citizens must seek God's voice. We must preach and teach from God's word – directly from His word revealed and written in Scripture. But we must also hear from Him ... deep in our spirits. God wants to speak directly to you – personally to you about yourself and your church members – for application and direction. God wants to speak into the pastors, prophets, teachers, evangelists, and really speak His own voice through them to His people on earth.

That is God's desire today and sadly, most believers are stuck in a feeling of disconnect from God because we somehow believe that, even though God went to all the trouble to put His divine Spirit inside of us, we can't actually tap into His Spirit and connect with Him in a real tangible, experiential way. Does that even make sense? Yet, in my experience, that is what most Christians believe.

    I believe that after a lack of faith, the main reason that we are disconnected from truly experiencing conscious contact with God is because of busyness and carnal lives. We've spiraled out of balance because we have replaced God's priorities with our own selfish desires. As Westerners, we are over-committed in our schedules, driven by materialistic pursuits to satisfy our fleshly desires of temporal gain. We seldom take time to truly stop and listen for God. How many of us take a true, legitimate, quality amount of time during each day to pray, read God's word, and sit in stillness or darkness in nature (or anywhere quiet) for an hour or more? Do you realize how much more potential God would unlock through each of us by His Spirit if we would practice this ancient art of living? Do you know how much clarity and direction we would receive from God's Word and His Spirit if we could substitute Bible memorization, stillness, and prayer instead of televisions, tweeting, and Facebook? Why don't we pray? Isn't prayer strategic? Isn't the Holy Spirit *the key power source for evangelism and discipleship*? Shouldn't we spend some quality time getting to know the Holy Spirit who actually lives inside of us? During these times of silence and solitude, I ask Him questions, and when I ask Him a question, I wait for a response. Why shouldn't we?

    Because I have a deep burden for what's going on in evangelical Christianity, I want to pull over and focus for a moment here. As I listen to pastors, teachers, and other Christian leaders, one of the key words I keep hearing being tossed out as *"the most important ingredient to success"* is having and communicating *"vision"* in your church. The new buzzword being propped up for great young leaders of the Church is the word, vision. We are being taught that we must "create a culture" of pure, dripping, seething "vision." Everyone in the Christian business/industry, including think tanks, panels, and networks of bright-minded top leaders, is rallied together to come up with the next new one sentence slogan or acronym, so they can become the next best-seller book in religion-land and make a lot of money. Sadly, that seems to be the truth when you get behind the scenes and see the reality. Sometimes when I attend evangelical conferences or pastoral gatherings, I vacillate between laughing hysterically and weeping like a lonely prophet when I leave. Why? Because, in my experience, most Christian leaders actually believe that they are supposed to *"create the vision"* for their church. The truth is that almost every spiritual leader I interact with in the Christian community actually believes that God does not directly speak to us as individuals. They tell us that God has left us His Holy book to scour, pick apart, learn, and memorize, so that *we as leaders of His Church* can use our brains and logic and determine the best possible strategy and system to accomplish the task of making disciples of all the nations and peoples of the world to bring glory and honor to Him. We're all familiar with the "textbook answer" that we rely on the Holy Spirit to direct and guide us. But instead of relying on Him, Christian leaders tell us that God really blesses those who *"sow the most seeds and the most seeds well,"* and therefore we must become expert experts in tactics and strategy when it comes to evangelism and witnessing. Don't believe me? Just look at the number of books written on evangelism and witnessing. That's exactly what they are telling us. This is a common thing – and most leaders would probably not admit this is true, but whether we agree to it in word or speech, the proof is always in the way we live our lives on a daily basis. Our actions (our works) really prove what we believe and put our faith in. Isn't that what James said in James 2?

You may be sitting there thinking, *"What's wrong with that?"* My answer is EVERYTHING! It's a lie from the pit of hell! How could we, as a spiritual community, have become so perverted, humanistic, and disrespectful to the Holy Spirit in the way we think? The job of *every believer* is to be a "witness" (Matthew 28:18-20; Acts 1:8). But the power source of a true witness is not logic, intellect, relevancy, strategic mapping, apologetics, or any other man-made idea or marketing ploy. The power and fuel of true evangelism which flows into disciple-making is the Holy Spirit of God Himself. It is possible for the Holy Spirit of God Himself to speak directly through us and work directly through us in our evangelism and discipleship methods. He Himself is the one who can save people – not us. When I feel led to speak to someone about Christ or share my faith, I close my eyes, take a deep breath, speak and pray to the Spirit of God, and then believe that when I open my mouth to speak to that person, the Spirit is moving my mouth like the wind moves a ship on the sea and He is intervening in my conversation to prick and prod the heart of the unbeliever. It is His power and wisdom and truth, not mine. Many of us just have never experienced that in reality and don't think it is realistic and practical in real life … but it is!

Jesus said *"I will build my church."* But *we* are the Church! If Jesus builds His church that means that we cannot, will not, and never have been able to make one soul part of Christ's collective body. Even more, the sanctifying work and progress that truly happens inside of us and all followers of Jesus Christ is the direct work of the power of God's Holy Spirit and God's Holy Word joining together in perfect harmony to actually change the spiritual composition of our being itself. Godliness, as we've already spoken of, slowly begins to change our inner life which in turn will slowly manifest drastic changes in our lifestyle, appearance, demeanor, "vibe," and other qualities seen and sensed by others around us. The same life, Spirit, and power which raised Christ Jesus from the dead, lives within our mortal bodies. He can lead us and guide us into supernatural and miraculous evangelistic encounters and conversations with people every single day of the week.

After His resurrection, Luke records Jesus telling the disciples to go back to Jerusalem and wait until you are *"clothed with the power from on high."* Jesus had just told them, *"I am sending forth the promise of My Father upon you"* (Luke 24:48-

49). That promise was the Holy Spirit, coming to fill, energize, empower, and change our lives. The Holy Spirit is the power (Greek, *dunamis*) which we are clothed with. He allows us to truly be effective witnesses in this world. His power, light, and truth speak through us, manifesting Christ to our dark world. Jesus, in *true, undeniable form,* is the One who opens the eyes of those who are spiritually blind, who brings hearing to the spiritually deaf, and then draws those people into the Kingdom of God. God's Kingdom is demonstrated not in word or speech, but in other-worldly power and authority which can be seen, felt, and experienced by a lost and dying world around us.

    The reason most of us are not truly experiencing power in our witness and not witnessing on a regular basis is that **(a)** we don't really have a filling and empowering relationship with the Holy Spirit; **(b)** we don't really believe we can interact with the Holy Spirit in such a direct way; and **(c)** we don't really believe He will give us *dunamis* power and anointing when we are witnessing to friends, family members, co-workers, and strangers. Again, it is a faith issue. There is a massive disconnect in what we say we believe and how we actually live out our lives. So what is it that we actually believe? Plain and simple, we've believed Satan's lies. There is no other explanation or valid excuse. If you don't like what I'm saying, then just tear those verses about the power of the Holy Spirit to be a witness out of your Bible. Please don't pervert, twist, and malign God's word to compensate for your unbelief or acceptance of a satanic lie.

    Is vision-casting effective in a corporation and business? Yes! Will articulating a clear and orderly vision and plan in your church actually get many people excited, unified, and most likely result in financial and numerical growth? Yes, of course! That is why everyone is so excited about it. Do we not think that corporations, companies, and Satan himself know the same tactics? Where do you think we got that from? They are, at best, carnal and worldly thinking empowered by human logic, and abilities, and can create large churches of up to 50,000 people without any need at all, whatsoever, on the Holy Spirit's power and presence. Vision-casting works so well because human beings move in a herd-type mentality. No matter what size the church (large, small or in-between), you need nothing more than a good business plan and marketing strategy, coupled with a decent communicator who can administrate. Add a decent music leader, and a cool website; name it anything you like, push the button and presto, you've got yourself the next new, exciting brand of church. Package it anyway you want, yada-yada-yada, it's all the same.

Please don't misunderstand me. I am not against *"casting vision."* That would be stupid! Vision casting is essential to all successful churches, organizations and ministries. What I am trying to say is that we must get the initial vision FROM GOD. We cannot create the vision ourselves. It must originate from Him.

Has it not occurred to anyone else that the more mega churches, church planting networks, missional books, and the more culturally-relevant groups and churches there are out there in the United States, the less effective Christianity as a collective group in America has become? Is it not clear, based upon cold, hard, scientific facts, that in general there is death and decay in our denominations and associations? Despite my own generation's strong reaction against hymns, Bible thumping, shouting, and choir robes, our society has become more and more sick and morally bankrupt with each passing day. How is that possible if our "strategic" and "philosophical methods" are so brilliant and well thought out? With all of the billions of dollars being pumped into cutting-edge churches and church planting strategies, why are we as a church body losing more and more influence over our society?

Why has the church lost the battle of reaching our generation? The very fact that people are actually creating "generation X" churches is PROOF that we are powerless over the spiritual powers of darkness. Let's be honest: does MTV have to develop creative ways to reach the youth of today because they're losing their clientele to those darn Christians? Do the CEOs of the world's social institutions gather around, scratching their heads about how to combat the Christian social and cultural forces which are taking away from their business and revenue (kind of like Demetrius did to Paul in the book of Acts)? Why has the church not put the pornographers and adult film industry out of business? We are having little-or-no appreciable impact on the moral integrity of our society.

The person and power of Jesus Christ manifested through His Church should be so powerful, revolutionary, and beautiful that we become a serious force even to the media and entertainment industry of the Western World. Despite how mad and angry you get at me for saying this, the bottom line is this: Satan is now pretty much ruling over the evangelical church. Satan began the process of infiltrating the evangelical church as early as the first century. *Why would he not do such a thing?* We Christians teach our people to infiltrate government, education, media, the scientific communities, for the purpose of gaining influence and to be "salt and light" in a darkened world.

For some reason, believers refuse to believe there are actually Satanists, occultists, men of reprobate minds and hearts, money hungry and perverted men who have slowly infiltrated our denominations, seminaries, Christian media outlets, church pulpits, and Christian publishing companies in the 21st century western world. It is unthinkable for most followers of Christ to believe that some of their most beloved men preaching on their podcasts or authors of their most beloved books, TV and radio programs are not really in it for the glory of God but for sex, money, and power. It is not by accident or mistake that the Church is being taken further and further away from the Gospel and true Bible teaching. It is being done by design, by sociological, psychological, and spiritual architects – because evil men and apostates have crept in unaware (read the epistle of Jude to see how it happened then and is happening now) and this is exactly what was predicted to happen by Paul and other New Testament writers from the beginning. A great apostasy is manifesting openly – and we are too asleep to see it. These men have crept into our pulpits, places of power and prominence unnoticed, and Satan's ultimate goal is to slowly assimilate more and more religious pluralism and religious syncretism (one degree at a time) because the ultimate goal of spiritual, political, and economic Babylon is globalism.

What I am about to say is difficult to prove and I admit that this could be more of a personal opinion as opposed to empirical, proven fact. However, as the years pass, it seems more and more clear that the Church and state are really not too separate. Many large Christian organizations and entities work directly with the Department of State, the Central Intelligence Agency, and other branches of governments, especially internationally. [109] I remember in Church History class hearing about a famous church father who cried, *"What does Rome have to do with Jerusalem?"* The idea was that the Church (represented by Jerusalem) had *nothing in common* with the political institutions of the day (represented by Rome). Today, I cry at the top of my lungs, *"What does Babylon have to do with Mt. Zion, the New Jerusalem? Come out of her, body of Christ. Do not be intoxicated by the lies and seduction, the power, the money, the fame, or the sexual immorality of mystery Babylon."*

This is not a rant against the institutional church. This is speaking the truth in love about what is real, tangible, and observable. Evil forces can be discerned and judged when dissected by the plumb line of God's Word itself. It doesn't take

---

[109] One such (non-Christian author) is Jeff Sharlet, *The Family: The Secret Fundamentalism at the Heart of American Power.* A second is Lt. Col. William Millonig, USAF (March 15, 2006), *"THE IMPACT OF RELIGIOUS AND POLITICAL AFFILIATION ON STRATEGIC MILITARY DECISIONS AND POLICY RECOMMENDATIONS"* (PDF). U.S. Army War College.– this is a PDF file online. Finally, Anthony Lappé, *"Meet 'The Family',"* Guerrilla News Network, June 13, 2003, (http://www.alternet.org/story/16167/).Many more could be listed, please note that these are just a few of dozens of books, newspaper articles, journals, magazine articles, etc… of the sometime unsettling "relationship" between church and state .

a prophet or a seer to see what is happening in front of all of us in real time. At its root, the institution of Christianity is really a religion called Protestantism, a sectarian off-shoot of Roman Catholicism. It has a form of godliness, but denies the power thereof. We talk about the power of God to change and transform culture, but at a macro level our talk is just that – it's talk. Instead of seeing Christianity thrive and flourish and take over the culture and institutions in America and the West, the world systems have influenced Christianity to the point where our churches are so seeker-driven, so seeker-inspired, so relevant, so non-abrasive in some contexts, that you could walk into a church and never feel the slightest bit of discomfort. How Satanic is that? How have we become so diluted and polluted by the toxicity of worldly and vain logic that we've drunk the cool-aid of pragmatic business models and called it "church"?

What we as a collective body are missing today is plain and simple: *the manifestation of true Holy Spirit, Kingdom Power demonstrated on a daily basis by a community of other-worldly people who are characterized by faith, hope, love, and united by the message of Jesus Christ and Him crucified and raised from the dead.* We have plenty of church buildings and resources in the Church to get all the homeless people off the streets in America and give them beds. We could feed all the hungry people in our country and take in all of the foster children. We could be doing Kingdom work to prepare the way for the arrival of our coming King who will be doing the same things on earth when He returns! All of the music, all of the technology, all of the strategies are just a shell, and a good shell at that. But it is a shell that must be empowered first and foremost by the Holy Spirit. Evangelism, discipleship, and every other type of strategy, program, or system is good and should be well thought out and Bible based. The only problem is we have created the infrastructure (the roads, the bridges, the sidewalks) and now we need fuel to make the bus move! The Holy Spirit and His power are the fuel that we need in our bus now, to make us move. But the only way to truly know and utilize the Holy Spirit's power is to know Him, learn to practice His presence on a daily basis, and allow Him to purify us and rid us of our carnal thinking and carnal living so God's power has room and space to manifest.

Let me give you an example. Recently, a graduate student from a well-known seminary came and did an interview and case study on our church's missional strategy. He had been given an assignment to study a real church's statistics and data to see how effective they were at evangelism and discipleship. I thought it was a great hands-on assignment. As we neared the end of our conversation, I told him about our missional DNA (which is "DMD" – *Disciples Making Disciples*) and leadership training.

During our conversation I began to feel the Holy Spirit prompting me to give my fellow brother in Christ some encouragement and exhortation. I noticed that he, like me when I was in his shoes, was going down a path of turning Kingdom work into some sort of scientific model or technique that was disconnected from the real resurrection power of the Holy Spirit working through Kingdom people. At that point, I asked him a question: *"Do you consider prayer a strategic element of missional discipleship and evangelism?"* He looked a little confused and replied *"Well, I know the answer is supposed to be yes ... but ... uh ..."* I said, *"Is prayer a major part of your everyday life in seminary?"* He put his head down and said, *"No ... I know that is a major need for improvement."* I said, *"No need to feel bad ... but why do you think you don't pray – or perhaps you feel the need to pray but you don't?"* *"I don't know,"* he said, *"I guess whenever I try to pray I get distracted, fall asleep, or my mind wanders off and I can't stay focused ... many times I wonder if God is even hearing me. And sometimes I forget things to pray about."*

I finally responded, *"Do you think that maybe you struggle with believing that God is really hearing your prayers, and that even if God did hear your prayers, He is not actually going to change anything ... and that because God is sovereign and in control over everything, prayer isn't really needed to actually see people get saved or see things happen?"* He agreed. I encouraged him that he could really truly have a real one-on-one relationship with Jesus right here and right now. We prayed and he confessed and cried out to the Lord. When we were finished, it was like I had given candy to a baby. I showed him how to *"know God,"* and He was thrilled. I have experienced this many times with similar people and never get over the amazement that our churches and seminaries are not teaching our religious leaders how to actually know and experience God. How is that possible? We must be truly "practicing the presence" of God in a tangible way. It can't be taught – it can only be caught.

Hebrews 11:6 tells us that *"Without faith, it is impossible to please God."* What an important verse for us today! Yes, you really can know God and talk to Him, experience Him, and have a real dynamic, awesome relationship and communication 24-7. He lives in us! He is waiting to speak to you, waiting for you to stop and listen, and in faith believe that He can help you in every specific need you have in your life. He is our Counselor. When we draw near to Him and experience Him, He will truly set us on fire! When that happens, people start to feel the heat – and either catch your flame, get ignited by your flame, or they get burned and stay away from you.

I tell you the truth: the fire Jesus promised is soon coming to this earth. You can call me a prophet of doom and gloom, but it's only doomy and gloomy if you have no hope and peace and no salvation through the blood of Jesus Christ.

Just like Jesus, God has given each one of us individually –

and all of us collectively – a mission. If you seek God you'll find Him. [110] When you find God, you'll find yourself in Christ and Christ in You. When you find yourself and God together, He'll reveal to you the mission He has for you!

All of us who follow Christ also have a "baptism" to undergo. And we will be distressed until it is completed. Brothers and sisters, if you're not weeping over your sins and the sins of your family and friends on a weekly basis, there is something wrong. Jesus wept with loud cries and groans. If we do not feel the burden of the world going to hell, there is something terribly wrong and we are not in line and fellowship with God and His Spirit. If our lives, thoughts, and joy are not centering around Jesus Christ and His cross, then something is wrong!

We have fallen asleep. We have allowed ourselves to become lukewarm, even to the point now where we have a form of godliness but not the power of godliness. And the power that comes forth from godliness is the surging resurrection life and power of Jesus Christ Himself manifesting in and through us.

What must we do? Repent! Revival starts right now! It starts here and now. We don't need to wait and talk about revival and an awakening. We must take the leap of faith, on an individual level, to put our money, our resources, and our entire lives where our mouth is, because talk is cheap. Luke-warmness at an individual level and corporate level is no longer acceptable for you, for our families, for our churches across the globe, or our nations.

Jesus Christ and the Gospel of His Kingdom is so important, so awesome, so glorious that it must take top priority in our lives, even above our own families. It is the Kingdom of God

---

[110] Deuteronomy 4:29; Jeremiah 29:13-14. I realize these promises were to Israel and should be exposited and interpreted in that particular historical context. However, if they apply to God's covenant people in exile how much more would they apply to His people, the people of the Messiah, part of His heavenly Kingdom, purchased by the blood of the Lamb?

on earth made available to anyone and everyone through the precious blood of the lamb of God. It is the glory of heaven shining through into our world … the intersection of time, space, heaven, and earth all at once. It is more than good news, it is a celebration and a way of life. A life characterized and experienced as joy, peace, love, freedom, and victory. Victory and deliverance from this world and its darkness is the song that the Kingdom citizens may chant together in unison today and forevermore. Jesus Christ, the Divider, is calling you, today, right now, to leave everything you know and pursue Him and His way of living. We have a great cloud of witnesses in heaven and a huge host of holy angels, as well as our elder brother and Lord, Jesus Christ, and a Cosmic God and Father as our united Family (see Hebrews 12). What an exciting adventure and movement to be a part of! Will you come and join us today?

Questions for Reflection and Response:

- How do you see church life today?

- What is your prayer life like today?

- Have you ever felt the Holy Spirit speak to you and/or work through you in a real way?

Chapter Sixteen

A Call to Kingdom Action!

Come and Join the Kingdom Unite™ Revolution!

The Power of Unity

Imagine an army of strong, skilled warriors dressed in indestructible armor. Each of these soldiers is equipped with weapons, uniform, and has come together with his fellow soldiers in preparation for a great war about to take place against a formidable enemy. However, when they come together, there is no organization, no pre-made plan, no "trumpet" to blow and unite the soldiers into formation when it is time to begin marching towards the battlefield. The result: *disaster!* What a waste of men, resources, and potential power to overcome a dangerous threat to a kingdom!

Now that you have read *God's Secret: The Gospel of God's Kingdom Unveiled,* it would be a tragedy and waste of your time if you put the book down and went on with life *as usual.* I would hate to see an army of God's Kingdom citizens ready to unite and do battle together but have no way to connect, come together in formation, and be prepared to face our spiritual enemy head on!

A Call to Kingdom Action!

God's Secret is not just a book. It is meant to be a call to action to God's Kingdom citizens, the remnant church on earth today, from the United States all the way to China ... and everywhere in between. It is a call to repent *("to think differently")* and begin to think with a Kingdom mindset and live life with Kingdom values.

Furthermore, this is a call to local churches everywhere to begin to move from an exclusivist mentality of focusing on *"our church"* and *"our family"* to focusing on God's Kingdom and the Kingdom citizens of your local city, county, state, and the rest of the world ... so that God's Kingdom citizens organized in *"Kingdom communities"* (that is, local churches) unite together as a unified army and fellowship of people empowered by the Spirit of Christ, storming the gates of hell hand and hand together in the love, truth, and power of God's Holy Spirit. What a beautiful sight that would be! Now, it is possible for Kingdom communities to come together through a new and exciting online social network called Kingdom Unite™, but before getting into the specifics on Kingdom Unite™, let us first address some pressing needs for the body of Christ right now.

You have already read in the previous pages the serious need of the church, especially the American Church, to rely upon the Holy Spirit's power for ministry, growth, and cultural transformation. We have also discussed the need for the Western church to get back to focusing on the Gospel of GOD'S KINGDOM as well as a renewed commitment to focus on the cross, the blood, and the resurrection of Jesus Christ for our salvation. Besides those important issues, another absolute essential need in the Church today is UNITY!

Psalms 133:1-3 *A Song of Ascents. Of David. Behold, how good and how pleasant it is for brethren to dwell together in unity! It is like the precious oil upon the head, running down on the beard, the beard of Aaron, running down on the edge* *of his garments. It is like the dew of Hermon, descending upon the mountains of Zion; for there the LORD commanded the blessing— Life forevermore.*

To be more specific, it is time to put denominational differences aside. No, I am not saying there are not useful elements within denominationalism, nor am I saying denominations themselves are inherently evil. If by "denomination" we simply understood and realized that certain groups of Christ followers have different doctrinal beliefs and interpretations of certain specific Biblical texts, that is fine and dandy. Furthermore, there is a broad diversity of methodology and traditions which are preferred more by some than others. We can all agree to disagree on certain points which are non-essential to *orthodoxy*.

However, if we are honest with one another and don't live in a state of denial, then we must admit that denominationalism is not simply different viewpoints, methods, and constructs within a globally unified "body of Christ" working together to spread the Gospel and attack the kingdom of darkness. Denominationalism, though well intentioned and sometimes useful, has become a means of fragmenting the body of Christ in an almost hopeless way.

Satan has worked strategically since the inception of the Church to do anything and everything in his power to divide the Church. He knows that if he can divide then he can easily conquer. Though the Church will not ultimately be defeated (because Christ is our Head), Satan has done serious damage to Christ's body on earth. In fact, from certain prophetic Scriptures in the New Testament it is clear that in the end the Christian "religion" as a whole, except for a godly remnant, will totally apostatize and fall away from the truth. It was Jesus himself in Luke 18:8 who asked *"Nevertheless, when the Son of Man comes, will He really find faith on the earth?"*

One way Satan has disabled and all but euthanized the Church of Jesus Christ has been to get us so focused on doctrine and dogmatic interpretations of God's word. We have become almost obsessive-compulsive and even paranoid at times about "right doctrine" that in the name of Jesus Christ and His Kingdom we have argued, slandered, hated, and divided (as a body) from one another over points of doctrine, many times non-essential doctrines, traditions, creeds, and dogmas which really do not determine orthodoxy.

It is almost as if *Christians have been plagued with a phobia – the phobia of heresy.* Why is slander not considered heresy? Why is division not looked upon with contempt as heresy? Why is it not considered "heresy" to not love and accept our Baptist, Pentecostal, Episcopalian, Lutheran, Methodist, Anglican, or other denominational brothers and sisters in Christ? Denominations are just labels to describe believers who interpret and act out certain Scriptures in a particular way – dogmatically on certain key issues. I am fine with Christ followers differing on points of Scripture. In fact it is healthy to challenge and debate (gracefully and lovingly) with one another sometimes, to keep one another sharp and accountable to fidelity to God's word. We all must be faithful to interpret Scripture to the best of our ability, with the aid of the Holy Spirit. Furthermore, we will all answer to God one-on-one for our stewardship of His Word.

My intention here is not to say "doctrine" or "Bible-study" and standing up for "God's truth" is wrong! Heaven forbid! Recently, a friend of mine challenged me to read the Pastoral epistles seventy-five times in a row and I did. One thing Paul instructed Timothy on was the protection of the sheep from false doctrine and false teachings. We agree!

However, many of the doctrinal differences which divide churches, associations, ministries and denominations are not related to the eternal Gospel of Jesus Christ and His Kingdom!

I wonder in amazement how pastors and teachers can fight and argue about doctrine and interpretation and then go days on end without praying. I wonder in amazement how Christians can fight and argue in anger and rage with other Christians about petty points of doctrine while not realizing that NOT LOVING YOUR BROTHER IN CHRIST is the ultimate HERESY (see 1 John)!

The division and "schism" (separation) [111] that many of us have participated in, gloated over, and patted ourselves on the back for, is in reality gross and displeasing to our Lord and Savior. Please, hear my words and test whether what I am saying is true. We must unite with one another. Satan and his dark kingdom know that unity and love among the brethren is the one thing that they cannot stand against. Unity and love among the brethren is what will set apart the Church from the world and be a true witness and light to a hopeless, dark, and divided world.

Now that you know my heart about uniting and coming together, I also want to warn you about a serious danger lurking beneath the surface in regards to really uniting and coming together. While Satan has fought his hardest to keep the church divided, he is also working on the other end of the spectrum to unite and "assimilate" the churches and denominations under the banner and leadership of people and organizations with an agenda not focused on Jesus Christ and the Kingdom of God. Some of the big "movers and shakers" in the Christian world that are influencing the "Christian masses" are not helping us but hurting us. Some even seem to be men of reprobate minds with seared consciences intent on bringing as many Bible-believing kingdom citizens under the umbrella of something that is anything but true, honest and Christ-centered.

---

[111] **Note:** The word heresy comes from the Greek word *hairesis* (Strong's Number 139) which is defined: "to choose, select. Heresy, a form of religious worship, discipline, or opinion…" In contrast to schism (G4978) which is an actual tearing apart, heresy may represent a divergent opinion but still be part of a whole. One can hold different views than the majority and remain in the same body, but he is a heretic (hairetikós [G141]). However, when he tears himself away (schízō [G4977]), then he is schismatic. Heresy may lead to schism which is when actual tearing off and separation occur…" Spiros Zodhiates, *Complete Word Study Dictionary of the New Testament*, (E-sword, electronic edition).

A Call to Kingdom Action!

People of God and shepherds of God's people, here me loud and clear. Stay clear and be suspicious – yes very suspicious – of any man, agency, church, or organization that is not FOCUSED AND ANCHORED SECURELY ON THE PROCLAMATION OF JESUS CHRIST, AND FAITH IN THE CROSS OF JESUS CHRIST, THE BLOOD OF JESUS CHRIST, AND THE RESURRECTION OF JESUS CHRIST. *Jesus Christ and Him crucified is the one message that should unite all Kingdom Citizens together.* The Gospel cannot be taken out of the verbiage and vernacular! Thus the unashamed proclamation of Jesus Christ and His Kingdom Gospel is one of the true "badges" of a Kingdom leader and a Kingdom movement! There are many groups and men in public view promoting everything except the cross, the blood, and the resurrection of Jesus Christ. They promote peace, love, unity, social justice, and everything else except the eternal Gospel of Jesus Christ and His Kingdom.

Now, moving from the *broad* to the *more specific*, how can individual Kingdom citizens, Sunday school teachers, youth leaders, pastors, seminary professors, denominational leaders, and evangelical para-church/ministry leaders come together and fight in a tangible way?

First, we must stop the competition. Being a pastor in a fairly large church, it often feels like "church growth" winds up being no more than a secular, competitive, capitalistic, survival-of-the-fittest marketing campaign! No offense, but if I have to hear about one more *church growth model*, I think I might lose it! *Do you want to know a real church growth model? Love one another, pray in the Spirit, be united in the fellowship of Christ, and be witnesses in the power and might of the Holy Spirit* (Acts 1:8)! I'm serious! What if larger churches worked tirelessly to help equip and train smaller churches in the nearby community to help them fill up their auditoriums on Sunday? Why can't they help them develop administrative and organizational needs? What if youth leaders in any given city banded together to reach the public high schools, not concerned about whether or not their youth group would benefit and grow, but rather, that an army of young men and women sold out to Jesus Christ would be raised up to capture their schools for the cause of the Gospel?

In most cities and towns across the country from California to New York City, there is really not that big of a need to build more church buildings. We could start by trying to fill up the already existing church buildings we have which are mostly empty! Furthermore, with the amount of Christians and churches already established in America there is no reason we should need to rely on local or national government institutions to help combat homelessness, childcare, stock food pantries, welfare, or any other such need. If we could somehow, someway, unite and become one (despite denomination, creed, dogmas, or man-made traditions which separate us) we could combat and defeat many of the social problems facing our country today.

There are an unlimited number of practical and simple ways for followers of Christ, as well as church leaders, to make a true Kingdom impact with little to no financial resources needed. All we need is the Spirit of God and intentionality to unite with one another and share resources together (man-power, time, financial and non-financial resources).

You may be sitting there reading this thinking it would be impossible to unite … but is that the voice of the Holy Spirit speaking to you? Is this not what Jesus prayed in John 17? Was Jesus unrealistic? Was Paul unrealistic when he wrote Ephesians 4:1-4? Is Revelation 5:9-10 unrealistic? I assure you, it is not God, but Satan who wants to keep churches hopelessly fragmented and divided. The great deceiver has spread a spirit of distrust, skepticism and pessimism among Christian leaders towards the thought of uniting with Baptists, Pentecostals, Presbyterians, Methodists and others in the Body of Christ.

Finally, another key tool to assist Kingdom citizens and Kingdom Communities is technology. For too long Satan has used technology against the world and the Church. In most cases, the Kingdom community is way behind the times in utilizing effectively and professionally the latest technology and tools available on the secular market. There are many individuals and groups out there in the United States and across the earth who are well aware of the power of technology. But for the most part, Christians are still living in the dark ages. It is time to take the internet away from the hands of the ungodly and take Satan's influence over the world and the Church and place it into the hands of God's Spirit-filled people representing the King of Kings and Lord of Lord's, Jesus Christ. One of the many new attempts to do just that is an initiative called Kingdom Unite™ (www.kingdomunite.net).

What is "Kingdom Unite™"? What Does It Have To Do With Me (or my ministry, my church, or church planting organization)?

Kingdom Unite™ is not just another website. It is a mission to connect each and every community of God's Kingdom Citizens on earth and UNITE! *The time is now!* As this entire book has sought to proclaim loud and clear, you are part of something much bigger than yourself. You are a citizen of the most prestigious and powerful organization in existence: The Kingdom of God! The Kingdom of God is not found in buildings. It is made manifest through people and communities when the Spirit and message of Jesus Christ live through them. God's Kingdom is made manifest on earth when His will is done in people, families, churches, and nations just as it is done in the heavenly dimensions. Every citizen of God's Kingdom has a mission to do which is God-given and God-empowered. Through unity with other Kingdom citizens, we can transform our individual worlds, spheres of influence, and domains together.

Further, each *community* of Kingdom Citizens working together possesses a corporate mission which is God-given and God-empowered. As God's Kingdom Communities get organized and join together, we can be the salt and light to the world Jesus Christ is calling us to be. Let us UNITE together and transform our communities, nations, and world together!

For starters, please know that the phrase "K*ingdom Community*" refers to local churches whether the church meets in a big building, small building, house, dorm room, under a tree, in a trailer park, in a store-front, or anywhere! Kingdom Unite uses the word "community" as opposed to "church" not to change things up for fun or irritate you. It is simply to start re-enforcing in your mind and construct that there really is just one Church after all … the word *church* simply means an assembled group of people. So we prefer to say "*community!*"

Kingdom Unite™ is NOT the next *Christian Facebook*. Though the site is useful and applicable for individual Kingdom Citizens, the foundational principle and purpose of the site is to allow any and all community leaders (church planters, pastors, house church leaders, and home "small groups" of any and all orthodox denomination, association, or affiliation) to have a profile page, (similar to having a Facebook profile page or a Twitter account) and then be able to network , form groups, interact, and join together for the purpose of doing Kingdom projects and missions with other Kingdom Communities nearby and around the world.

Each community leader will have a profile to represent his or her community of people who follow Jesus Christ as Lord and Savior. Individuals involved in each community represented by that profile will be able to follow and interact with their profile by "following" their page just as individuals can follow a Twitter account. Kingdom Unite™ is not a denomination or a church or church planting organization or anything like that! We are simply a social network to allow you to network with other kingdom minded communities. It is as simple as that.

There is much more to explain and describe about Kingdom Unite™ and its possibilities for you and your church, but you'll have to check it out for yourself at www.kingdomunite.net. Most important, this website and all of the resources available on the site are totally free! It will not cost you a thing. There is no catch at all!

It has major potential to not only bring God's kingdom remnant together, but also be a valuable tool for your own church or network you belong to (in regards to communication, networking, and logistics). It has been said that there is no such thing as a free lunch. However, that is only true for the world, not God's Kingdom!

God's Secret: The Gospel of God's Kingdom Unveiled

kingdom**unite**

Go ahead, Join the revolution.

visit www.kingdomunite.net

A Call to Kingdom Action!

Appendix 1

Becoming a Kingdom Citizen and Growing as a Kingdom Citizen:

Practical tips and help on how to "enter" the Kingdom of God and then grow as a Kingdom Citizen – through a real, authentic, and experiential relationship with God, through Jesus Christ.

First Step: Enter God's Kingdom!

Before you experience God's Kingdom, you must first become a disciple (or student, follower) of Jesus Christ! That is, you must become a Kingdom citizen. The time is now! Today is the day of salvation, if you are willing!

In order to really understand what God's word actually says about salvation and how to become a Christ-follower, read the following Scriptures carefully and prayerfully. Right now, close your eyes, take a deep breath, and speak to Jesus Christ, saying these words: *"Lord Jesus, I believe you are real and I want to* become a citizen in your Kingdom. Please open up my eyes and my heart to the truth in your Word below."

Matthew 4:17 From then on Jesus began to preach, "Repent, because the kingdom of heaven has come near!"

Mark 1:14-15 After John was arrested, Jesus went to Galilee, preaching the good news of God: "The time is fulfilled, and the kingdom of God has come near. Repent and believe in the good news!"

John 3:13-18 [Jesus' words speaking to a Jewish religious leader named Nicodemus] No one has ascended into heaven except the One who descended from heaven--the Son of Man. Just as Moses lifted up the snake in the wilderness, so the Son of Man must be lifted up, so that everyone who believes in Him will have eternal life. For God loved the world in this way: He gave His One and Only Son, so that everyone who believes in Him will not perish but have eternal life. For God did not send His Son into the world that He might judge the world, but that the world might be saved through Him. Anyone who believes in Him is not judged, but anyone who does not believe is already judged, because he has not believed in the name of the One and Only Son of God.

Acts 2:36-40 [The Apostle Peter preaching to Jews in Jerusalem on the day of Pentecost, 10 days after Jesus ascended into heaven] "Therefore let all the house of Israel know with certainty that God has made this Jesus, whom you crucified, both Lord and Messiah!" When they heard this, they were pierced to the heart and said to Peter and the rest of the apostles: "Brothers, what must we do?" "Repent," Peter said to them, "and be baptized, each of you, in the name of Jesus the Messiah for the forgiveness of your sins, and you will receive the gift of the Holy Spirit. For the promise is for you and for your children, and for all who are far off, as many as the Lord our God will call." And with many other words he testified and strongly urged them, saying, "Be saved from this corrupt generation!"

Acts 16:30-33 [Paul speaking here to a jailor] *Then he escorted them out and said, "Sirs, what must I do to be saved?" So they said, "Believe on the Lord Jesus, and you will be saved--you and your household." Then they spoke the message of the Lord to him along with everyone in his house. He took them the same hour of the night and washed their wounds. Right away he and all his family were baptized.*

Acts 17:30-31 [Paul preaching in Athens on Mars Hill to philosophers and educated Greeks] *"Therefore, having overlooked the times of ignorance, God now commands all people everywhere to repent, because He has set a day on which He is going to judge the world in righteousness by the Man He has appointed. He has provided proof of this to everyone by raising Him from the dead."*

Acts 26:14-20 [A conversation between Jesus and Paul] *When we had all fallen to the ground, I heard a voice speaking to me in the Hebrew language, 'Saul, Saul, why are you persecuting Me? It is hard for you to kick against the goads.' "But I said, 'Who are You, Lord?' "And the Lord replied: 'I am Jesus, whom you are persecuting. But get up and stand on your feet. For I have appeared to you for this purpose, to appoint you as a servant and a witness of things you have seen, and of things in which I will appear to you. I will rescue you from the people and from the Gentiles, to whom I now send you, to open their eyes that they may turn from darkness to light and from the power of Satan to God, that they may receive forgiveness of sins and a share among those who are sanctified by faith in Me.' "Therefore, King Agrippa, I was not disobedient to the heavenly vision. Instead, I preached to those in Damascus first, and to those in*

Jerusalem and in all the region of Judea, and to the Gentiles, that they should repent and turn to God, and do works worthy of repentance.

Romans 3:23-25 For all have sinned and fall short of the glory of God. They are justified freely by His grace through the redemption that is in Christ Jesus. God presented Him as a propitiation through faith in His blood, to demonstrate His righteousness, because in His restraint God passed over the sins previously committed.

Romans 5:6-8 For while we were still helpless, at the appointed moment, Christ died for the ungodly. For rarely will someone die for a just person--though for a good person perhaps someone might even dare to die. But God proves His own love for us in that while we were still sinners Christ died for us!

Romans 6:23 For the wages of sin is death, but the gift of God is eternal life in Christ Jesus our Lord.

Romans 10:9-13 If you confess with your mouth, "Jesus is Lord," and believe in your heart that God raised Him from the dead, you will be saved. With the heart one believes, resulting in righteousness, and with the mouth one confesses, resulting in salvation. Now the Scripture says, No one who believes on Him will be put to shame, for there is no distinction between Jew and Greek, since the same Lord of all is rich to all who call on Him. For everyone who calls on the name of the Lord will be saved.

Ephesians 2:8-10 For by grace you are saved through faith, and this is not from yourselves; it is God's gift – not from works, so that no one can boast. For we are His creation – created in Christ Jesus for good works, which God prepared ahead of time so that we should walk in them.

1 Timothy 2:3-6 *This is good, and it pleases God our Savior, who wants everyone to be saved and to come to the knowledge of the truth. For there is one God and one mediator between God and man, a man, Christ Jesus, who gave Himself--a ransom for all, a testimony at the proper time.*

Now, if you have never actually put your sincere faith in the Lord Jesus Christ, the power of His shed blood, the power of the cross, and His bodily resurrection, then I challenge you to do so right now. However, before you do so, you must also realize that following Jesus Christ, receiving His Spirit, and entering into His eternal Kingdom is no small decision. It does not happen by praying a magic prayer!

True acceptance of Jesus Christ and the Gospel of God's Kingdom always comes with repentance. No, you don't get saved by "doing" or "not doing" something. But if you truly understand God's gift to you through Jesus Christ, there will be a sincere desire in your heart of hearts to follow Him in obedience. The Gospel of Jesus Christ and His Kingdom will compel you to totally change your mind and way of thinking from a worldly and self-centered way of life, to a Jesus Christ and His cross way of thinking. *Jesus doesn't "come to live in your heart" just by you saying a simple prayer with the words of your mouth*. When you pray the following prayer in absolute faith, sincerity, and passion, and you're not ashamed to let the whole world know, God's Word says that you will be saved at that very moment. Then you will pursue a new way of life – a way of life which Jesus revealed to us in His own words in the Gospels (Matthew, Mark, Luke, and John). Pray this prayer out loud in full faith that God is hearing you and will respond to your request:

"Dear Father God in heaven, I thank You and praise You for making Yourself known to me through Your Son Jesus Christ. I believe in You, Jesus. I believe You are Messiah, Savior, and Lord. I put my full faith in You. I put my faith in

Your shed blood ... that Your blood is the only thing that can wash away my sins and allow me to be cleansed and forgiven. I believe that Your cross defeated the power of Satan, the power of death, and the curse of sin, and brings me victory over the kingdom of Satan.

"Lord Jesus Christ, I believe with all of my heart that You really did rise from the dead and ascended into heaven and are now sitting at the right hand of Father God. Please save me and deliver me from the grip of Satan and his evil kingdom right now! Please forgive me of my sins. I repent and give myself totally over to You. Now, please send Your Holy Spirit to come inside of me, change me, and make me a new creation. Bring me into Your Kingdom right now – I want to be a part of and represent Your Kingdom starting today! Thank you Lord Jesus Christ, Father God, and Holy Spirit. I worship you! Amen"

Now What Do You Do?

- Tell a friend or loved one! Do you have a friend or loved one that you know has been praying for you to make this commitment and take this step of faith? If so, call them immediately and let them know what has just happened! If you meant that prayer and believed then you will not be ashamed to let people know.

- Find a Kingdom Community! If you answered "yes" to the question above about a loved one or friend praying for you, you need to get connected with them and their church/Kingdom Community. You need to be in fellowship every week with other Kingdom citizens who are truly seeking to live a godly life and grow in their knowledge and experience of God. Hebrews instructs us to *"not forsake assembly"* which basically means GO TO

CHURCH! If you don't have a friend or loved one, or have a clue about what church to go to, I suggest logging onto www.kingdomunite.net to find a Kingdom Community in your local area. Note: it is important that you search for a community that is in a "network" which means they have been ordained and commissioned by an already existing church and have accountability and oversight. This is very important. Kingdom Unite™ is simply a social network for Kingdom Communities and does not validate or support any particular group over another.

- Get Baptized! Read Matthew 28:18-20, Acts 1:1-8 and Romans 6:1-5 to learn more about baptism. Baptism was not optional in Jesus' teaching – it was a command given from Him to every new disciple. You're are a new disciple and therefore need to understand the value, importance, and beautiful symbolic picture of what baptism means and how important it is. It demonstrates what happened to you at a spiritual level (spiritual regeneration), symbolizes your spiritual union with Christ Jesus (in His death, burial, and resurrection), your inclusion into the "Church" of Jesus Christ, and a public statement and testimony that you have come into God's Kingdom and are not ashamed of it! Baptism is a special, once in a lifetime experience that you do not want to miss out on!

- Grow! Begin to Grow in your knowledge of God's Word and your personal experience of God every day. Start your relationship with God right now! Read below for practical tips on "how to do that." Your new job and purpose is "to know God and make Him known to others."

Second Step: Grow!

Here are some practical tips on how to have and grow a real authentic relationship with God through Jesus Christ.

As you just read in the book several times, the essential elements of a true relationship with God are prayer, Bible study, meditation, and fellowship with other followers of Jesus Christ who are passionate and sold out to Kingdom living and experiencing God. One additional element regarding closeness with God is obedience to His Word and a pursuit of God's righteousness (Matthew 6:33). If we really love the Lord then we will obey His commandments (John 14:15). When we live life in a state of perpetual, known, and willful rebellion and disobedience to God's Word and God's Spirit, our fellowship with the Lord will become distant and stagnant. The "waters" that we once knew and cherished will become dried up because our willful sins act like a dam holding back God's waters from flowing in and through us.

However, you must also remember that you can pray, study your Bible, be still, and go to church all day, every day, until you are blue in the face and never really experience God in a tangible way. What do I mean when I say *"experience God in a tangible way?"* All my life I have heard from well-intentioned and sincere men and women of God that our relationship with God is not based upon "feelings" and "experiences" but upon the truth and knowledge of God's Word alone. Of course all truth and doctrine originate in God's word and His Word alone. However, to say that our relationship with God does not also involve experience and feeling is not only misguided, but it's not logical.

The Bible creates a boundary and limit which keeps God's children in line and in balance. For example, right now you are most likely sitting in an enclosed room. You are free to walk around anywhere and everywhere within that room. Yet, if you continue walking in one direction long enough, you're going to hit a wall – a barrier. God's Word creates a similar "room" for us to live in. Knowing God's Word, His truth, His promises, and His laws creates such a boundary for all Christ-followers to live in with liberty and freedom. His Word protects us from sin, false teaching, lies from the enemy, and lies of our own carnal mind. At the same time, the life of every Spirit-filled believer is to be lived in experiential knowledge of God as we stay within the boundaries of God's written and inspired Word passed down by the Apostles and Prophets of old.

When someone makes a statement like *"we don't base our relationship with God on feelings or experiences,"* the point that is usually being made is that God has spoken to us and revealed Himself to us in Scripture and that *we do not need to physically feel God or actually hear His voice directly.* This point is usually made by "mature Christians" who have seen God's truth and written Word perverted by good-intentioned but immature believers who placed "experience" over God's written Word. Many Bible-believing Christians feel that one cannot trust and know for sure that certain experiences, thoughts, or ideas actually originate in God Himself, therefore we should steer clear of basing decisions and pursuits in our lives purely based upon emotions we're feeling or ideas we *think* might have come from God.

There is good reason for this. Anyone and everyone can say *"God told me this"* or *"God wants you to do that."* Only God knows the amount of damage and abuse which has been experienced by church goers and Kingdom citizens due to the ignorance, self-absorbed thinking, and puffed up imaginations of pastors, teachers, and church leaders who believed they knew God better than anyone else on earth. Super-spiritual Christians. Surely, you have met more than a few people who believed themselves to be "the next Moses" or "a twenty-first century John the Baptist" or "Joshua leading people into the promised land." Therefore, we must practice extreme discretion and caution in ever saying *"God told me this"* or *"God wants you [or me] to do this/that."* Instead, when we feel God speak to us in a real way and we encounter His living Word, we should write it down in our prayer journal and begin to pray for confirmation to validate the word given to us, and then instead of shouting it on the roof-tops, we get on our knees and begin to pray.

Let me give you an example. I have had encounters with the Lord when I felt God gave me a real vision or special knowledge about a particular person, friend, church member, or co-worker. Ignorantly, when I began having these experiences and insight from the Lord, I would go to that particular person and say, *"Brother, I want you to know that God told me about [such and such problem or issue] in your life and I want to help you out."* Instead of helping comfort or solve a particular problem in that person's life, I was often met with skepticism, doubt, and questioning from the individual who immediately had a red flag and put up a wall of defense.

I have had spiritual mentors and others warn me about the "danger" of believing I'm actually hearing from God directly. The most common response I receive when delivering such a "word from the Lord" is *"Well, if God wants me to know that or if He wants me to do something, then He'll tell me. I don't think He would tell you. He would speak it to me."* Thus, through personal experience and immaturity, I learned a valuable lesson. Serve and love others through prayer. Instead of telling someone you have a word for them, simply get on your knees and pray and intercede for that particular individual, and plead with the Lord for a "divine encounter" with the individual. Maybe they will approach you for help and counsel regarding that particular issue in their life.

I cannot count the number of times I have experienced such a scenario. There is no need to run around and tell everyone that *"God gave me a word of knowledge"* or *"I have a special insight"* about someone. That is between the Lord and me. We share those moments together. They are private and it is unnecessary for the whole world to know God really spoke to me. I know and have empirical, undeniable, tangible proof and evidence to validate that fact. I have recorded those events in my personal prayer journal time and time again, and I have seen how God orchestrated and fulfilled exactly what He said He would. You can have the same confidence in your relationship and communication with God – every Kingdom citizen is free and able to know God in such a way.

The Essentials of Having an Authentic, Vibrant Relationship with God

Now, we went off on a bit of a tangent there, but I want to get back to the essentials of having an authentic, vibrant, and experiential relationship with God Almighty. I noted a few paragraphs above that you can pray, read your Bible, be still, and go to church until you are *"blue in the face"* and still never really experience God. Essentially, all of these activities could be likened to parts of an engine. An engine has many parts and components which work together to make the whole engine run. However, if you forget to put fuel in the engine, you'll never be able to get the thing started! FAITH is the fuel which makes "the relationship" with God work.

Living a life of faith is really just following in the footsteps of Jesus Christ. In God's Kingdom, faith is the currency which makes all things work and function. Without faith, a relationship with God is really just a series of daily religious acts which will most likely help you live a moral and decent life. Essentially, a person who is dedicated to Bible study, prayer, and fellowship with other Christians at church will almost always experience a REFORMATION in his/her life. There will be a noticeable change in that person's lifestyle … but still, without faith, this "reformed life" becomes nothing more than another empty religious person, worshipping the idea of God, obeying a book with God's revelation in it, and finding comfort in the whole idea of a relationship with God, but never really experiencing God. Religious pursuit, however well-intentioned and sincere, without faith will turn all of its victims into nothing more than empty, cracked cisterns, unable to receive and be filled with the life-giving waters of God's Spirit.

Seeking God's Presence

So then, what is the difference between doing these religious things without faith and doing them with faith? How do we actually "do it"?

First, you must believe God is real and He rewards those who earnestly seek Him IN FAITH (Hebrews 11:6). You must whole-heartedly believe that God can be felt and experienced. It is not a metaphor or mere *talk*. We are spiritual beings and can connect at a real spiritual level with God who is also Spirit … not to mention His actual, real, living Spirit lives inside of our own spirits! What that means is that you can and should be able to *experience and feel God's literal presence in a tangible, experiential way, and communicate back and forth with Him.* Now, this is where the eyebrows begin to rise by regular, dedicated, church-goers, who do pray and read their Bible every day and seek to live a godly life.

When teaching on this most important aspect of experiencing God, I usually ask a series of questions like this to prove the logic and soundness of such a belief: *"Do you remember the first time you experienced the reality of God or felt God in a real way at some point in your life?"* Usually the answer is "yes."

Then I'll ask the following, *"When you first encountered God, what did it feel like … that is, how did God make you feel when you received salvation through the gift of faith in Jesus Christ (Eph. 2:8-9), or had another intimate experience with the Lord?"* I always get answers like the following "extreme joy," "warm fuzzy feelings," "goose bumps/cold chills up and down my spine," "the feeling of pure ecstasy," "I felt the love of God *all over me," "I felt the urge to jump up and down and shout glory," "I began to weep when I felt God's presence," "God gave me an overwhelming sense of peace and serenity that cannot be explained," "God's presence felt heavy and thick, almost like it could be touched."* The list could go on and on. Most likely you're able to relate with such feelings and experiences. Is that not also many of the same reactions we see in people in the book of Acts and other narratives in Scripture who found Jesus Christ and the truth of His Gospel?

Are the emotions of joy, peace, love, and forgiveness not experienced as feelings? If they're not things we feel, then how do we know when we do or do not have them? How do you know when you're happy? How do you know when you're sad? How do you know when you have peace? Yes, they are theological truths and ideas to talk about and study, but they are also experiences and feelings that we can have and *feel* which are many times the direct results of encountering God's presence in a real, tangible way. Even more, the *glory* or *presence* of God is something that can be felt – physically.

For some of you, that's a hard pill to swallow. I challenge you to be open-minded. Read God's Word from Genesis to Revelation and make a note of every time someone encountered the real, live, actual presence of God. How did people respond? Many times, even being in the presence of an angel knocked godly men like Daniel, Ezekiel and John down on their faces. As they encountered the living God, men's bones would rattle and shake because of the awesome power and energy which accompanied God's Shekinah glory. I need not even cite Scripture references because this is a well-known fact for all who have read and studied God's Word.

Now, let me ask you another question: *Is God's Spirit and glory which dwell within your body any less "God" or "real" than His glory and presence in the days of "the Bible?"* Is God's Spirit living in you right now somehow different or less than God's Spirit Who hovered over the face of the waters in Genesis 1? If your answer to that question is yes, I challenge you to explain why. What is the difference? What scriptural reference or precedent do you have for believing that way?

When we individually and corporately seek God with all of our hearts in consistent prayer, praise and worship (with our hearts, our hands, our minds, and our entire lives), God's presence will at times "manifest" in a way which can be felt and experienced by our physical bodies. It's almost as if God rewards us for our earnest pursuit of Him when done in faith. *"He is real and rewards those who earnestly seek Him."*

God's presence is everywhere and is always around us. So you may ask, if that's true, why don't we always feel and sense His real tangible presence? Honestly, I wish I could give you a "nuts and bolts" answer about how God's presence "works" in our lives. But it would be foolish for me to even try. I don't think such mysteries should even be uttered.

The only way I understand His omnipresence is like the "dimmer light switch" we have in our dining rooms or living rooms at home. When you walk into the dark room, you take the dimmer knob and slowly turn it. The light turns on very dimly but gets brighter and brighter as you continue to turn the knob. In my experience, as I earnestly seek God in faith day after day, I sometimes feel absolutely nothing. I believe in faith that I am in God's presence and He is near to me. I must walk in faith. I ask God to shine His face upon me and reveal Himself to me … and yet there is nothing tangibly experienced. But nonetheless, I know in faith that I am in God's very throne room, seated with Christ in heavenly places (Eph. 2:6), receiving in faith every spiritual blessing from the Spirit of Christ within me as promised to us in Ephesians 1:3. If I need wisdom, in faith I ask God believing He is giving me all knowledge and insight needed. It will manifest in due time. If I'm feeling unhappy, I believe in faith and ask that God's Spirit release within my soul unspeakable joy and gladness as I willingly release any fear, stress, resentment, or ungratefulness to the Lord in repentance. If I need love, I ask and believe in faith that God's Spirit is blessing me … and in pure and total faith I receive those things from God; spiritual blessings which originate from God Himself in the Spirit.

At special times in my daily time of prayer with the Lord, *He "turns the dimmer switch" of His Shekinah glory up a little bit.* I am more attuned to His Spirit in me and His presence around me. I have experienced times of prayer with my friends where I have physically felt the presence of God fall on us like a spiritual blanket. Sometimes we prayed for three or more hours, enthralled by God's goodness and presence, only to get up and feel as if we only prayed twenty minutes. We had no clue we prayed for such a long time. There have been times when I have prayed in my office with other men of God. When we ended our prayer time, I've heard more than a few of them exclaim, *"Jesse! Are you seeing what I'm seeing?! Is it is just me or is it extremely bright in your office? I've never seen light like this. Everything seems kind of foggy and hazy!"* I just smile and say *"Yeah, I think God has blessed us with His manifest presence! Thank you Lord!"*

I have had personal times of prayer when I have sought the Lord all night long, deep into the next morning, until I could pray no more. I simply longed for His presence more than life itself. There have been times when the manifest presence of the Lord has become evident, at which time my body begins to quiver and shake as if I was freezing cold. A feeling of dread and holiness comes over me. In times past when God has made His reality and presence known to me, it first terrified me, as if I had a lump in my throat and I felt totally exposed and naked and filthy in His presence. But soon His sweet, soft, gentle voice whispers in my ear to tell me I am loved and cherished by Him, that I am His son, at which time I have become overwhelmed in praise and worship.

When we really encounter God's true manifest presence, all we can really do is do what the angels in heaven do: shout out in words and songs of worship: *"Holy, Holy, Holy, is the Lord God Almighty! Worthy is the Lamb Who was slain!"* When God's presence and Shekinah glory is made manifest to us, we sing songs of joy and laughter, and get up and jump and dance in overwhelming joy. Sound bizarre? Sound out of balance or "disrespectful?" I challenge you to read the Psalms, because if that seems *irreverent* or *uncouth* to you, then you would've had a really bad feeling about King David and other great men of the faith.

I'm not sure what King David, Jesus, Paul, Peter, and the others would have to say about most "prayer meetings" that take place today. I think they'd say, *"What are you guys so depressed about? Where is your joy? Where is your excitement? Where is the celebration?! Don't you know how great it is to be able to approach the Throne of grace to find help and mercy in time of need (Hebrews 4:16)?"*

Before moving along, please know that my intent in sharing personal encounters with the Lord is not meant to impress you or act like I'm *"Mr. Spiritual."* That is a joke. You are able and should be having the same experiences with God. We are all God's children! God loves me no more than He loves you.

I also want to caution you that as you seek God's presence, you must stay balanced. My father, David Nelms, has taught me that the key to the Christian life is BALANCE. I thank God for that wisdom he imparted to me many years ago. *We must never seek only feelings, gifts, signs or manifestations from God.* It may seem that way to you after reading the above paragraphs, but I assure you, that was not the intent or purpose. We must stay focused on seeking God and God alone. God is our joy! God is our portion! God is our bread and our water! God Himself and His face are what we seek!

My point is that we really can and do experience God in a real way when He is our first priority and He is more important to us than anything and everything else. When we earnestly seek Him that way in faith, He will, I repeat, He will reward us with His manifest presence. His presence is experiential and results in bearing fruit for the edification and strengthening of other Kingdom citizens in our fellowship and network. God will shine His light in you and through you in order to edify and minister to other believers which will ultimately bring glory and honor to His name. Praise the Lord!

Practical Steps in Experiencing God

So then, here are some practical tips to assist you in your daily spiritual disciplines:

1. Prayer

I found a very simple formula to keep me effectively focused in prayer called *The Three P's*:

First, **Prepare!** Prepare your mind and heart by contemplating on the majesty, power, and holiness of the God you're preparing to speak to. One way that has helped me to do this is to read passages such as Isaiah 6, Daniel 7, or Revelation 4 which describe the Throne Room of God. After reading those passages, I visualize God's throne room and imagine myself, in spirit, actually kneeling down directly in front of God's Throne with God sitting on it in inapproachable light. I imagine the setting, with myriads of angelic beings and the twenty-four elders encircled around God's heavenly throne room. Then I recognize that I now have the privilege to talk directly to my Lord, face to face.

Second, **Pause!** Before I speak, I try to put myself in the throne room setting above. I don't speak. Many times when we pray, we pray in the flesh. We blurt out the first thing that comes into our mind, rather than speaking with consideration and reflection. Can you imagine walking into God's heavenly court, in front of thousands of angels, who are covering themselves with their wings from God's light and glory, and then simply saying something like:

"Dear God. Thank you for this day. Thank you for my family. Please help me to have a good day. Please help me not sin [in such and such way] and please provide the money I need for my bills. In Jesus name I pray, Amen." I doubt it! Pause and reflect. I challenge you as you begin, to even set a timer – set the timer for three to five minutes – and be still, focusing your mind on God's character and attributes. Don't empty your mind like eastern meditation and New Agers do. Anchor your mind to Scripture.

Finally, **Pray!** Once you are in a reverent state of being and right "mind-set," simply open your mouth and speak to the Father. Speak to Him as your heavenly Father and God, knowing that He cares for you and listens to you.

Here are some other practical tips that I have found helpful in developing a prayer life that is alive and effective:

- *Turn off your cell phone!* You wouldn't answer your phone while in a job interview or in a meeting with an important person. Don't interrupt your time with God either.
- *Turn off your music – even worship music!* Wait and talk to God in silence.
- *Pray in a secret place.* That is, pray in a place with little to no distractions or loud noises.
- *Pick the time that you set aside for prayer and conversation with the Lord when you can give full energy and alertness to God.* He deserves the best part of our

day (whether that is morning, noon, or evening), not our left-overs and "yawns." If you're not a morning person, don't pray in the morning. Who says you have to pray in the morning if those are not your best and most alert moments in the day? I personally enjoy praying in the evening time before I go to bed.

- *Schedule a daily time (or meeting) with the Lord.* Don't let *anything* interrupt that scheduled appointment. If you are a fairly busy person, you probably depend upon some sort of calendar to manage your day. I have had to actually set a daily appointment in my Microsoft Outlook Calendar with God. If someone wants to meet with me or do something which conflicts with that time, I just say, *"You know what? I'm sorry. Can we find a better time? I have an appointment already set for that time which I really cannot change."* It's true! Why should I move my time with God to meet with another human being? Now, there are always exceptions to this rule, but in general if we don't create and manage our own schedule and daily agenda, other people will gladly do it for us!

- *Make a prayer list.* I will touch on this a little bit more below, but at the start of each new year, I make up a two-tiered list. One column is for personal prayer requests and goals, and the second tier is composed of prayers for my church. For you it may be your job, ministry, and a diversity of work and ministry related goals. I review and pray over this list, if not daily, at least weekly. I also leave space next to each item where I write notes and the date in which that particular prayer was answered. Just about every prayer I pray in faith is answered … many times it is not the way I envisioned, but nonetheless it is answered! This can be verified with many of my friends and brothers in Christ at Grace Fellowship who pray with me on a weekly basis! We give God all the glory for His power to do anything and everything He pleases according to His will!

- *Make a Matthew 18 prayer covenant.* This may be one of the most important prayer principles I've ever learned. It was taught to me by Dr. Rick Amato, one of my closest friends and mentors in the Lord. So I saved the best for last.

In Matthew 18:19-20, Jesus said: *"Again I say to you, if two of you agree on earth about anything they ask, it will be done for them by my Father in heaven. For where two or three are gathered in my name, there am I among them."*

I like what Vernon McGee said about Jesus' words here: *"Does He mean that if we agree on anything, He will hear us? Yes, but notice the condition: 'where two or three are gathered together in my name.' He will hear any request which is given in Christ's name—that is, a request that Christ Himself would make. Or, we could say that asking in His name is asking in His will."*

Further, an additional stipulation on this fantastic promise from the Lord and Head of the Church is unity in our relationships with fellow brothers and sisters in Christ. When we are in close fellowship with the Lord and with each other, and in constant prayer and meditation, we will be connected with Jesus Christ and will more easily discern His will for us, our church, our families, our friends, and our needs. We know many things which are the will of God: peace, unity, personal sanctification, to attack and tear down strongholds that the enemy has over us, our families, and the list goes on.

Therefore, a Matthew 18 covenant is a mutual agreement and covenant we make with one another to not gossip and slander one another. Instead of *talking about one another,* we must *talk with one another.* A Matthew 18 prayer covenant is really about keeping relationships strong and healthy so that our prayers may be answered by the Father.

When we have a problem or have been offended by a brother or sister in the church, we need to go to them in love and follow the precedent Jesus mandated for His people in Matthew 18:15-18. You need to get well accustomed with those verses in Matthew 18. Memorize this passage. When we live in a Matthew 18 way of life with one another, there truly is the power to ask for ANYTHING in Jesus' name (things we know are according to His will, His purposes, His desires, which he has revealed to us personally or in His Scripture) and know in full faith and confidence that it will be done.

2. Stillness, Meditation, and Journaling

I have decided to talk about these spiritual disciplines directly after prayer tips, because stillness and meditation go hand and hand with prayer. In prayer, we speak to God. It is in intentional times of stillness and meditation that we wait and seek God's response and answer to our prayers, questions, and concerns. It is in the stillness and serenity of our mind and heart that God reveals important truths to us regarding sins we may be unaware of, direction and specific tasks He desires for us to do, His plan and purpose in our life and ministry, instructions about how to help, minister to, or intercede for a brother or sister in Christ, and many other specific personal issues relating to our spiritual growth and daily sanctification.

You may be thinking: *"What is the difference between stillness and meditation?"* Well, that depends on who you ask! The two could be put together as a unit, but for clarification I am treating them separately. Again, there is no right way, rhyme, formula, etc.. Therefore, though stillness and meditation are inseparable, you can be still without truly *meditating*, but you cannot really meditate without being silent.

Silence is terrifying to many. If you ever stop and think about it, it is virtually impossible in many parts of the United States to avoid noise. We are a noisy society! However, it is in the still and total silence that we can practice the presence of God. As we exercise the discipline of silence day after day, it will begin to get easier and easier to discern the voice of the Lord from other voices which may come into our mind.

What other kinds of voices are there? There is our own carnal thinking – and there are the thoughts from the enemy which get projected into our minds daily. They are lies and false ideas which are "fiery darts" from demons. There is a song by *Casting Crowns* called *"The Voice of Truth"* which beautifully illustrates this particular truth. The song speaks of many different voices that speak to us, but the "voice of truth" tells us a different story. Amen, that is the truth! Therefore, take the step of FAITH today and began to still your mind in silence. Believe you are truly in the presence of God, and sure enough, in faith you shall surely experience the Lord!

Mediation is a spiritual discipline seen throughout the Psalms. David was a man deeply committed to prayer, stillness, meditation, singing, and dancing before the Lord. In fact, reading his songs to the Lord, it seems he was more passionate about prayer and meditation than almost anything else in his life!

There are several Hebrew words used in the Psalms which are translated *"meditation"* in English. The general idea is to *"ponder in one's heart"* (Psalm 49:3). It includes *"thoughts or internal musings, specifically, thinking in the heart as opposed to speaking (particularly in Psalm 19:14)."* [112]

Another interesting Hebrew word (*siyach*) translated in English as "meditation" is found in Psalm 104:34. This word means *"contemplation, meditation, prayer, talk, utterance, babbling. The primary meaning of the word is a complaint ... Elijah mocked the*

---

[112] Spiros Zodhiates, *Complete Word Study Dictionary of the New Testament*, (E-sword, electronic edition).

prophets of Baal, telling them to cry louder because their god might be deep in thought [meditation] (1Kings 18:27). The word is also used to denote Hannah's prayer containing words of great anguish (1Samuel 1:16). The psalmist used the word to depict meditation that he hoped would be pleasing to the Lord (Psalm 104:34)." [113]

Here are some examples of meditation in the Psalms:

Psalm 5:1 *Give ear to my words, O LORD, Consider my meditation.*

Psalm 19:14 *Let the words of my mouth and the meditation of my heart be acceptable in Your sight, O LORD, my strength and my Redeemer.*

Psalm 49:3 *My mouth shall speak wisdom, and the meditation of my heart shall give understanding.*

Psalm 104:34 *May my meditation be sweet to Him; I will be glad in the LORD.*

Psalm 119:97 *Oh, how I love Your law! It is my meditation all the day.*

Psalm 119:99 *I have more understanding than all my teachers, for Your testimonies are my meditation.*

I have found that few people have ever really thought about meditation; much less practice it as a valuable and strategic form of connection and communication with God. The key in meditation can be seen clearly in the two verses in Psalm 119 above. We see that God's "law" and "testimonies" are David's focus in meditation throughout the day. Our meditation should be focused on God's revealed Word. How do you meditate?

---
[113] Ibid.

Meditation is simply *"focused thinking on God, God's character, His personal attributes, or His written words of truth, law, promise, or prophecy. "*

Many people are a little nervous about meditation because Hinduism, Buddhism, Yoga, transcendental meditation, and other religious practices come to mind. Many non-Christians around the world are experts at meditation because it is an important aspect of their religion. However, such meditation is often focused on doing the opposite of what God's Word teaches. Such ideas about meditation are usually to *empty the mind totally of all thoughts and basically open up oneself for interaction and communication with any "spiritual thought" which may come into your mind from within or from without.* This is NOT what I am instructing you to do. Biblical meditation is Word-centered. It is content-focused.

Start with God's Word. Perhaps it is a key phrase that has spoken to you; maybe it is a passage of Scripture like Revelation 4 that talks about the throne of the Lord; maybe it is simply a verse written on a note card that you have been thinking about. Use these words as an "anchor" in your mind.

As we try to calm down, be still, listen, and then meditate, we realize how addicted to noise we really are. It's hard being still – but that is exactly what we need. Many of us are actually scared of total silence. We have to have music or the TV constantly turned on. But it is in the silence that we are able to begin to feel and hear the small, gentle voice of God speaking to us at a spiritual level. We are also faced head on with our own thoughts, which sound like a megaphone in our minds, when we sit in total silence. We seek to focus, not on our own thoughts, but on God's thoughts and His ways which we find solely in Scripture. It will be natural to drift away from focusing on God and to think about anything else. Therefore, we must be intentional and focus like a laser beam on God and His Word, anchored there so we don't drift.

Tips to Effective Meditation:

- *Find a comfortable place to sit, lay, or kneel on your knees where you feel relaxed and safe.* This is also the place where you should pray. It is your personal secret place that you share intimately with God. (A word to the wise: if you're going to kneel on your knees and elbows find a couple pillows to put under your joints.)
- *Minimize the distractions.* Turn off the lights or just have the room dimly lit.
- *Begin to meditate after you pray and read the Bible.* During my time of prayer I usually seek God's advice, counsel, and direction. I bring various needs before His throne for which I need help. I also pray according to my prayer goals I've set for myself and for the church for that year and ask God to continue to work to accomplish the goals. Thus, after my prayer time I seek to hear back from the Lord in response to my prayers offered to Him already. I also suggest meditation after Bible study as well because often, as I read Scripture, a particular passage or verse will hit me squarely between the eyes. I'll feel in my gut that it is God speaking to me. I'll write that Scripture in my journal or on a note card to memorize. Then, during my time of stillness and meditation, I will focus my mind on that passage.
- *Close your eyes.* Why? Simply because with your eyes closed it is easy to keep from being distracted by things in the room or wherever you are. In addition, God sometimes communicates to us visually (through images or scenes, which are not "divine revelatory visions" to be interpreted as scripture or doctrine). God sometimes will bring memories to our mind, or show us applications

about His Scripture in a visual way in our mind, which is easy to perceive with the eyes closed. This should be natural to us as we also are accustomed to praying with our eyes closed. God and His Kingdom can almost never be perceived with the natural eye but with the eyes of our heart. *"Open the eyes of my heart, Lord,"* is a song we often sing in church. It has been said that we can see things much better with our eyes closed than with our eyes open. I have found that to be true.

- *Reflect.* When you focus your mind on God's Word in meditation, you do not need to repeat the verse over and over in your mind. That may be how your start for the first few minutes until you've got it memorized. You think about that passage, what it means, you ask questions about the implications of the verse itself, you think and contemplate on how that verse can apply directly to you in your present walk. Essentially, you let the words from God soak and marinate in your mind. This is what it means to *"hide God's word in your heart."*

- *Reserve a good amount of time for quality meditation.* Ideally, that would be thirty minutes, but you may need to start out with shorter times. As I was starting out, I found it helpful to actually set a timer or an alarm on my cell phone to indicate when thirty minutes was up. At first, it felt like eternity, but soon it seemed to pass by in moments.

Meditation falls right in line with journaling. Essentially, in my practice, I journal 3 things: (1) key verses that stick out to me in my Bible study and reading, (2) prayers and prayer requests relating to key events occurring in my life, and (3) ideas, thoughts, "downloads," insight, applications, and words spoken to me by the Lord during times of stillness and meditation.

During your time of focused stillness and meditation, you're most likely going to be battling your own flesh and mind. You will wonder, *"Are these my thoughts or God's thoughts coming to me? How do I know?"* Don't worry, everyone experiences that, and we should not assume that every little thought and idea which passes through our mind is from God! That would be very unwise! However, if we are diligent IN FAITH to seek God in the stillness and meditate on His Words of truth, He will reward us. He will give us wisdom and insight and depths into the multiple layers and dimensions of a particular verse or passage of Scripture. If you will be faithful to meditate on a story in the Old Testament or a doctrinal truth in Romans, and you truly still your mind and seek God's presence and Spirit to illuminate truth to your mind, He will reward you. You will know when the Lord speaks to you. Trust Him and rest on His Spirit to guide you. Like sitting in an inner tube on a lazy river, drifting downstream, He will lead and direct you. That is God's desire! He wants to teach us and give us wisdom and insight freely.

> **James 1:5-8** *If any of you lacks wisdom, let him ask of God, who gives to all liberally and without reproach, and it will be given to him. But let him ask in faith, with no doubting, for he who doubts is like a wave of the sea driven and tossed by the wind. For let not that man suppose that he will receive anything from the Lord; he is a double-minded man, unstable in all his ways.*

3. Bible Study

If we are going to "think right" about God and God's will, then we must be fully immersed and ingrained in His Word! My mother-in-law, Sande Oliver, is currently writing a wonderful book for women (which she has allowed me to preview and read before completion) *Train My Spiritual Hands for War*, about effectively fighting and winning the spiritual war every day. The title of her book comes from Psalm 144:1, which says, *"Blessed be the Lord my Rock, Who trains my hands for war, and my fingers for battle."*

In the opening of her book she gives simple, helpful tips on Bible reading and Bible study. I'm obliged to quote from her wisdom and advice regarding Bible study:

> Make a commitment to read your Bible every day. You can begin today by following a yearly Chronological reading plan of the Scriptures. If you are very type 'A' and starting in the middle goes against your grain, then begin at the beginning: either in Genesis or Matthew (or any of the Gospels). You may also choose to read from your favorite epistles or Old Testament prophets or Psalms. The important thing is that you make a commitment, decide what the commitment is – what book and number of chapters each day – and stick to it. If you are crunched for time, try setting your alarm fifteen minutes early and read only one chapter or a few verses. And if you do miss a day ... just pick up your Bible the next day and get back into the reading!
>
> Begin journaling, if you are not doing so already. Purchase a blank book and begin. Currently, I am reading and journaling with three specific questions in mind: Who is this God I am reading about (His character, Nature); What has He done for us; How am I to respond?
>
> I have tried other journal prompts in the past, but I am enjoying these three simple yet direct and thought provoking prompts. You don't have to write the great American novel, just a few thoughts. This is a great focus builder for those of us who tend to be divergent and easily distracted (as well as a memory keeper for the forgetful learner)." [114]

Practical Tips on Reading Scripture

- *Maintain the right mindset.* Don't fall into the trap of

---
[114] Sande Oliver, *Train My Spiritual Hands for War* (unpublished).

thinking that reading your Bible is somehow a reason to give yourself a pat on the back. On the other hand, don't start believing that when you don't read your Bible that God is keeping a checklist up in heaven and is angry with you.

Bible study is not some religious duty that makes God smile. Reading God's word should be so fun, so exciting, and so addictive that you have a hard time putting your Bible down. Why? Because it's God's actual words! If in FAITH we simply believe with all of our hearts that God is real, He is as big as we say we believe He is, He has all of the answers to life, and we have His collection of ancient, inspired writings by real prophets and apostles, then reading His Word would not be a burden or a chore to us. The Bible is the most precious resource and invaluable piece of history, wisdom, truth, and knowledge in the world. Thank the Lord for preserving His written Word and testimony for His children, the Kingdom citizens on earth.

- *Get a Study Bible in a translation you can read and understand.* I personally enjoy many different translations: the King James Version, New King James Version, NET Bible (my personal favorite), the English Standard Version, the New American Standard Version, and several others. When you read a particular book in the Bible, take the time to read the "synopsis" or "review" of that particular book in the Study Bible. It is like "cliff notes" to help you understand the overall story. It will provide you with important historical, cultural, and other contextual issues which will help you understand the plot and story of what is happening to prevent confusion as much as possible.

- *Read the Bible as a whole...look at it as one story with one theme throughout the entire book.* It is the record of God's plan to destroy His enemy and save a "holy nation" of people, first starting in Israel then spreading to every nation of the world, through the sacrifice of Jesus Christ and His shed blood on the cross. When you read the Bible, remember that the story is not over yet and we are living in the final days and final "pages" of God's story. Because of that, make the commitment to read the entire Bible from Genesis to Revelation. Though the Bible is definitely not a novel, if you picked up a novel and decided to read it, you would not open it 2/3 of the way through and try to figure out what is going on. The Old Testament will tell you where we came from and the New Testament tells us where we are now and where we are headed as an assembly of "called out" people.

- *Read the Bible to learn – Study it!* Many people read the Bible in a leisurely, devotional way. I tend to be the exact opposite. I personally love to discover truths, correlations, patterns, and connections. I anticipate finding a precious pearl of truth and hidden gold nugget just waiting to be discovered every time I read. When reading, I place myself in the story and plot and read it as if I was truly experiencing what I'm reading. That's especially helpful when reading narratives and stories in Scripture.

Furthermore, I suggest that you not only read God's word but that you STUDY it, too! Treat the Bible like a user manual or a textbook that you're studying. Try to comprehend and learn it in the same way you would to ace a final exam for an important course. When you don't understand a word, look it up and discover the meaning. Take notes, make observations. In every book you read, seek to answer the questions: who, what, when, where, why, and how does this book fit in with the rest of the Bible? You would be surprised at what you can learn and discover about God's Word by simply making observations from the text itself without even trying to interpret the meaning.

For example, I challenge you, as a practice test to turn to James chapter one and make twenty-five observations. **I'll give**

you an idea below of what an observation is and what an observation is not:

> **James 1:1-3** *James, a bondservant of God and of the Lord Jesus Christ, To the twelve tribes which are scattered abroad: Greetings. My brethren, count it all joy when you fall into various trials, knowing that the testing of your faith produces patience.*

Here are some observations to get you started:
The book of James was written by James (duh!). James considered himself to be a bondservant of God. James also considered himself to be a bondservant of the Lord Jesus Christ. James addressed his letter to the "twelve tribes" which are scattered abroad. This means that James, in its original context, was sent first and foremost to Jewish Christians. James first opened up by sending His Jewish brothers (that is those of the twelve tribes scattered abroad) greetings. We should count it all joy when we fall into various trials. Christians will fall into trials – we are not exempt from various trials once we get saved. Trials test our faith. The testing of our faith produces patience. Difficulties in our lives should not be resented because whatever we suffer and overcomes only makes us stronger with patience and strengthened faith.

In addition to observations we make directly from the text, many people make "interpretations" or "assumptions" which are not found in the text itself. Steer clear of this. Let the Bible speak for itself. **Though the following points may be true they are NOT observations from the text**. James was the most prestigious and respected Apostle to the early Christians (not stated in text). James gave up everything to follow Jesus Christ (nowhere is this stated in the text). James wrote his letter to all Christians everywhere (not stated in the text, this is an assumption that cannot be provided by the text alone). James was the biological brother of Jesus.

You get the point. When it gets right down to it, Bible study is pretty basic stuff. It is not rocket science!

- *Record what you learn.* I recommend, instead of journaling everything you read and study in the Bible, to keep the journal more focused on prayer, meditation, and insight given directly to you from the Lord relating to certain key verses and key texts. When it comes to making notes and observations from your Bible reading, I suggest creating a computer file that you save on your desktop. If you use a PC like me, make a "Microsoft Word file" entitled something like *"Bible Devotions, Reflections and Study."* Open it each day as you start your Bible study. Read your Bible close by your computer. In doing so, simply type in your notes, thoughts, reflections, and important observations, under the heading of each book you read, under the chapter number, listed with the verse numbers, as a kind of outline. Later on, as you begin to make your way through the Bible, you'll have your own personal work and study record. It's amazing how much God will teach you. You'll begin to make "cross-references" and put verses together. The Bible, instead of seeming like a confusing puzzle, will begin to fit together like a beautiful mosaic and it will just begin to "make sense." Furthermore, as you make new disciples, you can help them out in their own personal study of Scripture, and you can teach them the same principles! It is so simple if we will just be strategic and intentional about how we study and use the precious time God has given us.

4. Fellowship with Other Kingdom Citizens

This last and final point for key aspects of developing your personal relationship with Jesus Christ is not so much focused on your "personal relationship with God" but is the glue that will hold everything together. Kingdom life is a life meant to be lived in community with other believers. We really cannot do it alone. We need one another desperately. Finding a solid Kingdom Community is of the utmost importance for you.

There is neither time nor space to go into the all of the reasons why community life is so important for you . I will simply list a few:

Encouragement and edification is a huge key. We constantly encourage one another and inspire one another to stay committed to Jesus Christ and His Kingdom when life gets tough. Many of us have realized the practical benefit to having a workout partner to exercise with. The same is true in the spiritual realm. We all need to be part of a team because once we get isolated we are an easy target for Satan. The Holy Spirit of God has empowered each of us with spiritual gifts which are meant to be used for one another to build up and strengthen God's church.

Community with other believers in smaller type groups (guys with guys, women with women, as well as corporate gatherings) also provides much needed accountability. We all must be accountable to other believers. We keep each other in line. If we're going to stay on the path God desires us to be on, we need to humbly submit ourselves to the leadership and spiritual officers in a Kingdom Community. Authority is very important in God's Kingdom – it is a foundational issue. If you reject authority, then you have no authority. We are all equal and one in the Body of Christ – but God has called certain men to function as leaders, such as deacons and elders. We also come together with one another in community for the purpose of observing the

Lord's Supper. The Lord's Supper or Communion is not only a memorial of the broken body and shed blood of Jesus Christ, but a reminder that His Spirit really does live in us and we're joined together as one body with Christ. Furthermore, Communion is also a means for corporate "cleansing" and renewal as we must be committed to confessing sins and repenting of any wrong way before observing the meal.

Finally, community assemblies are meant for a time of worshipping the Lord together in unity and love. It is also a time to be equipped by leaders whom God has raised up to teach and preach His word. God wants to speak and give direction to each community of Kingdom citizens through His "spokesmen" who are pastors, apostles, prophets, evangelists, and teachers. These men are responsible not only to train and equip each Kingdom citizen *to do the work of ministry out in the world*, but also to dedicate their time to reading God's Word, teaching His Word carefully and clearly to the people, and speaking prophetically to the people about what God is saying to the group as a whole. Pastors are to protect, shepherd, and nurture their community as a whole. An entire volume of books could be written on this subject alone, but this is only meant to be a brief summary.

To find a local Kingdom community near you visit **www.kingdomunite.net** to get connected to a group of Kingdom people who you can join in with and contribute to the family and mission of God's Kingdom in your city right where you are!